Early Childhoods in the Global South

Early Childhoods in the Global South

Local and International Contexts

Jacqui O'Riordan, Deirdre Horgan and Shirley Martin (eds)

PETER LANG
Oxford • Bern • Berlin • Bruxelles • Frankfurt am Main • New York • Wien

Bibliographic information published by Die Deutsche Nationalbibliothek
Die Deutsche Nationalbibliothek lists this publication in the Deutsche Nationalbibliografie; detailed bibliographic data is available on the Internet at http://dnb.d-nb.de.

A catalogue record for this book is available from the British Library.

Library of Congress Control Number: 2013936579

Cover image by Clíona Scully.

ISBN 978-3-0343-0879-3

Peter Lang AG, International Academic Publishers, Bern 2013
Hochfeldstrasse 32, CH-3012 Bern, Switzerland
info@peterlang.com, www.peterlang.com, www.peterlang.net

Printed in Germany

Contents

DEIRDRE HORGAN, JACQUI O'RIORDAN AND SHIRLEY MARTIN
Introduction 1

SECTION 1 Children's Lives and Livelihoods 9

KAREN WELLS
1 Mobility and Social Reproduction: Key Issues for Early Childhood Research in Developing Countries 11

ANGELA VEALE, SUSAN MCKAY, MIRANDA WORTHEN AND MICHAEL WESSELLS
2 Children of Young Mothers Formerly Associated with Armed Forces or Groups in Sierra Leone, Liberia and Northern Uganda 27

UNA MURRAY
3 Child Labour: A Complex Problem Requiring 'Joined Up' Responses 47

SAMUEL OKYERE
4 An Assessment of the Impact of Hazardous Work on Children's Educational Attainment 67

SECTION 2 Early Years Policy and Practice 83

HELEN PENN

5 Does International Aid Work? The Example of Early Childhood 85

JOHANNA DAVIS

6 Values in Early Childhood Development: A Venture into the Field of Childhood Aid 107

ROSARII GRIFFIN AND JACQUI O'RIORDAN

7 Early Childhood and Primary Education in Sub-Saharan Africa: The Impact of HIV and AIDS on Education in Lesotho 131

JACQUI O'RIORDAN, JAMES URWICK, MATEMOHO KHATLELI, STELLA LONG, GRACE NTAOTE, FLORENCE NYAKUDYA AND NTHABELENG MAKETELA

8 Identification of Disabilities in Young Children in Lesotho: The Role of the Early Childhood Sector 145

MAHIMA MITRA

9 The Take-Up of Government Early Childhood Education and Care Services in Developing Countries: Evidence from India and Theoretical Frameworks for Guiding Research 161

ANNIKA PISSIN

10 Migration in China: Floating Mothers and Fathers, Left-Behind Girls and Boys 181

BARNEY SHIELS

11 The Equity Approach to Early Childhood Development and Accomplishing the Millennium Development Goals 203

SECTION 3 Language and Culture: Working with Children 219

MARY KELLETT

12 Research Methods with Young Children: Extending the Canvas 221

JACQUI O'RIORDAN, DEIRDRE HORGAN, SHIRLEY MARTIN AND MICHAEL BLANEY

13 Day-To-Day Transitions for Children of People Seeking Refugee Status Living in Ireland 235

JOY CHALKE

14 Supporting Children with English as an Additional Language in the Early Years Foundation Stage (UK): Meeting the Challenges 255

ANNE M. DOLAN

15 Critically 'Reading the World' through Picture-Books 271

PAMELA MACKENZIE

16 A Mother Tongue Based Multilingual Curriculum as a Means to Quality Education. Lessons from Minority Language Communities in India and Bangladesh 289

SARAH QUINN AND SUE KRAFTSOFF

17 Maintaining the Mother Tongue: An Exploratory Study of Russian-Speaking Immigrant Parents' Opinions on Maintaining their Primary Language in their Children 311

Notes on Contributors 329

Index 339

DEIRDRE HORGAN, JACQUI O'RIORDAN
AND SHIRLEY MARTIN

Introduction

The overall aim of this book is to deepen our understanding of children's lives in the Global South, drawing particular attention to early childhood as well as the importance of including local traditions, culture and knowledge in developing professional practices in Early Childhood Care and Education (ECCE).[1] We acknowledge that all the terms used to depict global divisions, for instance, developed/developing, majority/minority worlds, north/south, are problematic. The title of this publication uses the term Global South, which stresses socio-economic, cultural and political divisions between lower income, largely southern hemisphere countries, known collectively as the Global South, and wealthier high income countries, mostly located in the northern hemisphere, and known collectively as the Global North.

This is an innovative book that attempts to examine a number of important issues in the new and emerging area of ECCE from a global development perspective. Together, the contributions in each section draw on topics identified for discussion at the Early Childhood in Developing World Contexts International Conference that was held at University College Cork in April 2011. As the conference progressed it became increasingly apparent that the discourse on issues surrounding early childhoods was very exciting, with lots of contributors involved in active research, much of which was not sufficiently recorded. We thus began to look at a meaningful way of bringing together the many discussions which took

1 Various terms are used to refer to early years care and education throughout the publication. These reflect the manner in which thinking about the sector is changing as well as localized emphases.

place over the two days of the conference and in its aftermath. Included in this publication, then, are chapters developed from presentations given at the conference as well as others identified in further discussions with contributors. Importantly, it incorporates key authors in the field of global childhoods, bringing together a mixture of high profile international academics in this area, for instance Helen Penn and Karen Wells. When the full tranche of submissions was collated, it became clear that the book would have wide ranging themes which all connected with one or other of the following sections, around which the book is structured: livelihoods and childhood; early years policy and practice; and language and culture: working with children.

Increased attention has recently been given to the role that ECCE can play in global development. Some key themes include: the argument that ECCE is an essential component of overall poverty reduction strategies; that children who participate in ECCE *and* have positive early learning experiences *may* make better transitions to primary school, and *may* be more likely to begin and remain in primary school; that ECCE is considered to be an important instrument for promoting gender equality; and that children who attend quality ECCE are more likely to have better educational outcomes when they attend school, whereas low quality ECCE can be detrimental to children's development and wellbeing (UNESCO 2007).

A central aim of this publication is to equip readers to understand localized contexts of childhood and to challenge a more euro-centric perspective that is, largely, offered through current research and practice. It is in keeping with Grantham-McGregor's (2007) argument that such an approach to ECCE is important in reaching Millennium Development Goals One and Two on eradicating extreme hunger and poverty and achieving universal primary education. Penn (2004) is critical of an over-emphasis on Euro/American models of early years programmes that are not easily translatable into traditional communities. This is exemplified in Penn's chapter, 'Does International Aid Work? The Example of Early Childhood', where she states that while early childhood aid projects are increasingly based – in theory at least – on a concept of children's rights, and children's rights to basic services, often such projects reflect the needs and beliefs of the funder rather than the needs and beliefs of local women and children.

So the process of funding international aid is a very complicated business and the visibility of such transactions warrants much more attention. Penn argues that if international aid is problematic, often wasteful and complex, then it matters a great deal that those involved in early childhood programmes should understand the complexities of aid; the macro and micro issues involved. Instead, NGO and charitable discourses about early childhood very often draw on ideas and knowledge from the Global North, in particular from North America. They assume that ideas and knowledge constitute universal precepts which are applicable everywhere. They tend to minimize contextual issues, in particular the adverse effects of inequality, and hold few expectations of government intervention.

All three themes – livelihoods and childhood; early years policy and practice; and language and culture: working with children – bring a critical focus on social constructions of childhood and developments in ECCE globally. The book provides space for interrogation of the concepts of 'childhood' which are largely adult-centred, with children often represented as dependant and innocent beings who should be protected and cared for by adults (Breuil 2008). These discourses of childhood are normative, and fail to recognize the historically and culturally specific experiences of children. The consequences of such constructions of 'childhood' are critiqued throughout the book in relation to associated assumptions about children's agency. The book aims to explore how researchers and policy makers can build on the experience of children/young people to develop more appropriate policies and professional practices in early years care and education.

In light of this, and of the importance of understanding local contexts, Mary Kellett argues for children's voices to be heard and acted upon in the shaping of services. She states that children's participation should be integral to any decision-making that affects their lives, including the planning and evaluating phases and not just the implementation. Such participation requires a fundamental rethinking of children's capabilities, experiences and contributions. Crucially, this necessitates a reappraisal of the research methods employed with young children to ensure there is genuine engagement and active participation. Kellett's chapter, 'Research Methods with Young Children: Extending the Canvas', maps some examples of valuable activities developed by NGOs and childhood organizations globally with regard to young children's participation. One such is the Phila Impilo project in South Africa which uses puppetry as part of a participative methodology to generate data that assists us in accessing and understanding the lived experiences of children who have chronic diseases, such as HIV and TB. Such understanding is essential in adequately developing provision for their needs *vis-a-vis* long term hospital care.

Mobility in early childhood is another key theme of the book. Wells' chapter, 'Mobility and Social Reproduction: Key Issues for Early Childhood Research in Developing Countries', aims to show how social reproduction and mobility intersect and how mobilities of children and adults impact on early childhood. She argues that such impacts on children, especially those left behind by global domestic workers, are not fully acknowledged or analysed. She points out that 'children's mobility is generally organized by their families in a complex economic, social and cultural nexus. Some of these mobilities will lead to the formation of transnational families [and that] [o]ther, more local mobilities, especially of young children, might strengthen social ties between the multiple households to which children become attached through these movements' (p. 4 this volume). Annika Pissin, in her discussion on migration in China, offers a nuanced analysis of children of migrant workers in China. She questions assumptions that are often made about grandparents, mothers, and children 'left-behind', as well as assumptions about rural and urban lives.

Attitudes towards early childhood policy and provision differ widely around the world. While the twentieth century was dominated by developments in the provision of education, we still see significant inequality in children's access to education. Millennium Development Goal Two seeks to achieve universal primary education. In this regard, early years care and education is crucial in combating inequality. In many developed countries now there is a focus on children's experiences before school, with increased government commitment and expenditure in the area of early years care and education. In Ireland, for example, the government introduced the Early Childhood Care and Education Scheme in 2010 that provides universal access to a free year of pre-school for every child in the state. Investing in quality ECCE is crucial, as it is thought to be at this stage that the foundations are laid for subsequent learning and achievements, and because it is shown to contribute to breaking cycles of disadvantage. Globally, however, there are significant variations between countries as regards enrolment rates, supply, quality, resources, approaches and governance of ECCE. Johanna Davis, in chapter six, provides critical comment on the development of Early Childhood Development (ECD) in Majority World contexts where the focus has been on the economic argument. She argues that this offers one concept of childhood that often reflects neither childhoods in the Global South nor outside of the mainstream in the Global North.

In more recent years the quality of ECCE provision has started to feature on the policy agenda in many countries. For example, until a few years ago, the focus of most EU level action was on providing more childcare places to enable parents to join the labour market. More recently, the European Commission's Communication on ECCE, adopted in February 2011, sets out key policy areas for cooperation within the Open Method of Cooperation, in order to improve the accessibility and quality of ECCE across Europe. It calls for well-integrated services that build on a joint vision of ECCE, for effective curricular frameworks and for the development of staff competences and governance arrangements necessary to deliver that vision. However, while there appears to be a broad consensus on the importance of ECCE, most of the evidence on which policy is based comes from the English-speaking countries of the Global North. Research is, therefore, needed that takes account of the heterogeneous nature of ECCE in a broader global context.

The Organisation for Economic Co-operation and Development (OECD), among others, has outlined the importance of investment in this area, including facilitating parental participation in the labour force as well as the social, emotional, cognitive and economic benefits of quality early intervention in children's lives. In its recent report *Starting Strong III* (2012), it argues that child, parent and societal benefits of ECCE are conditional on 'quality'. It recognizes that expanding access to services without attention to quality will neither deliver good outcomes for children, nor long-term productivity benefits for society. It outlines five policy levers that can enhance ECCE, including: setting quality goals and regulations; curriculum and standards; improving qualifications, training and working conditions; engaging families and communities; and improving data collection, research and monitoring (3). This book looks at policy and practice across Europe, India, China and Africa, with contributions from authors who have specific research interests in this area. It provides an analysis of interconnections between national policies and practices. Partner countries have different histories/cultures of childhood and are at different junctures in national policy development and implementation with regard to early childhood care and education.

Issues of child abuse and exploitation more broadly are discussed in the context of globalization and its impact on children and childhoods. The contribution of Angela Veale and her colleagues in chapter two brings our attention to the specificity of issues arising for young mothers who were former child soldiers in re-integrating into their home communities. Their children are often a stark and very visible reminder of conflict and its associated pain and suffering. Re-integration into communities raises issues of cultural expectations of mothers and generational (dis)continuity in, often, very complex and differing ways for the young mothers and their children. The examples that Veale and her colleagues discuss show how interventions that draw on the mothers' own priorities and capacities can contribute positively to their status and thus their acceptance, and that of their children, within their communities.

Child labour is both a cause and consequence of poverty and is addressed in a number of chapters throughout the book, which aims to mainstream the issue into the development debate. The book features a discussion of the ILO Convention 182 on the Worst Forms of Child Labour (WFCL), ten years after its coming into force. The current global economic crisis threatens progress made on the elimination of child labour. Una Murray, in chapter three, provides a discussion of child labour that draws our attention to the different ways it is defined and conceptualized as well as associated problems. It examines differing views on child labour, and looks at the differences between children helping out in family farms/businesses/homes and work that is hazardous to children. It discusses the view that child labour is necessary for economic development and the fact that economic development is often associated with increased levels of child labour. Finally, it looks at the conflict between access to and participation in education and work for children.

The book has an interdisciplinary approach, with the involvement of key international NGOs in this area and academics and researchers representing a variety of disciplines including social work, social policy, sociology, justice, early childhood studies, international development, education and psychology. Many of these contributors are involved in the training of social professionals and policy makers, thus enabling direct transfer of knowledge from research to professional education.

References

Breuil, B. (2008). '"Precious Children in a Heartless World"? The Complexities of Child Trafficking in Marseille Children and Society', *Special Issue: Child Slavery Worldwide*, 22 (3), 223–34.

European Commission (2011). *Early Childhood Education and Care: Providing all our children with the best start for the world of tomorrow. Communication from the Commission.* COM (2011) 66 final.

Grantham-McGregor, S., Yin Bun Cheung, Cueto, S., Glewwe, P., Richter, L., Strupp, B., and the International Child Development Steering Group (2007). 'Developmental Potential in the First 5 Years for Children in Developing Countries, Child Development in Developing Countries 1', *Lancet*, 369, 60–70.

OECD (2012). *Starting Strong III – A Quality Toolbox for Early Childhood Education and Care.* Paris: OECD.

UNESCO (2007). *Strong Foundations – Early Childhood Care and Education.* Education for All Global Monitoring Report. Paris: UNESCO.

SECTION I

Children's Lives and Livelihoods

KAREN WELLS

1 Mobility and Social Reproduction: Key Issues for Early Childhood Research in Developing Countries

Introduction

The aim of this chapter is to show how the exigencies of social reproduction shape mobility in developing country contexts and how these mobilities of children and adults impact on early childhood. Many of the reasons why children move (or are moved) from one household to another, sometimes across international borders, are tied to transitions from childhood to adulthood, albeit in complex ways. The migration of youth, for example, is often central to their attempts to make a successful transition to adulthood. However, for young children, the focus of our concern in this book, children's mobility is generally organized by their families in a complex economic, social and cultural nexus. Some of these mobilities will lead to the formation of transnational families. Other more local mobilities, especially of young children, will strengthen social ties between the multiple households that children become attached to through these movements. An exception to the generally local character of the migration of young children is that of transnational adoption, which is discussed here from the perspective of sending families. The chapter begins by outlining the concept of social reproduction and its relevance to children. I then discuss how social reproduction relates to the formation of global care chains. I then discuss other strategies that families deploy to manage social reproduction in precarious times, focusing on 'child circulation' and transnational adoption.

Social reproduction

Social reproduction is 'life's work' (Mitchell et al. 2004). It refers to the physical and emotional work that is necessary for life to continue, including biological reproduction. It is related to production but it locates it in relation to social reproduction; that is, it understands the purpose of production from the point of view of the labourer, rather than of the owner of the means of production. From the perspective of the owner of the means of production (land, machinery, factories) the point of production is to increase profit. From the point of view of the labourer the purpose of production is to generate the means to make life materially and symbolically possible: to buy or make food, homes, culture. Social reproduction is, as Bakker and Gill (2003) argue, analytically distinct from capitalism; all societies need to be reproduced, not only capitalist societies. But the rule of capital will obviously shape the context in which social reproduction occurs. Specifically, much of the stuff that is needed to make the work of social reproduction possible is commoditized and the costs of social reproduction will be unequally shared between capital, labour and the state. Specific, concrete political settlements, themselves fashioned out of political struggles between classes, will determine how the costs of social reproduction are shared between these three actors (Bezanson 2006; see also Pearson 2004).

The development of social reproduction theory was intended to give recognition to the social character of labour. Whereas capital wants to treat workers as unencumbered, independent individuals this is, of course, a distortion of how workers are enmeshed in wider social and cultural worlds. They need wages, not only to pay for their own individual needs but to contribute to the material costs of sociality: the costs of maintaining families, friendships and other social networks, in short, the costs of social reproduction. Some of these costs are met for 'free' by other people, typically mothers. Indeed, the emergence of social reproduction theory was intended to identify the central role of women's labour in social reproduction and the economic contribution that women make through cooking, cleaning and caring for children and others (Dalla Costa and James 1972, cited in Trotz 2010). Feminist theorists, in developing these arguments wanted to show that the private/public distinction between family and work belied the importance of political economy in shaping family life and determining the gendered inequalities inscribed in the family (Bezanson 2006).

Place of children in social reproduction theory

Children have had a paradoxical position in social reproduction – theoretically and empirically. On the one hand, definitions of social reproduction theory gesture towards the child. So, for example, Bakker and Gill define social reproduction as: biological reproduction; labour reproduction – that is both the subsistence costs of labour but also the costs of education and training; and provisioning. The latter includes the provision of food, but also of housing, clothes, warmth, water, etc.

In each of these elements of social reproduction there is clearly a place for children: they are the subject being biologically reproduced and educated and a lot of the work of provisioning is done for children (and often also by them). Similarly, the focus in social reproduction literature on 'care chains' or on how people, especially women, manage the work of social reproduction, often at a distance, recognizes that it is children who are being cared for and left behind, and children who are, to use the phrase Parreñas coined, being 'mothered from a distance' (Parreñas 2001: 361). However, for the most part, social reproduction theory has focused more on women than children. When theorists do include children in the work of social reproduction, they tend to be interested in older children and young adults who are doing the actual work of social reproduction (and even production) – looking after younger siblings, fetching water, herding animals and doing general domestic work.

Global care chains

One of the ironic effects of the integration of women into productive work in the developed countries under the sign of gender equality is that this work, the work of social reproduction, caring or emotional labour is increasingly being done by domestic workers, many of whom are migrant women (Chang 2000; Ehrenreich and Hochschild 2002; Hondagneu-Sotelo 2007). Some of the caring labour that used to be done in families, principally by women, has been moved out of the family and into institutions. The cost of providing care in institutions may be met by governments or by individuals buying services. In either case somebody has to do the work and increasingly that work is being done by low paid women workers, many of whom are migrants. It is because of this expansion of the costs of social reproduction into the public sphere that some theorists prefer to speak about global care chains rather than social reproduction (Yeates 2009).

Global care chains and children left behind

Important though a focus on global care chains is in showing how the productivity of developed economies depends on the work of low paid migrant women, it does shift attention away from the impacts of uneven development and global capitalism on children. Increasingly, the literature on global care chains acknowledges that there are material and emotional costs of migration on children left behind (Hondagneu-Sotelo and Ernestine 1997; Wolf 1997; Parreñas 2005; Coe 2011). However, these costs are quickly glossed over, partly out of a desire not to criticize women domestic workers. The still very small literature on the impacts of parental migration on separated children acknowledges that there has been little research done on the effects of transnational migration of parent(s) on children left behind (Graham and Jordon 2011).

Global care chains have mostly focused on two regions: Latino/a migration to the USA and the migration of Asian domestic and health workers, with a particular focus on the Philippines. These migrations are important and have captured the imagination of researchers, not least because of the challenge they represent to social categories like family and nation. However, migration across international borders represents a very small part of all migration. Most people migrate within their country or into border zones. Many more children are 'left behind' as a consequence of this scale of migration than global migration. In China, for example, around 20 million children are without parental care. In a study conducted in Hunan Province, central China in 2006, nearly 2.5 million children (27.3 per cent) of the under-fifteen population were without parent care, the majority of whom (74 per cent) were being cared for by their grandparents (Fan et al. 2010). The phenomenon of children left behind is tied to the migration of rural workers to urban centres. This is creating a large population of children left behind by one (usually the father) and, sometimes, both parents. This has produced a new research agenda (Liu et al. 2009) on early childhood in rural China and on populations of left behind (children and elderly) through these migrations (Liem et al. 2006). This research has produced some interesting insights into the impacts of being 'left behind', in particular on negative psychological and health outcomes, especially for younger children if their mother migrates. There is not, as yet, sufficient disaggregation of this work by type of care; for example, whether children fare better when left in the care of kin than in the care of strangers.

It may be that wellbeing outcomes for children left without parental care because of internal migration are different to those for children who are left behind because of international migration. However, to date there has been no comparative work done on the impact of different kinds of parental migration on children. This could be an interesting area for future research, for example do children imagine parents to be further away when they migrate to another country than if they migrate to another region in the same country; are the financial benefits of international migration greater than for internal migration in the Global South?

Child circulation

One exception to the elision of children in the work of social reproduction is the anthropology of child circulation in sub-Saharan Africa and, in particular, Esther Goody's seminal work on social reproduction and fostering in West Africa (Goody 1982). Goody herself, says that the fostering of children below the age of around seven years is exceptional in West Africa, and generally only done if there is a crisis in the child's natal family. However, other studies show even quite young children being fostered. These practices of fosterage or child circulation or child fosterage have a long-standing history in many regions of sub-Saharan Africa.

Research on this practice in Africa has mostly focused on West Africa (Isiugo-Abanihe 1985; Bledsoe 1990; Castle 1995; Eloundou-Enyegue and Stokes 2002; Notermans 2003; Alber 2003, 2004) but there are now some studies on Central (Whitehouse 2009), East (Archambault 2010; Archambault and de Laat 2010) and South Africa (Madhavan 2004). Child fosterage or child circulation, despite a superficial similarity – the movement of children from natal to non-natal households, usually of kin – is quite diverse. In particular, there are multiple reasons why children move (or are moved) from one house to another. They may move to help out another household, in which case the sending family is likely to be better off than the receiving family. They may be moved in order to construct or thicken a relationship between two households; suggesting that in these cases the sending household is likely to be worse off than the receiving household. The effect of child circulation may be to equalize the size of households that make up an extended family, or to give the child easier access to schooling or to an apprenticeship. In some cases, the motivation is to improve the child's health and nutrition. In migrant families, children may be sent to other families 'back home' to ensure that they are familiar with cultural practices and are fluent in their mother tongue.

These movements are often temporary and maybe multiple, with a child moving to different households throughout his or her childhood (Archambault 2010). This reflects local ideas about what children need in their best interests. Among fostering families in Africa, being attached to multiple households is seen as beneficial to children and their families. Generally, the point of circulation is that it is temporary, since it is this that creates a web of connection between the two or more households that the child has lived/is living in. However, some children may stay in their new home throughout their childhood and may be adopted. Although most children circulating in this way are not in their 'early childhood', infants and young children are also fostered and adopted.

These movements are clearly related to sharing the costs of social reproduction but it is also noteworthy that underlying them is a conception of children as being adaptive. The idea that the young child has a singular attachment to his or her birth mother seems to be largely absent in cultures where fosterage is practised on a wide scale.

This does not mean that children are not valued. They clearly are and, indeed, social personhood is deeply tied up with child rearing. For this reason, infertility is a common reason for a child to be given to another household (Archambault 2010: 233). Alber, in his ethnographic study of Baatombu child circulation in Northern Benin, notes that it is *because* children are highly valued that they are given away:

> [A]s many people explained to me, if one gives one's child away, one gives the most valued thing one could give. Hence, the person who takes a child will be forever grateful for having received the most precious gift one could possibly receive. The great value of children makes the gift of a child particularly precious. It is this great value attributed to children that qualifies them as ideal *objects of exchange*. (Alber 2003: 499, emphasis added)

Alber's use of the term 'objects of exchange' in the above quote brings into focus the implicit question of what precisely it means to make a 'gift' of a child. A gift implies reciprocity and also ownership. The child is the parents' to give and in making of the child a gift there is, according to the theory of the gift, a reciprocal obligation to return the gift. The failure to return the gift obligates the recipient (see Yngvesson 2002). This should not be understood as a direct, acknowledged obligation of reciprocity since it is precisely the character of a gift that it obscures the obligations inscribed on/in it. At the very least, however, it confirms the sense that the gift of the child creates social networks or webs of relation between giver and recipient.

The fosterage of children around puberty is prevalent in West Africa. In most cases the child is sent to help with chores, to look after younger children and to get an education or training. In these instances, the child will obviously remember his or her birth family, and may even arrange the fostering by themselves, particularly in the case of boys migrating for work (Hashim and Thorsen 2011). However, young children are also fostered and adopted and the adoptive and birth parents presume that the child will not remember their natal family or may be harmed by making new attachments (Alber 2003). Of course, this is in sharp contrast to prevalent ideas in the West of infant attachment to the birth mother.

Although fostering and adoption continue to be practiced, the norms of social parenthood are changing. Western discursive norms about what constitutes a family – circulated by NGOs, churches and schools – are influencing adults' and children's perceptions about where children belong. Both Archambault's Maasai informants and Alber's informants in Northern Benin, claim that 'we are less social now' and fostering, which in the past created kinship and bound more distant kin together, is now increasingly restricted to close family.

However, although local fosterage and adoption may be restricted to near kin, long-distant fosterage seems to be more flexible in the choice of who the child may be sent to live with. This is unsurprising given that the choice of relatives to place a child with is likely to diminish the further away a child is placed.

International fostering

Globalization is stretching practices of child circulation across national borders and regions (Øien 2006). As with child circulation in West Africa, most children who are sent to Europe to live with relatives or family friends are older children, although that can mean they are as young as seven. To European policy-makers sending young children to live with distant relatives in Europe is incomprehensible except as a clear sign of parental neglect. Children who arrive in Europe without parental care are viewed as *at risk* and often presumed to have been trafficked for the purpose of economic exploitation – especially benefit fraud and domestic work. However, it is more likely that what we are witnessing is the stretching of a local cultural practice of child fosterage or child circulation across international borders.

Transnational adoption and 'social orphans'

It may also be possible to view the giving of children into transnational adoption through these local conceptions of who children are and who they belong to and what the relations are between biological and social parents. Alber, for example, reports that:

> During my field research my rural Baatombu friends have often offered small children to me. My acceptance of the gift of one of their children, whom I could take to Germany with me, would have meant for them not only that I accept a very deep friendship but also that I would then become a real relative to them. (2003: 501)

In 2007 a French NGO took 103 children from their parents in Chad with the intention of bringing them into France for adoption. The parents of the children claimed that they gave the children to the agency because they had no school in their village and were told that they would be educated at a school in a nearby Chad town. The NGO intended to fly the children out of Chad, claiming that they were war orphans from Dafur, Sudan. The focus of reporting on this case has been on the misrepresentation by the NGO of the circumstances in which it took control over the children. The workers were charged in Chad with child trafficking and sentenced to seven years hard labour but were released in March 2008 after the President of Chad pardoned them (Bergquist 2009). At the time of the court case there were demonstrations in Chad against the NGO and child trafficking. Press attention on this issue has focused on the illegality of the NGO's action, which is certainly important. However, there is no suggestion that these adults took the children by force, although they did, apparently, give 'inducements' to their parents.

The much publicized high-profile adoption by the singer Madonna of two children from Malawi raised similar concerns about children being made available for adoption extra-legally. The first child was adopted as an orphan but it subsequently became clear that the child had a father. The second child was adopted after Madonna appealed against a court decision that ruled against the legality of international adoptions.

Both of these highly publicized cases illustrate some interesting issues about the connections between precarious social reproduction, globalization and child mobility. In both instances the question of what makes a child an orphan in global and local contexts is at the heart of decisions about whether child mobility is in the child's best interests. The International NGO (INGO) practice of calling children orphans who have lost one parent, has played an important role in the discursive construction of children living in poverty as 'orphans'. In this context, or so the argument goes, the loss of a parent can make the already precarious household economy unviable, rendering children vulnerable to homelessness, malnutrition, and exploitation. In other words, whether a child loses one parent or both parents does not make a significant difference to their material conditions. The problem with this argument, leaving aside the lack of empirical data to support it, is that even if materially the child is in a similar position, socially and symbolically they are not. To be an orphan in any context implies that a child has no adult who is emotionally invested in advocating for and protecting the child; this is even more so in the context of sub-Saharan Africa where wealth in persons is as important as wealth in things in determining social position and protection. The discursive construction of poor children as 'orphans' has made children vulnerable to being 'rescued' by NGOs.

The growing literature on transnational adoption (Volkman 2005; Dorow 2006; Howell 2007), as with global care chains, tends to focus on the adoptive parents rather than their children. Research that has addressed the impacts of transnational adoption on adoptive children tends to look at issues related to identity and cultural assimilation in the receiving country, eliding the transnational character of the child's history (Yngvesson 2010: 58) or dealing with it only to the extent that it shapes their cultural identity.

Although these are, of course, legitimate and interesting research questions, it is essential that transnational adoption be considered as a specific kind of child mobility that impacts especially on early childhood and is a direct consequence of global inequalities. This is the case whether parents give their children up for adoption or the child is released for adoption by state authorities. There is growing policy evidence, for example, that governments use transnational adoption to solve the crisis of care caused by poverty and conflict. The rapid expansion of transnational adoption from Ethiopia is indicative of this trend. This is an echo of practices in Brazil where parents who place their children in care in periods of familial crisis, with the intention of taking them back home when the crisis passes, often find that the child has been adopted overseas without their consent (Fonseca 2002). Conversely, as seen in the highly publicized attempt of a group of USA missionaries to organize the adoption to the States of Haitian children, parents may give their children for adoption believing that it is in their best interests to do so.

The availability of children for adoption from one country to another is a consequence of a crisis in social reproduction in child-sending countries. Most transnational adoptions are arranged because natal families do not have the material means to provide for their children. This lack of resources is often a consequence of exceptional structural circumstances, for example war. However, for many families their inability to provide for their children is not exceptional but is a persistent consequence of structural poverty.

To bring the discussion full circle, David Eng (2006) has provocatively argued that transnational adoption should be considered as part of global care chains. Here the work that is expected of the 'migrant labourer', that is the adopted child, is not cooking and cleaning, but the affective or emotional labour of completing the white middle class family in the heartlands of global capitalism.

Conclusion

This chapter has considered how the mobility of parents and children are shaped by wider economic forces in specific cultural contexts. It illustrates the close connections between economic conditions and cultures of parenting. The migration of parents, especially mothers, to meet the increasing demand for caring labour in the advanced capitalist countries has generated global care chains that raise questions about the wellbeing of 'children left behind'. Similarly, economic development in China has created a very large population of left-behind children. In both cases the migration of parents can be seen as strategies to meet the costs of social reproduction in the absence of welfare states.

Conversely, the migration of children or child circulation can be seen as a response to the precariousness of social reproduction in the context of rural communities in sub-Saharan Africa. These different strategies for managing social reproduction challenge many deeply held beliefs in the West, derived from development psychology and psychoanalysis, about what the young child needs to thrive emotionally or psychologically, and also physically. In cultures where fosterage is widely practiced there seems to be no presumption that infants and young children need a primary attachment to their birth mother and to a singular family. Indeed, it seems that creating webs of support for children that make multiple families responsible for their care, is regarded as more in their best interests than thickening the bond between the natal mother and her children.

From this perspective sending children to live with adults they barely know, in more or less distant places (from local to international migration), does not seem so suspect or neglectful as it does from the point of view of parenting cultures where to protect your child is to keep them close. This different perspective on the best interests of the young child further complicates the already rather complicated practice of transnational adoption. These are generally done as clean-break adoptions, again relying on presumptions about the importance of the singular family and close (adoptive) parent-child bonding to the wellbeing of children. However, it maybe that (natal) parents view adoption as part of the practice of extending webs of support and creating new networks to supplement, rather than replace, the networks that the child is already attached to. We urgently need more research on this topic. It is somewhat ironic that as adults, who were transnationally adopted as children, are making public the considerable emotional costs of these displacements, the expansion of international adoption from the Global South to the Global North continues unabated.

The research agenda on early childhood in developing country contexts has been shaped largely by development psychology. The child and parent mobilities discussed here, point to the need to expand the research agenda to consider the connections between economy and culture and to recognize the multiplicity of parenting cultures without assuming, for instance, the primacy of the mother-child dyad to the wellbeing of young children.

References

Alber, E. (2003). 'Denying Biological Parenthood: Fosterage in Northern Benin', *Ethnos*, 68 (4), 487–506.

Alber, E. (2004). 'Grandparents as Foster-Parents: Transformations in Foster Relations between Grandparents and Grandchildren in Northern Benin', *Africa*, 74 (1), 28–46.

Archambault, C. (2010). 'Fixing Families of Mobile Children: Recreating kinship and belonging among Maasai adoptees in Kenya', *Childhood*, 17, 229–42.

Archambault, C. and Laat, J. (2010). 'Social Mobility in Children's Mobility: Child circulation among the Maasai of Kenya'. In Marisa O. Ensor and Elzbieta Gozdziak (eds), *Children and Migration: At the crossroads of resiliency and vulnerability*, pp. 187–208. Basingstoke and New York: Palgrave Macmillan.

Bakker, I. and Gill, S. (eds) (2003). *Power, Production, and Social Reproduction: Human insecurity in the global political economy*. Basingstoke: Palgrave Macmillan.

Bergquist, K. J. S. (2009). 'Operation Babylift or Babyabduction?: Implications of the Hague Convention on the humanitarian evacuation and "rescue" of children', *International Social Work*, 52, 621–33.

Bezanson, K. (2006). *Gender, the State and Social Reproduction: Household insecurity in neo-liberal times*. Toronto: University of Toronto Press.

Bledsoe, C. (1990). '"No Success Without Struggle": Social mobility and hardship for foster children in Sierra Leone', *Man*, 25 (1), 70–88.

Castle, S. E. (1995). 'Child Fostering and Children's Nutritional Outcomes in Rural Mali: The role of female status in directing child transfers', *Social Science & Medicine*, 40, 679–93.

Chang, G. (2000). *Disposable Domestics: Immigrant women workers in the global economy*. Cambridge MA: South End Press.

Coe, C. (2011). 'How Children Feel about their Parents' Migration'. In C. Coe, R. R. Reynolds, D. A. Boehm, J. M. Hess and H. Rae-Espinoza (eds), *Everyday Ruptures: Children, youth and migration in global perspective*, pp. 97–114. Nashville: Vanderbilt.

Dalla Costa, M., and James, S. (1972). *The Power of Women and the Subversion of the Community*, (2nd ed.), Bristol: Falling Wall Press.

Dorow, S. (2006). *Transnational Adoption: A cultural economy of race, gender, and kinship*. New York: New York University Press.

Ehrenreich, B. and Hochschild, A. R. (eds) (2002). *Global Woman: Nannies, maids, and sex workers in the new economy*. New York: Metropolitan Books.

Eloundou-Enyegue, P. M. and Stokes, C. S. (2002). 'Will Economic Crises in Africa Weaken Rural-Urban Ties? Insights From Child Fosterage Trends in Cameroon', *Rural Sociology*, 67 (2), 278–98.

Eng, D. L. (2006). 'Political Economics of Passion: Transnational adoption and global woman', *Studies in Gender & Sexuality*, 7 (1), 49–59.

Fan, F., Su, L., Gill, M. K., and Birmaher, B. (2009). 'Emotional and Behavioral Problems of Chinese Left-Behind Children: A preliminary study', *Social Psychiatry and Psychiatric Epidemiology*, 45 (6), 655–64.

Fonseca, C. (2002). 'The Politics of Adoption: Child rights in the Brazilian setting', *Law & Policy*, 24 (3), 199–227.

Goody, E. N. (1982). *Parenthood and Social Reproduction: Fostering and occupational roles in West Africa*. Cambridge: Cambridge University Press.

Graham, E. and Jordan, L. P. (2011). 'Migrant Parents and the Psychological Well-Being of Left-Behind Children in Southeast Asia', *Journal of Marriage & Family*, 73 (4), 763–87.

Hashim, I. and Thorsen, D. (2011). *Child Migration in Africa*. London: Zed Books.

Hondagneu-Sotelo, P. and Ernestine, A. (1997). 'I'm Here, but I'm There: The Meaning of Latina Transnational Motherhood', *Gender and Society*, 11 (5), 548–71.

Hondagneu-Sotelo, P. (2007). *Doméstica: Immigrant workers cleaning and caring in the shadows of affluence*. Berkeley: University of California Press.

Howell, S. (2007). *The Kinning of Foreigners: Transnational adoption in a global perspective*. New York: Berghahn Books.

Isiugo-Abanihe, U. C. (1985). 'Child Fosterage in West Africa', *Population and Development Review*, 11 (1), 53–73.

Liu, Z., Li, X. and Ge, X. (2009). 'Left Too Early: The effects of age at separation from parents on Chinese rural children's symptoms of anxiety and depression', *American Journal of Public Health*, 99 (11), 2049–54.

Madhavan, S. (2004). 'Fosterage Patterns in the Age of AIDS: Continuity and change', *Social Science & Medicine*, 58 (7), 1443–54.

Mitchell, K., Marston, S., and Katz, C. (2004). *Life's Work*. Oxford: Blackwell.

Nguyen, L., Yeoh, B. S. A., and Toyota, M. (2006). 'Migration and the Well-Being of the "left behind" in Asia', *Asian Population Studies*, 2 (1), 37–44.

Notermans, C. (2003). 'Nomads in Kinship: Fosterage and the self in Cameroon', *Focaal*, (42), 89–103.

Øien, C. (2006). 'Transnational Networks of Care: Angolan children in fosterage in Portugal', *Ethnic and Racial Studies*, 29, 1104–17.

Parreñas, R. S. (2001). 'Mothering from a Distance: Emotions, gender, and intergenerational relations in Filipino transnational families', *Feminist Studies*, 27 (2), 361–90.

Parreñas, R. S. (2005). *Children of Global Migration: Transnational families and gendered woes*. Stanford Calif.: Stanford University Press.

Pearson, R. (2004). 'The Social Is Political', *International Feminist Journal of Politics*, 6 (4), 603–22.

Trotz, D. A. (2010). 'Shifting the Ground Beneath Us', *Interventions: The International Journal of Postcolonial Studies*, 12 (1), 112–24.

Volkman, T. (2005). *Cultures of Transnational Adoption*. Durham N. C.: Duke University Press.

Wolf, Diane L. (1997). 'Family Secrets: Transnational struggles among children of Filipino immigrants', *Sociological Perspectives*, 40 (3), 455–82.

Whitehouse, B. (2009). 'Transnational Childrearing and the Preservation of Transnational Identity in Brazzaville, Congo', *Global Networks*, 9, 82–99.

Yeates, N. (2009). *Globalizing Care Economies and Migrant Workers: Explorations in global care chains*. Basingstoke: Palgrave Macmillan.

Yngvesson, B. (2002). 'Placing the "Gift Child" in Transnational Adoption', *Law & Society Review*, 36 (2), 227–56.

Yngvesson, B. (2010). 'Transnational Adoption, Technologies of Exclusion, and the Promise of "Home"', *Suomen Antropologi: Journal of the Finnish Anthropological Society*, 35 (4), 56–62.

ANGELA VEALE, SUSAN MCKAY, MIRANDA WORTHEN
AND MICHAEL WESSELLS

2 Children of Young Mothers Formerly Associated with Armed Forces or Groups in Sierra Leone, Liberia and Northern Uganda

Introduction

Children born to girls and young women associated with armed forces or armed groups face many challenges. Often referred to as 'rebel babies', 'tomorrow's rebels' (McKay and Mazurana 2004) or 'children of bad memories' (Twum-Danso 2003), their survival, health and wellbeing are threatened by the circumstances of their lives. These children born of war often live in unsafe and insecure situations with mothers who have experienced multiple stressors because of their association with armed groups or fighting forces. Typically, when they return from war zones with their mothers, their mothers have difficulty providing for their needs because of community social prejudice and economic marginalization (Robinson and McKay 2005). These children may be amongst the most vulnerable of war-affected children (McKay and Mazurana 2004).

Interventions to target the children of formerly associated young mothers need to also target their young mothers and, where appropriate, her broader family network. Developing interventions that address the needs of the child, while also addressing those of the young mother, and supporting the dyadic child-mother relationship within a web of relationships made more complex by the stigma of war, remains a persistent challenge. In order to understand the situation of the child of a young mother, we must first understand the situation facing the young mother herself.

Brett and Specht (2004) found returned young mothers have more limited economic opportunities available to them. Annan and colleagues (2008) found that in Northern Uganda returned young mothers were severely restricted from returning to education or were unwilling to return; as a result they had a third less education than other returnees. In Sierra Leone, Baldi and MacKenzie (2007) interviewed fifty formerly associated mothers and found the care received by their babies and children was affected by their own often limited experience of good maternal care, as many were raised by extended family and/or by rebel groups. Family reunification is made more complex as a returning daughter now has a child or children of her own. In such circumstances, the challenge is how to engage with former children associated with armed forces or armed groups (CAAFAG), who return as young mothers, to learn their views on how to best support their social reintegration and that of their children. In this, it is important that interventions avoid recreating dynamics of disempowerment and lack of control that they may have experienced in fighting forces and armed groups (Coulter 2008).

In developing world contexts, the Global Child Development steering group found that the most effective early child development programmes provide direct learning experiences to children and their caregivers.[1] They are of longer duration and are integrated with family support, health, nutrition and other systems in children's lives (Engle et al. 2007). This chapter describes a community-based participatory action research study that took place over three years and may offer an example of such an approach. It involved over 600 war-affected young mothers and 1,200 of their children in Liberia, Sierra Leone and Northern Uganda. It aimed to empower young mothers to engage in social actions for their wellbeing and that of their children, and in turn to inspire those who care for them in their extended networks, and those in positions of leadership, to advocate and act on their behalf. We explore how the health and wellbeing of babies and children

1 The Global Child Development Group is a group of researchers and policy makers which authored the *Lancet* series on child development in developing countries in 2007 and 2011. See <http://globalchilddevelopment.com/lancet_series>.

were mediated through their mothers' meaningful participation in self-identified activities to address priorities of health, livelihoods, education and social (re)integration.

The overall goal of the study was to learn about what successful reintegration means to young mothers themselves and to enable them to plan, implement and evaluate social actions they initiated to support their reintegration. Two thirds of study participants were former CAAFAG and a third were other vulnerable young mothers. In this study, we use the terminology 'young mothers' because 80 per cent of the participants were between sixteen and twenty-four years of age but all young women in the study conceived or gave birth to children while they were themselves minors (under eighteen years). Through this targeted intervention with young mothers, we learnt about the situation of their children. In this chapter, we describe what we learnt about the children and how working with young mothers was effective in mediating change in the lives of their children.

War-affected young mothers

Research suggests that formerly associated girls are at greater risk of post-traumatic stress disorder (Phan et al. 2009) and exhibit higher levels of depression and anxiety and lower levels of confidence and self-esteem compared to boys (Betancourt et al. 2010), largely as a result of gender-based violence. In Sierra Leone, 70–90 per cent of females who were abducted by fighting forces were estimated to have been raped (Baldi and MacKenzie 2007). In Northern Uganda, Carlson and Mazurana (2008) found that forced marriage was widespread within the Lord's Resistance army (LRA) controlled areas. A quarter of all abducted girls were given to LRA commanders as forced wives and half bore children. They experienced more sexually violent events than either abducted males and never-abducted community peers, both male and female. In their study, forced wives and forced mothers experienced the highest rates of sexual violence and, on return to civilian communities, reported greater distress than other former abductees. This was explained by their increased exposure to violence during extended stays with the LRA. Returned young females therefore have particular experiences and needs that justify specific attention. The vast majority did not enter formal disarmament, demobilization and reintegration (DDR) programmes. In many cases, DDR planners were unaware of the presence and role of CAAFAG girls and they were marginalized or excluded from participation in formal DDR programmes (United Nations 2006; Worthen et al. 2011). Some girls sought to re-enter quietly to communities without seeking formal recognition of being a former CAAFAG. In interviews with returned young mothers in Northern Uganda in 2003, one young mother explained her decision to return directly to her family rather than going through a rehabilitation centre by saying that she just wanted to be a normal girl (Veale and Stavrou 2007).

What does it mean to be a 'normal girl' in war-affected communities such as Northern Uganda, Sierra Leone, and Liberia? In such contexts, adolescent girls are particularly at risk of sexual violence and exploitation as they are considered less likely to carry sexually transmitted diseases or the HIV/AIDS virus. Their social status as young unmarried girls can also contribute to their sexual vulnerability (Machel 2001). There is evidence that during the civil war in Teso, Uganda, unmarried girls were specifically sought by government soldiers for sexual purposes (De Berry 2004). In Northern Uganda, while the horrors experienced by abducted girls received significant attention, girls in displacement camps were frequently used for sexual purposes by Uganda People's Defence Force soldiers; subsequently, many of these girls became pregnant, although they were invisible within international non-governmental organization psychosocial programming (Shanahan and Veale 2010).

A key factor placing girls at risk of early pregnancy in war-affected communities is extreme poverty that can result in girls resorting to transactional sex to gain resources such as food or money to ensure their personal survival or that of their family. Baldi and MacKenzie (2007) have argued that in working with war-affected young mothers in Sierra Leone, it is misleading to focus on the place of conception – such as within armed groups – as the only signifier of vulnerability, and that it is important to focus attention on the complex relationship between paternity and stigma. They identify that children born to CAAFAG young mothers and those born from exploitative and unrecognized relationships such as through sexual violence, prostitution or transactional sex are also likely to experience marginalization and isolation. Children regarded as illegitimate by the family and community are likely to be rejected or abandoned by the paternal clan or, in the case of many CAAFAG young mothers, they wish to keep their children separate from the paternal kin. The situation of girls becoming pregnant in these circumstances described above is arguably a consequence of the inability of war-affected communities to protect adolescent girls. These young mothers have been identified in various war-torn contexts and given different labels: 'filles meres' in Democratic Republic of Congo (Save the Children 2004), 'child mothers' in Northern Uganda (Esaku 2009) or 'girl mothers' more generally (Robinson and McKay 2005).

Children of war-affected young mothers

The United Nations Study on Women, Peace and Security (UN 2002) identified one of the major impacts of armed conflict on young women and communities is the increase in children born of forced pregnancy. Yet little is known about how these children socially integrate and fare over time. Available evidence suggests that the children of these young mothers are generally accepted by the maternal family (Annan et al. 2008). In Sierra Leone, 78 per cent of young mothers reported that their families were welcoming of their children, although with a recognition of their status as 'illegitimate children' (Baldi and MacKenzie 2007). In Democratic Republic of Congo, Save the Children (2004) noted that children of CAAFAG young mothers were often physically accepted back to live with the maternal family, but the child was regarded as 'an extra charge' that they could not afford due to extreme poverty. In such cases, the responsibility for the sustenance and survival of the young child lay with the young mother, who was also responsible for her own upkeep. In Northern Uganda, families were generally welcoming of returned abducted young mothers and their children. This occurred in the context of Acholi customary law whereby children born outside of marriage would tend to become part of their mother's clan. However, there seem to be shades of difference between acceptance and belonging over time as familial tensions arose in relation to inheritance, access to communal clan land or economic pressures, and the identities of children born of forced marriage were sometimes contested and challenged (Shanahan and Veale 2010).

Despite the hardship of motherhood, little evidence exists that many young mothers abandon their children. Save the Children (2004) found that most CAAFAG young mothers wanted to keep their children and that their interest in and commitment to their children were evident. In reception centres in Northern Uganda, Jareg (undated: 2), a child psychiatrist with Save the Children, Norway, noted that in some cases where girls return with several children, some young mothers exhibited ambivalent attachment but that 'in most cases, mothers gave their babies a lot of affection and attention'. In Northern Uganda, Apio found that 36 per cent of a total of sixty-nine girls experienced motherhood as positive, while 64 per cent said it was negative; this was mainly due to the burden of responsibility of feeding, clothing and caring for a child in circumstances of extreme deprivation, that often resulted in illness and fears for the survival of the child (Apio 2008). As far as can be ascertained from the absence of reporting in the literature, very few children of CAAFAG young mothers are informally fostered. This is noteworthy because in many African contexts, child fostering is a normative response to family disempowerment due to war and poverty (Okunola and Ikuomola 2010).

Burman and McKay (2007) suggested that for CAAFAG young mothers, one of the biggest obstacles to social reintegration is extreme privation which can induce experiences of psychological, social, and economic marginality. The importance of livelihoods to social reintegration can be seen in a longitudinal study that followed former child soldiers and their children into adulthood. In Mozambique, Boothby et al. (2006) followed thirty-nine male former child soldiers for sixteen years after return. Most reported that they and their children were in either good or excellent health.

Fears that, after the war, these former child soldiers would be incapable of providing for their offspring were unfounded. Rather they desired a better childhood for their children than they themselves experienced and 75 per cent of their school-aged children were in education, which was significantly above the average of 60 per cent school attendance. One of the most important factors that supported these successful outcomes was livelihoods training as this enabled them to generate money. Economic resources in turn translated into social resources as the ability to earn an income made them socially valued in an informal economy where extended family is the main form of social security. Mbekenga et al. (2011: 98) examined under what conditions informal support was provided to first time mothers in a low income suburb in Tanzania and found '[i]nformal support was provided conditionally, where poor socio-economic status and non-adherence to social norms risked poor support'. This would suggest that an intervention, which would enhance economic status and strengthen identities linked to social norms (as a mother, daughter, valued community member), would impact positively on social support.

The PAR Study

The Participation Action Research (PAR) study sought to promote community participation with a focus on girl mothers (formerly associated with armed groups) and their children and other vulnerable young mothers in their communities. The study involved a partnership between community-based non-governmental organization partners working at grass-roots levels with war-affected communities in the three countries and national and international academics.[2] In total, 66 per cent of participants were formerly

2 Agency partners were Liberia: Save the Children, UK in Liberia; THINK; Sierra Leone: Christian Brothers, Christian Children's Fund, Council of Churches in Sierra Leone, National Network for Psychosocial Care; and Northern Uganda: Caritas, Gulu Archdiocese, Concerned Parents Association, Transcultural Psychosocial Organization, World Vision. National academics were Dr Stella Neema (Uganda), Dr Samuel Weekes (Sierra Leone), and Dr Debey Sayndee (Liberia).

associated young mothers and 33 per cent were other vulnerable young mothers. In Liberia, Sierra Leone and Northern Uganda, 111, 266 and 281 young mothers participated in the study and their average ages during the study were twenty years, twenty-two years and eighteen years respectively. With respect to household types, only 5 per cent of young mothers lived alone. The majority either lived with their boyfriend or husband (41 per cent, n=273) or with their parent or a guardian (36 per cent, n=234). Of the total, 22 per cent had one child, 44 per cent had two children, 25 per cent had three children and 9 per cent had four or more children when the study began. There were twenty sites across three countries; 60 per cent were rural and 40 per cent were urban sites. The majority of CAAFAG young mothers returned to their communities of origin, although this proportion varied across contexts; 35 per cent of young mothers in Liberia, 44 per cent in Sierra Leone and 21 per cent in Uganda were in communities where they had *not* previously lived.

Non-governmental organization partners identified war-affected communities with large numbers of formerly associated young mothers, held community meetings and met with local leaders to describe the study and solicit interest and involvement. Upon agreement to participate, community leaders and NGO field staff identified vulnerable young mothers, and as girls joined the project, these girls also invited others to be involved.

Over three years of the study, the young mothers met regularly in groups of approximately thirty participants. They slowly shared their problems and experiences, identified their priorities and developed 'social action' projects to address the challenges they faced. Their main concerns were poverty, stigma, marginalization and their poor health and that of their children. An innovative feature of the study was including a budget-line for as-yet unspecified social actions that would later be identified by participants. First, however, their groups engaged in discussion about the problems and challenges they faced and generated solutions in the form of social actions they could take to address their priority needs. Later, funds were made available to each group of young mothers to develop their activities, some of which needed financial resources and others which involved mobilizing their group for collective actions but did not depend on the use of money. Emergent social actions included individual and group livelihood initiatives, agricultural projects, micro-credit and micro-grant activities, community dramas, and pro-social activities such as community cleaning or helping at funerals (see McKay et al. 2011 for a fuller description). Throughout the project, emphasis was placed on developing linkages within their communities through advisory groups for each site, reaching out to community members through poetry and drama performances, visiting each other's homes, and with the support of their NGO field staff, communicating with community leaders about the young mothers' situations and needs. Over time, this resulted in community leaders in some areas donating land and material support, or issuing proclamations to protect and support them in cases of jealousies or negative feelings about the support they were receiving, and giving advice, support and encouragement. A wide range of training and skills education was provided across the study sites depending on the challenges encountered by participants. A key concern at a number of sites was the health of their children. Given high levels of privation, children were often very ill, and the cost of attending the health clinic exhausted meagre resources or the small profits from their livelihoods. They identified health training as a priority and this was delivered by community-based organizations at a number of sites. In Northern Uganda, for example, participants engaged in a participatory health assessment and then developed a health education programme for young mothers at all sites.

Towards the end of the third year of the study, a participatory evaluation was undertaken. In total, 434 participants completed the survey, which was implemented by country-based academics who privately surveyed each participant in her home community (see McKay et al. 2010 for further information). Several of the questions related to the health and care of their children. When asked to respond to a survey item 'How has the health of your child or children changed since you joined the project?' in total, 83.7 per cent of young mothers reported the health of their child or children was better; 14.3 per cent reported child health was the same, and 1.9 per cent reported child health was worse than before the project. In response to the survey item 'Involvement in the PAR has made me and my children more liked or loved by my family', 86.5 per cent responded positively to this statement, 2.6 per cent said sometimes and 10.8 per cent responded negatively. Also, when asked to respond to the statement 'I can take better care of my child than I could before I joined the group', 83.8 per cent of participants reported that they could take better care of their child or children, 7.1 per cent reported sometimes and 9 per cent reported that they could not take better care compared to before the project. Those who were formerly associated were more likely to report that they were better able to care for their offspring since joining the PAR (94.2 per cent) than those never associated (84.5 per cent), and this difference was significant (Cramer's V was .16, $p < .001$). What accounts for the shifts that took place over the course of the study with respect to the lives of these children that resulted in better health, greater family acceptance and enhanced child-raising experiences? Drawing on Carsten (2000, 2004), we argue that through young mothers' participation in self-identified activities to promote their social reintegration, they enhanced their own and their children's belonging and relatedness within the family and broader community. This is explored more fully in the next section.

Belonging and relatedness

Carsten (2000, 2004) has argued that notions of kinship and relatedness are undergoing a transformation as new family types emerge due to socio-cultural changes across the world. She has redrawn attention to the complex relationships between biology and broader political and cultural forces in definitions of kinship as she focuses on the extent to which kinship is given by birth and is unchangeable or how kinship may be something that is not pre-given but that is shaped through engagement 'in the ordinary, everyday activities of family life' (2004: 7). This offers an interesting lens to explore belonging in social reintegration as the identity of the young mother and her child may have been impacted upon by her time in the bush. There may be multiple ways in which war infuses the relational space between the family of origin and formerly associated young mother-child dyad, in which the 'natural order of things' ceases to be natural and has now to be negotiated. When CAAFAG young mothers come back with children, they are not automatically claimed as 'daughter' by the family and, in some cases, are rejected. In fact, the young women in our study experienced a full continuum from full and warm welcomes to abandonment and rejection. The return of a daughter with a baby or children was recounted as an emotional event filled with answered or unanswered questions or imaginings. In a separate study in Northern Uganda, elders talked about the abuses of girls during war such as 'being taken outside and slept with in the bush', thereby violating cultural taboos and positioning girls as external to and outside of cultural norms associated with women, as daughters and wives (Shanahan and Veale 2011: 121). Across the three countries, some CAAFAG young mothers experienced rejection by their biological family on return, as is captured in the following example:

> Young mother (Sierra Leone): I am Fatuma and sometime back in 2000 the rebels captured me. I went to the bush I stayed there for 4 years.[3] I have 2 children and the person I married was killed. One day I escaped and came back home. Now in Freetown everyone calls me a rebel, and they don't understand. People are always beating my children. There are only two people in this community who help me with my problems. My mother is very old and weak but when I go to her she helps me and takes care of my children. My father has rejected me and does not accept my children.

The most common response to young women seems to have been conditional acceptance. Many reported that their families welcomed them back and were glad to see that they were alive but the daily realities of extreme privation meant that a daughter returning with children of her own was an added responsibility within the family economy. Another young mother described how her mother said she could either care for her daughter or for her child but did not have the resources to care for them both:

> I have two children, five years and four years. My mother says I won't support you and at the same time support your children, you must choose one. I appeal to her to support my children first. (Liberia)

> (They tell me) you and your child are eating all our food. (Sierra Leone)

3 All names have been changed to pseudonyms.

Biological relatedness, that is, being claimed as a daughter and as a grandchild may happen, but it is not a given. For many of the children of young mothers, their claim to paternal kinship – and thereby extended family support – was weakened in cases of having an unknown father or where no formal or traditional marriage had taken place, no dowry, no compensation or other such cultural symbols that gave entitlement to paternity. On the maternal side, we found relatedness was more readily acknowledged and in some cases was strong but in other cases, it was tenuous at this initial point of return.

Across the PAR sites in three study countries, the economic marginality of CAAFAG and other vulnerable young mothers in the study, was a shared experience, and this manifested in the poor health status of their children. In spite of the challenges faced, overall it also seemed that young mothers were engaged with and loved their children. A key, repeated motivation for engaging in the study was to secure a better future not just for themselves, but even more so, for their children. A young mother in Northern Uganda noted: 'What I wanted from this project was to earn income to help my children [...] send my child to school'. This refrain was echoed across the other sites in the three countries.

It might be tempting to see enhanced income-generation capacity as a key transformational element that facilitated young mothers to address the needs of their children. However, an analysis of the study process indicates moments of transformation happened at multiple levels. Rather than an income-generation or a microcredit project, this was a community-based, collective process that involved exchanges of information, resources, and support, firstly, within the girls' groups and their families, and then through feedback loops, to others in the community including husbands and boyfriends. Bonds of 'relatedness' were constructed, as Carsten notes, through everyday activities of engaging, sharing stories, giving and receiving support. We can describe this strengthening of relatedness at different levels: within the young mother-child dyad, between the young mother and her intimate relationships (parents, boyfriends or husbands), and between the grandchild-grandparents.

A common observation by family and community members was that as young mothers engaged with their group processes and their social actions, they were 'fussing' less (community member, Sierra Leone) and their minds became 'more settled' (Northern Uganda). Recent developmental and neuropsychological theory would suggest that such maternal 'calming' would have important implications for babies and young children (Shore 2008). Modern attachment theory shows how infant development is highly relational and neuro-behavioural organization and emotions are initially regulated by the caregiver externally and then become transformed into 'internal' regulatory capacities. The more the regulatory capacities of the caregiver are appropriate and attuned to the needs of self and then other (baby), the more growth-facilitating is the relationship as over time the young child becomes increasingly self-regulatory (Shore 2008). For the young mothers, we saw that if their babies and young children were healthier, cried less often and became more emotionally regulated, mothers were more likely to experience themselves as good mothers. In terms of attachment theory, this would likely strengthen their own internal working model as an effective and nurturing mother which in turn would further support their children's early development. As one agency staff member observed: 'The socialization that happened through the PAR was transmitted to their children'.

Changes in the wellbeing of the young mother created change in other parts of the family system. As the capacity of girl mothers to care for their children was enhanced, transformations occurred within the atmosphere of the family home. Enhanced functioning in the young mother-child dyad had ripple effects on other relationships in interesting, even profound ways:

> GRANDMOTHER A: Now there is a difference since before. She can buy clothes for the baby. The baby used to remain dirty and is now well-dressed. She can go to the health center, buy drugs, she has a business, hygiene is well-kept, she knows preventative measures such as she has learnt about the care of her baby, the best type of food, and now the baby is less sickly.

> GRANDMOTHER B: There is a difference now, she did not know what kind of food was good for the child, she has learnt a lot and it's good for the babies for growing. The child looks healthy.

GRANDMOTHER C: There is no more tension about the baby like before – my daughter can know how to take care of her.

INTERVIEWER (AV): Has it changed the atmosphere in the family?

GRANDFATHER: Development will come to their family as the girl has seen new things by coming to the group. I see my grandchild playing, which means that the child is healthy, well, growing, now I no longer have to buy small things for the baby, Ayot (his daughter) she even buys for the family. No one blames each other like before. Now I can attend to the other children. (Focus group discussion with family members of participants, Northern Uganda)

The everyday activities by young mothers of feeding, cleaning, dressing and generally caring for their children effectively, what Carsten (2004: 7) refers to as 'the everyday activities of family life', arguably strengthened relatedness between the grandparents and their children so rather than the grandchild being a source of tension between members of the household, grandparents were happy to see their grandchild as healthy, well-cared for and playing as is appropriate for a young child. Previously weak bonds of kinship were arguably re-constructed and enhanced through these social practices. In their responses, there is an evident sense of pride in their daughter and grandchildren as daughters take on roles and identities of being good mothers, which is a valued and respected social role. Furthermore, they maintained that daughters had a greater capacity to engage in reciprocal relationships of care, both material and emotional – a quality which has been noted to help create relatedness (Nyambedha 2008). Engagement in the different social actions of the study – community dramas, individual and group livelihoods, community cleaning, home visits, support and encouragement of other vulnerable young mothers – facilitated a developmental transition, not (only) as an internal change but as a cultural community event as they changed position from dependents of their family members, with further dependents of their own, to mothers who have the capacity and resources to be responsible for their child. The ability to be responsible, to be independent, to give as well as receive support are the practices of assuming adult status. These qualities were also evidenced in changing relations with community members:

> One way I have learned about being integrated is the fact that I now have the confidence to leave my children at home, in my community. I had the fear that I would not be able to leave them. My mother is old and can't really take care of them. I know my community members will help her take care of them. (Sierra Leone)

> Before the project, the girl mothers' children were seen as different, but now they're seen as positive, and other members allow their children to befriend them. (Liberia)

Relationships between the children and the husbands or boyfriends of their mothers were more complex. Among all participants, 33 per cent reported that their boyfriend or husband was supportive of them and their children while 16.2 per cent said he was sometimes supportive and 50.6 per cent said he was not supportive. The number of young mothers who said their boyfriend/husband was not supportive was significantly higher in Uganda than the other two countries. This may be because of the younger age of participants and that more study participants lived with family members instead of boyfriends or husbands compared to Liberia and Sierra Leone. Also, the conflict in Uganda was still ongoing at the time of the study, and 'rebel' fathers may have remained in the bush, or were unknown or lived elsewhere. This is an important area for further research.

Conclusion

Effective early development programmes are those which interact with the biological (health), familial and community systems in which children and their mothers are embedded. This chapter has outlined a community-based participatory action research intervention that aimed to engage formerly associated young mothers and other vulnerable young mothers in their communities in meaningful participation to address the challenges they faced in their lives. Participatory evaluation highlighted that over 80 per cent of young mothers judged that the self-assessed health of their children had improved since they joined the study, that they could take better care of their children, and that their children were more loved by their families and by the communities. Approximately 15 per cent of young mothers reported that their circumstances on the above indicators had not changed substantially, in their opinion. This is also an important finding as it highlights that a cohort of young mothers and their children continue to be vulnerable. Ethnographic observations in Northern Uganda indicate that young mothers who were particularly isolated at the start of the project, who were experiencing very significant suffering, trauma or ill health, or who had difficulty utilizing the material resources offered through their groups fared less well. Advisory group members and field staff as well as peer group members were available to support young mothers. For those who failed to experience changes in their life circumstances, the support given through the study may have been insufficient for their complex needs. Overall, however, this analysis demonstrates how an intervention that empowered young mothers to develop social actions that addressed their priorities and were supported by communities mediated the wellbeing of their children in important ways. A key emergent finding is the inter-relatedness of change in one domain of life (community admiration, livelihoods, wellbeing, capacity to support) which stimulated transformations in family relationships, reciprocal support, mutual respect and community networks.

References

Annan, J., Blattman, C., Carlson, K., and Mazurana, D. (2008). *The State of Female Youth in Northern Uganda: Findings from the survey of war-affected youth – phase II*. USA: Feinstein International Center. <http://chrisblattman.com/documents/policy/sway/SWAY.Phase2.FinalReport.pdf> accessed 28 November 2012.

Apio, E. (2008). *Bearing the Burden of Blame – the Children Born of the Lord's Resistance Army, Northern Uganda*. London: Coalition to Stop the Use of Child Soldiers. <http:/www.child-soldier.org/psychosocial_report_reader.php?id=301 accessed> 28 November 2012.

Baldi, S., and MacKenzie, M. (2007). 'Silent Identities: Children born of war in Sierra Leone'. In R. Carpenter (ed.), *Born of War: Protecting children of sexual abuse survivors in conflict zones*, pp. 78–93. Bloomfield, CT: Kumarian Press.

Betancourt, T., Agnew-Blais, J., Gilman, S., and Ellis, B. (2010). 'Past Horrors, Present Struggles: The role of stigma in the association between war experiences and psychosocial adjustment among former child soldiers in Sierra Leone', *Social Science and Medicine*, 701 (1), 17–26.

Betancourt, T., Borisova, I., de la Soudiere, M., and Williamson, J. (2011). 'Sierra Leone's Child Soldiers: War exposures and mental health problems by gender', *Journal of Adolescent Health*, 49 (1), 21–8.

Boothby, N., Crawford, J., and Halperin, J. (2006). 'Mozambique Child Soldier Life Outcome Study: Lessons learned in rehabilitation and reintegration efforts', *Global Public Health*, 1 (1), 87–107.

Brett, R., and Specht, I. (2004). *Young Soldiers: Why they choose to fight*. Boulder, CO: Lynne Rienner Publishers.

Burman, E., and McKay, S. (2007). 'Marginalization of Girl Mothers during Reintegration from Armed Groups in Sierra Leone', *International Nursing Review*, 54 (4), 316–23.

Carlson, K., and Mazurana, D. (2008). *Forced Marriage within the Lord's Resistance Army, Uganda*. USA: Feinstein International Center. <https://wikis.uit.tufts.edu/confluence/download/attachments/14553676/Forced+Marriage+within+the+LRA.pdf?version=1> accessed 28 November 2012.

Carsten, J. (2000). *Cultures of Relatedness: New Approaches to the Study of Kinship*. Cambridge: Cambridge University Press.

Carsten, J. (2004). *After Kinship*. Cambridge: Cambridge University Press.

De Berry, J. (2004). 'The Sexual Vulnerability of Adolescent Girls during Civil War in Teso, Uganda'. In J. Boyden and J. de Berry (eds), *Children and Youth on the Front Line: Ethnography, armed conflict and displacement*, pp. 45–62. Oxford: Berghahn Books.

Engle, P., Black, M., Behrman, J., Cabral de Mello, M., Kapiriri, L., Martorell, R., and Young, M. E. (2007). 'The International Child Development Steering Group. Strategies to Avoid the Loss of Developmental Potential in more than 200 Million Children in the Developing World'. *The Lancet*, 369 (9557), 229–42.

Esaku, S., and Boyer, R. (2009). *Ugandan Child Mothers Get a Second Chance*. Kampala: World Vision. <http://www.worldvision.org/news.nsf/news/child-mother-education-200907-enews> accessed 28 November 2012.

Honwana, A. (2006). *Child Soldiers in Africa*. Philadelphia: University of Pennsylvania Press.

Jareg, E. (undated). *Girls Associated with Armed Groups*. Norway: Save the Children Norway.

Machel, G. (2001). *The Impact of War on Children*. London: Hurst and Company.

Mbekenga, C., Pembe, A., Christensson, K., Darj, E., and Olsson, P. (2011). 'Informal Support to First-Parents after Childbirth: A qualitative study of low-income suburbs of Dar es Salaam, Tanzania', *BMC Pregnancy and Childbirth*, 11, 98.

McKay, S., and Mazurana, D. (2004). *Where are the Girls? Girls in Fighting Forces in Northern Uganda, Sierra Leone and Mozambique*. Montreal: International Centre for Human Rights and Democratic Development.

McKay, S., Veale, A., Worthen, M., and Wessells, M. (2010). *Community-Based Reintegration of War-Affected Young Mothers: Participatory Action Research (PAR) in Liberia, Sierra Leone and Northern Uganda*. <http://www.uwyo.edu/girlmotherspar/> accessed 28 November 2012.

McKay, S., Veale, A., Worthen, M., and Wessells, M. (2011). 'Building Meaningful Participation in Reintegration Among War-Affected Young Mothers in Liberia, Sierra Leone and Northern Uganda', *Intervention*, 9 (2), 108–24.

Nyambedha, E. (2008). 'Sharing Food: Grandmothers and the Children of Today in Western Kenya'. In E. Alber, S. van der Geest, and S. White (eds), *Generations in Africa: Connections and contrasts*, pp. 91–114. Münster: Lit Verlag.

Okunola, R., and Ikuomola, A. (2010). 'Child Labour in Fostering Practices. A Study of Surulere Local Government Area Lagos State, Nigeria', *The Social Sciences*, 5, 493–506.

Phan, P., Vinck, P., and Stover, E. (2009). 'Returning Home: Forced conscription, reintegration, and mental health status of former abductees of the Lord's Resistance Army in Northern Uganda', *BMC Psychiatry*, 9, 23–37.

Robinson, M., and McKay, S. (2005). *A Conference on Girl Mothers in Fighting Forces and Their Post-War Reintegration in Southern and Western Africa*. Bellagio, 12–18 April 2005.

Save the Children (2004). *No Place like Home: Children's experiences of reintegration in the Kailahun District of Sierra Leone*. United Kingdom: Save the Children.

Shanahan, F., and Veale, A. (2010). 'The Girl is the Core of Life: Violence and the sacred in social reintegration, Northern Uganda'. In B. Maeland (ed.), *Culture, Religion and the Reintegration of Former Child Soldiers in Northern Uganda*, pp. 115–31. New York: Peter Lang.

Shore, J., and Shore, A. (2008). 'Modern Attachment Theory: The central role of affect regulation in development and treatment', *Clinical Social Work Journal*, 36 (9), 9–20.

Twum-Danso, I. (2003). *Africa's Young Soldiers: The co-option of childhood*. Pretoria: Institute of Security Studies. <http://www.iss.co.za/Pubs/monographs/No82/Content.html > accessed 28 November 2012.

United Nations (2002). *Women, Peace and Security*. New York: United Nations. <http://www.un.org/womenwatch/daw/public/eWPS.pdf> accessed 28 November 2012.

Veale, A., and Stavrou, A. (2007). 'Former Lord's Resistance Army Child Abductees: Exploration of identity in reintegration and reconciliation', *Peace and Conflict: Journal of Peace Psychology*, 13(3), 273–92.

Wessells, M. (2006). *Child Soldiers: From violence to protection*. Cambridge, MA: Harvard University Press.

Worthen, M., McKay, S., Veale, A., and Wessells, M. (2011). 'Gender-Based Insecurity and Opportunities for Peace: Supporting the reintegration of young war-affected mothers', *Disarmament Forum*, 3, 35–6.

UNA MURRAY

3 Child Labour: A Complex Problem Requiring 'Joined Up' Responses

Introduction

Out of the estimated 1.586 billion children in the world, at least 215 million children are under pressure to provide for their own or their family's livelihood from a very early age. As a result many such children have to forgo chances of education. While an estimated 306 million children are engaged in 'work', 215 million are described as being engaged in 'child labour'. This is because 'they are either under the minimum age for work, or above that age and engaged in work that poses a threat to their health, safety or morals, or are subject to conditions of forced labour' (ILO 2010: 7).[1]

This chapter provides an overview of the problem of child labour. The mainstream view is that child labour is unacceptable and must be abolished, as it deprives children of their childhood, and condemns communities into cycles of poverty (Hindman 2009). The international policy framework condemns child labour, and seeks to immediately eliminate the worst forms of child labour. A competing viewpoint maintains that as long as children's labour contribution is essential for survival, rather than seeking to abolish child labour, the emphasis should be on supporting child labourers. Dissension with regard to definitions of 'child labour' and notions of 'childhood' is important in this evolving debate, as well as what is defined as 'hazardous work' for children. Children's rights are also an important consideration, particularly when work is juxtaposed against the right to a basic education. Although the majority and legal framework viewpoint is

1 This figure refers to children aged five to seventeen years.

against child labour, there are also different strands within this viewpoint (i.e. phasing out child labour; the relative importance of education; the need for poverty reduction efforts).

Where are children working?

Children are found working in domestic labour, home based enterprises or workshops, street selling, shoe shining, scavenging rubbish, quarrying, fishing, in underage prostitution, and make up a large proportion of the agricultural workforce. Working children everywhere tend to be located in the informal sector.

The International Labour Organization (ILO) estimates that 60 per cent of all child labourers are found in the agricultural sector, with a quarter in services, 7 per cent in industry, and with over another 7 per cent not specified. Only one in five children globally are in paid employment, the majority of children are unpaid or unpaid family workers.

About 5.7 million children worldwide are estimated to be in forced and bonded labour (ILO 2005). Bonded child labour occurs when labour is demanded as a means of repayment for a loan and individuals become trapped into working for no pay (ILO 2005). Findings from a study on bonded labour of the Kamaiya system in Nepal indicate that children can begin work as early as four in the morning and finish at seven in the evening, with 70 per cent in this sample, working over twelve hours per day, and one third suffering accidents at work (Sharma et al. 2001). Several Indian reports have highlighted the use of bonded girls for cottonseed production (ICAC 2008).

Forced labour is work extracted under the menace of a penalty and undertaken involuntarily (ILO 2005: 5). Sometimes a child's work is included within the forced labour provided by the family as a whole. Many children are forced into prostitution and trafficked. Horrendous trafficking of children takes place for the sexual gratification of adults. Trafficking also takes place for other types of work, for example for cocoa production in West Africa (Manzo 2005).

What do we mean by 'child labour'?

Apart from the most extreme forms of abuse (such as bonded labour, trafficking), having precise terminology and definitions regarding other forms of child labour is difficult. This is because what exactly constitutes child labour is not that easy to identify and measure. The ILO states that the term 'child labour' can be defined as work that deprives children of their childhood, their potential and their dignity, and that is harmful to physical and mental development.[2] The ILO further states that child labour refers to work that is mentally, physically, socially or morally dangerous and harmful to children; and interferes with their schooling by:

> depriving them of the opportunity to attend school;
> obliging them to leave school prematurely; or
> requiring them to attempt to combine school attendance with excessively long and heavy work.[3]

On the other hand, UNICEF defines child labour as work that exceeds a minimum number of hours, depending on the age of a child and on the type of work (UNICEF, 2008).[4] A wide range of child labour studies may use different age references and numbers of hours worked.

An ILO Convention (No. 182) defines the worst forms of child labour, categorizing them into 'unconditional worst forms of child labour' and

2 The ILO refer to child labour amongst children aged between five and seventeen years. Article 1 in the UN Convention on the Rights of the Child refers to a child as below the age of eighteen years unless, under the law applicable to the child, majority is attained earlier. When childhood ends can range from between thirteen and twenty-one years, depending on culture. Indeed, social class, caste, gender rites, physical size, maturity, sexual activity and employment can be more important than age.

3 From ILO-IPEC webpage, <http://www.ilo.org/ipec/facts/lang--en/index.htm> accessed 6 November 2011.

4 UNICEF use the following indicators: Ages 5–11: At least one hour of economic work or twenty-eight hours of domestic work per week; Ages 12–14: At least fourteen hours of economic work or twenty-eight hours of domestic work per week; Ages 15–17: At least forty-three hours of economic or domestic work per week.

'hazardous work'. *Unconditional worst forms of child labour* include slavery, trafficking of children, debt bondage, use of children by armed forces, the prostitution of children, use of children for pornography, use of children for illicit activities and work which is likely to harm the health, safety or morals of children. *Hazardous child labour* is work in dangerous or unhealthy conditions that could result in a child being killed, or injured and/or made ill as a consequence of poor safety and health standards and working arrangements (ILO 2002: 9). Children are vulnerable to the same dangers faced by adult workers, but because children are still growing, they can be affected by different workplace hazards and risks. For example, younger tissues and organs can be more vulnerable to chemicals or heavy weights. Hazards and injuries that do not show up immediately in the workplace are easily ignored, yet may manifest as health or psychological problems later in life. Child labour hazards are defined by the national authorities (i.e. the government, trade unions and employers' organizations), who decide what is included on the national hazardous list for children above or below designated ages (ILO 2011).[5]

The minimum age for employment in most countries is usually around fourteen or fifteen years. However, fifteen- to seventeen-year-olds are classified as child labourers if they are in hazardous work. Global estimates indicate that over half of the 215 million child labourers are in hazardous work.[6] For the age group five to fourteen years, 153 million are classified as being in child labour, and about one third of those in hazardous work.[7] For the age group fifteen to seventeen years (legally allowed to work, so long as it is not hazardous), 62 million are in hazardous work and thus classified as child labourers (ILO 2010).

'Child work' is the term often used for work that is considered suitable for children in comparison to 'child labour', which is considered unsuitable or dangerous. Acceptable work for children is work that does not affect children's health, morals, or personal development, or interfere with

5 For example, some forms of agriculture work may or may not be nationally identified as a type of work that falls within the category of 'hazardous work' as outlined in the ILO International Convention (182) on the Worst Forms of Child Labour.

6 115 million.

7 53 million.

schooling – for example, helping parents on a family farm outside school hours or during school holidays. Such work contributes to children's development and helps families.

Sometimes acceptable work can deteriorate into child labour depending on the child's age, the type of work performed, the conditions under which it is performed, the objectives of the person giving the work, and whether the work is supervised by an adult or not (ILO-IPEC 2005). The question of whether to include children working in agriculture as child labourers remains confused as many view agricultural tasks as non-harmful. Yet, it can deteriorate into child labour when it interferes with schooling or when children develop musculoskeletal problems, are exposed to toxic substances, or deprived of sleep because of work, or work under forced conditions and so on. About two-thirds of children in hazardous work in sub-Saharan Africa are unpaid family workers (ILO 2010).

A key concern is how child labour is defined, including what are deemed hazardous tasks for children. Another concern has been the previous neglect of domestic work in child labour measurements. Domestic chores take many hours in countries where children must help with water and fuel collection and can affect schooling (Kane 2004; Kolomiyets 2004; Birner and Horowitz 2008; Cook 2008). It is likely that estimates of girls working are under-reported because of unclear distinctions between household chores and domestic work in third party households.

Another issue is that many children work sporadically or during particular seasons (harvesting months or tourist seasons). Intermittent employment of children means that standard employment measures (e.g. based on a single reference week) can miss important aspects of children's work. The intermittent nature of children's work has major significance for education provision.

Hence, defining child labour is complicated. It depends on whether or not particular forms of 'work' can be called 'child labour'; it depends on the child's age; the type and hours of work performed; the conditions under which it is performed; and the national hazardous work list. Whether child work is considered to be child labour or not varies from country to country, as well as among sectors within countries. The *worst forms of child labour* (such as bonded work, child soldiers, prostitution) are more easily identified as harmful, but these children are often concealed in society.

The international child labour framework

The international conventions dealing with child labour illustrate the progression of children's rights and standards with regard to children working (OHCHR 1989; Noguchi 2002). 193 countries have ratified the 1989 UN Convention on the Rights of the Child (CRC). Protecting children from economic exploitation and from performing any work that is likely to be hazardous, or interfere with the child's education, or is considered to be harmful to the child's health and physical, spiritual, moral or social development (Article 32), as well as the right to education (Article 28), are some of the rights set out in the CRC.[8]

The notion of setting a minimum age for work has existed since the first decade of the twentieth century (ILO 2011). 161 countries have ratified the ILO Convention 138 on Minimum Age of Workers (1973), implying that ratifying states must determine a minimum age for employment. This age should not be lower than the age at which compulsory schooling ends and it should not be less than fourteen or fifteen years. Regarding ILO Convention 182 on the Worst Forms of Child Labour (1999), there have been 174 ratifications. A new Convention on Domestic Work was agreed in June 2011, and a minimum age for domestic work will be set out by nation states that ratify it.[9]

Upon ratifying conventions, governments should take immediate steps to put into action what they have signed. Some countries have a national policy, which deals specifically with child labour elimination. Other countries develop an action plan for the elimination of the worst forms of child labour. Numerous programmes that have removed children from work have documented how children have reported that they are happier and

8 The African Charter on the Rights and Welfare of the Child adopted by the Organisation of African Unity (OAU) in 1990 also outlines issues around child labour in Article 15. At least forty-five of the fifty-three countries in Africa have ratified the Charter.

9 Convention 189 Domestic Workers Convention, 2011: <http://www.ilo.org/ilolex/cgi-lex/convde.pl?C189>.

better off not working (ILO 2007, Winrock International 2008). Yet, child labour still thrives in many regions in an unabated manner.

Legislation does not automatically ensure rights, and rights do not always translate into concrete benefits. For example, children quickly removed from the Bangladesh garment industry were reported to have ended up worse off than when they were working.[10] Many displaced child workers could not avail of education and ended up in jobs that were more hazardous and exploitative than garment production such as stone-crushing, street hustling, and prostitution (Myers 2001a; Hanson and Vandaele 2003; UNICEF 2007).

Critiques of definitions and terminology

A number of authors criticize international child labour policy instruments, questioning the abolitionist paradigm, their perceived North American-European ethnocentric origins and construction of children's rights (Myers 2001b; Bourdillon 2003; Hanson and Vandaele 2003). McKechnie and Hobbs (1999) indicate that we need to distinguish between 'good' and 'bad' work, and also whether children's work is consumption driven or occurs out of necessity. Eliminating the worst forms of child labour seems to be more acceptable than enforcing minimum ages for work.

There is confusion regarding the distinction between 'child labour' and 'child work', which in many languages is not obvious (Bourdillon 2006; Bhukuth 2008). Some international NGOs, such as Save the Children, prefer to use the term 'child work' to cover all forms of children's work. Accuracy in language is important, because it is the abuse of children that must be eliminated. Bourdillon (2003) defines abuse as work for long hours, low pay, health hazards at work, deprivation of sleep, education or

10 Because of a response to the proposed United States Harkin Bill banning the import of goods produced wholly or in part by child labour.

leisure. However, it can be argued that 'harmful' work can be interpreted in different ways. A child labour abuse in one culture may not be regarded as an abuse in another (Ajayi and Torimior 2004).

Other criticisms relate to the focus on the definition of 'childhood'. Issues such as whether 'childhood' is a social construct, or where childhood ends (somewhere between thirteen and twenty-one years) in different cultures are questioned (Woodhead 1999; Myers 2001a; Ennew 2002; Bourdillon 2003; Steinberg and Kincheloe 2004; Jones 2005; Hinton 2008). Hinton (2008) argues that particular notions of 'childhood' are alien to many communities, particularly when children take on social and economic roles, and where children are given more responsibility and obligations early on in life.

The importance of training as a socialization process in particular cultures is often stressed (Ajayi and Torimior 2004). For example, in Indian cultures and in many cultures in Africa, children earn responsibility early, and are exposed to risk early, learning essential life skills. Liebel (2003) argues that children's responsibilities are not strictly separated from playful forms of action. Yet, it is necessary to ask whether girls are inclined to be given less freedom or fewer opportunities for *playful forms of action* due to gender roles dictating repetitive household duties. Gender roles and birth order distinguish the type of work done by girls and boys, the number of hours worked as well as who gets an education (Burra 2001; Basu and Tzannatos 2002; Amorim et al. 2004; Cook 2008).

Evidently children do work. A question then arises as to whether children have a right to work, and if so, should they have rights to protection the same as other types of workers? On the other hand, would a right to work contradict their right to education?

Working children's social movements and organizations have emerged since the 1980s seeking improved working conditions and fair pay.[11] They demand the right to work for children in a protected environment and the right to participate in decision-making processes that relate to their work.

11 Child Workers in Asia is one such example. It is an umbrella organization which furthers the rights of working children and provides a support group for child workers in Asia: <http://www.cwa.tnet.co.th/about-cwa.html>.

With the focus on the elimination of child labour, children who are working illegally cannot discuss their rights. However, a few examples indicate that children's organizations have been recognized by local administrations. In Nicaragua, for example, Liebel (2003) reports that agreements between the Ministry of Health and the national police were forged for street children. In Peru, a contract with city authorities gave paid work under 'dignified conditions' to children (Liebel 2003).

'Mainstream' trade unions will not represent child workers, for obvious reasons – they are legally underage workers and they may accept reduced wages. Child labour is, in any case, mainly in the informal sector. Evidently children's organizations cannot solve the structural causes of exploitation, rather 'only' ease the difficulties children face and reduce risks a little. The threat of death or permanent injury hangs over many working children. The dilemma is whether a right to work is in the 'best interest of the child' in the long run, or violates a child's right to education. It is plausible that energy and resources may be better focused on realizing rights to education rather than the right to work.

The right to education

The Universal Declaration on Human Rights, in Article 26, states that everyone has the right to education.[12] Education is not something children or families should be grateful for, but it is their right to at least complete a full course of primary school. Many of the strongest proponents of children's right to work do not stress the potential of education to be in the long-term best interest of the child. This may be due to the quality of education in many countries (Guarcello et al. 2008). When guardians do not expect children to learn much in school they can decide that 'informal' education through work experience is the better option.

12 The UDHR is available at: <http://www.un.org/en/documents/udhr/index.shtml>.

Child labour and education are linked in many ways, with some children reporting they work to pay for education for themselves or their siblings; and other children being unable to attend school because of work. But does child labour hinder future employment opportunities, or build skills? Obviously it depends on the kind of work. Harriss-White (2010) highlights the strong correlation between illiteracy and casual contracts. Casual contracts, over a life cycle, in turn forfeit rights to social security. It is well documented that a lack of education perpetuates cycles of poverty. Without an education, individuals are less empowered to voice their views politically and realize other rights later in life.

Many studies asked children themselves their views on schooling and working. A study of 350 girls in Maiduguri, Nigeria, found that 89 per cent of the respondents would like to go to school (79 per cent were not attending school) (Audu et al. 2009). Tabassum and Baig's (2002) study in Pakistan revealed that 79 per cent of working children did not like to work. In India, 94 per cent of working children in one study preferred to be able to attend school (Mathews et al. 2003).

A myriad of factors affect education quality and attendance. Improving education provision is often a central strategy to reduce child labour. When education is compulsory, free and of good quality, it can greatly help to reduce child labour. Many programmes have documented what has worked to prevent and eliminate child labour through education (see for example ILO 2007; Murray 2003; UNICEF 2007; Winrock International 2008; UNESCO 2009).[13] Good teaching staff, bridge courses for children lagging behind and cash transfers for school attendance have resulted in children remaining in education.

Accommodating work with school attendance is another strategy although such combinations can leave children too tired to learn, and they

13 For example, the CIRCLE project reached over 24,000 children who were withdrawn from or prevented from entering the workplace. Awareness of the importance of education and mobilizing many actors to improve and expand education infrastructure; skills training for older children; teacher training; use of community monitoring systems; developing bridging education options; and strengthening national institutions and policies on education and child labour were all important strategies.

lose interest (Heady 2003; Blanco and Hagemann 2008). When advocating for combining work with school, there must be clarity on the form of work. For instance, in agriculture, children may not be able to travel to both school and work. The seasonality of work is also an important factor, as are gender roles. The more hours that children work, the less likely they are to receive schooling (Blanco and Hagemann 2008).

In summary, the assertion of education rights implies responsibility and duties by duty bearers. Governments must implement policies and allocate resources to improve education provision, particularly in rural areas, and guardians have a duty to encourage or facilitate children's school attendance.

Supply and demand reasons for working children

The reasons behind child labour must be known before anything can be done about child labour. According to Salmon (2005) empirical studies have identified at least four types of supply factors:

> Child specific factors such as age, gender and the child's existing level of schooling, number and sex of siblings.
>
> Parental/guardian characteristic factors, such as the schooling of parents and the nature of their employment, whether regular, or irregular, formal or informal, agricultural or non-agricultural; the presence or absence of both parents, and whether the household is female- or male-headed. Children are less likely to work when parents are better educated.
>
> Poverty and wealth variables, such as whether land and livestock are owned.

Context specific factors such as the cost of schooling for the area, labour market opportunities, cultural norms and children's wage rates.

With respect to demand factors, the non-pecuniary characteristics of children make them attractive for work. Children are less aware of their rights; more easily exploited; considered less troublesome; more willing to take orders; and will do monotonous work without complaining (Levison 1996). Children are often preferred for technically simple tasks (Fyfe 1989, 2009). Children are perceived to have nimble fingers and a small physique which can bend and perform repetitive tasks. Children can pluck delicate jasmine flowers without breaking branches, or cross pollinate plants or weed small plants. Children undertaking domestic work free up adults' time to undertake economic or agricultural activities elsewhere.

Within the agricultural sector, where 60 percent of child labourers are located, context specific empirical studies indicate that poverty, although highly significant, is not the only supply/demand factor. Levy (1985) stresses the effect of mechanization, changing cropping patterns and farming profitability in reducing child labour in Egyptian agriculture. In Ethiopia the participation of children in economic activity increases with increasing wealth, to a certain comfort zone (to a maximum financial sum per month) before households are prepared to substitute with hired labour (Woldehanna et al. 2008).[14] In Himachal Pradesha and Uttaranchal states in India, a specific acreage of land (four acres) must be reached before there is a decline in child labour (Basu et al. 2010). Some studies suggest that child labour initially increases with economic growth, because of labour demands, but gradually decreases (Swaminathan 1998; Kambhampati and Rajan 2006). Children's work is closely linked to a mother's labour (Eldring et al. 2000). A study in Andhra Pradesh (India) indicated that a female agricultural labourer earns about forty rupees per day, and her child will add about twenty to thirty rupees per day (ICAC 2008: 56).[15]

14 Ethiopian Birr 100–300 or €4–€12.

15 40 rupees = €0.57.

Tackling child labour

Some consider that child labour should be progressively eliminated (Heady 2003; Tabatabai 2003; Betcherman et al. 2005), while others believe that child labour is essential to survival in many regions of the world (Bourdillon 2006; Hesketh et al. 2006) and that children have the 'right' to work. Some organizations stress trade boycotts for products that were made with children's labour, while others turn to historic evidence from industrialized economies as to how child labour gradually decreased. Views range from those who consider child labour as unacceptable and something that must be abolished, to views that highlight children's economic contribution as essential for survival. Many argue that the absence of child labour is a luxury that a poor country cannot yet afford, particularly in subsistence agriculture, and that to prohibit it is to prevent the overall economic growth necessary to eventually relieve a society of the need for child labour.

Evidently education can broaden children's minds and their opportunities for the future. Yet, such an argument assumes that education is neither indoctrinating nor intimidating and employment opportunities are available. Sending all children to school will decrease a family income. Yet, arguments around the lost income of children's work sometimes neglect to stress that only one in five children are in paid employment, the majority are unpaid family workers.

With economic growth, child labour does not necessarily automatically decrease. Indeed, child labour is still evident in industrialized countries such as amongst migrant families who harvest crops in North America and Europe (White 1994; McKechnie and Hobbs 1999; Fyfe 2009) and the sexual exploitation of children is still rampant worldwide. While different forms of child labour may wane, others can persist.

Arguments around children's rights and culture raise the question of how to develop approaches that fulfil universal concepts of human rights and children's rights but do not embrace cultural relativism. Can there be a more culturally inclusive and flexible formulation of children's rights standards? Whether global policies on children's rights can be adapted to local conditions is challenging conceptually as well as in terms of implementation.

Clearly, due to poverty, many children have no other choice than to work. Thus, any banning of child labour must be accompanied by poverty alleviation mechanisms. The fact that the majority of children exploited are in the informal sector requires further analysis in terms of approaches to tackle child labour (and also the relevance and cost/benefit of child labour free product initiatives). Given the relatively high numbers of children described as child labourers in agriculture (60 per cent of 215 million children), the sector has received relatively less attention.

All the above indicate that more joined-up thinking is required to respond to child labour anomalies and incongruities. As far back as the 1980s there have been calls for integrated approaches to address child labour (Beguele and Boyden 1988; Jensen 2001; Masum 2002; Murray 2003; Tabatabai 2003). Statements and guidance of inter-governmental development bodies advocate for integrated type approaches for combating child labour.[16] Multi-faceted interventions including the adoption of poverty reduction strategies; the introduction of labour-saving technologies for agricultural production; improvements in access to and the quality of education; community or social awareness raising; the adoption of child labour legislation and financial incentives and food for school programmes. In some cases, combining work and school can be possible as long as certain conditions are met.

National governments are responsible for improving coherence of their labour legislation, and for its enforcement as well as for improving access to, and the quality of, education (which is a human right for all children). Jones et al. (2007) recommend that there should be child sensitive budget analysis and monitoring initiatives, so that there is an adequate funding focus for child poverty. From field programme experiences (particularly from the ILO Child Labour Programme, IPEC), there is a strong awareness that prevention of child labour is preferable, and more efficient, than post-hoc approaches to treat the symptoms (ILO 2006: 53).

16 For example ILO-IPEC, the OECD, and international movements such as the 'Global March against Child Labour' also call for integrated responses to child labour.

Conclusion

Currently, divergent views on the issue of child labour are clearly evident. The distinction between child labour and child work causes confusion rather than clarity and is difficult to translate into other languages. The intermittent employment of children is often not measured and whether certain activities gradually digress into child labour is not always evident. All institutions, policy stakeholders and communities must be clear with regard to what 'the rights of the child' actually means and understand possible contradictions that can emerge, for example, the right to work versus the right to education. The right to education for all children seems to be a more acceptable policy measure than banning children from working, although how child labourers can enjoy such a right is not always clearly articulated. Some view economic development as being the key driving force towards child labour elimination, as opposed to a legislative top-down approach to remedying the problem. Yet, child labour does not immediately decrease with economic growth.

However, most individuals and organizations agree that the 'worst' forms of child labour are unacceptable (prostitution, slavery, child soldiers) and agree with goals to reduce such abhorrent forms of child labour. Although many countries have legally agreed to implement children's rights agendas, policy actors and guardians may not share prescriptions of norms around children working, nor be convinced that it is a desirable goal. Legislation is difficult to implement in the informal sector, unless those in the informal sector are fully on board. Rules, physical and material conditions affect the outcome of a policy measure. A complexity of variables (often linked to poverty) result in children working rather than attending school. Child labour mitigation requires a child focused context specific response, which also respects the rights of the child. More examples and evidence of how 'good' intentions for children actually get translated into action on the ground in an integrated manner are required.

References

Ajayi, A. O., and Torimior, D. O. (2004). 'Perspectives on Child Abuse and Labour: Global ethical ideals versus African cultural realities', *Early Child Development and Care*, 174 (2), 183–91.

Amorim, A., Murray, U., and Bland, J. (eds) (2004). *Girl Child Labour in Agriculture, Domestic Work and Sexual Exploitation: Rapid assessments on the cases of the Philippines, Ghana and Ecuador*. Geneva: ILO IPEC.

Audu, B., Geidam, A., and Jarma, H. (2009). 'Child Labor and Sexual Assault among Girls in Maiduguri, Nigeria', *International Journal of Gynecology & Obstetrics*, 104 (1), 64–7.

Basu, K., and Tzannatos, Z. (2002). 'The Global Child Labor Problem: What do we know and what can we do?', *World Bank Economic Review*, 17 (2), 147–73.

Basu, K., Das, S., and Bhaskar, D. (2010). 'Child Labor and Household Wealth: Theory and empirical evidence of an inverted-U', *Journal of Development Economics*, 91 (1), 8–14.

Beguele, A., and Boyden, J. (eds) (1988). *Combating Child Labour.* Geneva: ILO.

Betcherman, G., Fares, J., Luinstra, A., and Prouty, R. (2005). 'Child Labor, Education, and Children's Rights'. In P. Alston and M. Robinson (eds) *Human Rights and Development: Towards Mutual Reinforcement*, pp. 173–200. Oxford: Oxford University Press.

Bhukuth, A. (2008). 'Defining Child Labour: A controversial debate', *Development in Practice*, 18 (3), 385–94.

Birner, R., and Horowitz, L. (2008). 'Gender and Agricultural Livelihoods: Strengthening governance module overview'. In World Bank (2008) *Gender in Agricultural Livelihoods Sourcebook*, pp. 23–35. Washington: World Bank.

Blanco Allais, F., and Hagemann, F. (2008). 'Child Labour and Education: Evidence from SIMPOC surveys'. *Working Paper*. IPEC Statistical Information and Monitoring Programme on Child Labour (SIMPOC), Geneva: ILO.

Bourdillon, M. (2003). 'Author response to Reviews of "Earning a life"', *Children, Youth and Environments*, 13 (1). <http://www.colorado.edu/journals/cye/13_2/responses/BourdillonResponse.htm> accessed 20 October 2012.

Bourdillon, M. (2006). 'Children and Work: A review of current literature and debates', *Development and Change*, 37 (6), 1201–26.

Burra, N. (2001). 'Cultural Stereotypes and Household Behaviour: Girl child labour in India', *Economic and Political Weekly*, 36 (5–6), 483–8.

Cook, K. (2008). 'Gender Issues in Agricultural Labor'. In World Bank (2008) *Gender in Agriculture Sourcebook*. Washington: The World Bank, FAO and IFAD.

Eldring, L., Nakanyane, S., and Tshoaedi, M. (2000). 'Child Labour in the Tobacco Growing Sector in Africa'. Report prepared for IUF/ITGA/BAT conference on the elimination of child labour, October 2000. Fafo Institute for Applied Social Science – paper.

Ennew, J. (2002). 'Outside Childhood: Street children's rights'. In B. Franklin (ed.), *The New Handbook of Children's Rights: Comparative Policy and Practice*, pp. 388–403. London and New York: Routledge.

Fyfe, A. (1989). *Child Labor.* Cambridge: Polity Press.

Fyfe, A. (2009). 'Worst Forms of Child Labour: Agriculture'. In H. Hindman (ed.), *The World of Child Labor: An historical and regional survey*, pp. 82–5. USA: Sharpe. Inc.

Grisewood, N., Brand, S., and Ruiz, H. (2008). *Best Practices in Preventing and Eliminating Child Labour through Education.* Arlington: Winrock International.

Guarcello, L., Lyon, S., and Rosati, F. (2008). 'Child Labour and Education for All: An issue paper', *Journal of the History of Childhood and Youth*, 1 (2), 254–66.

Hanson, K., and Vandaele, A. (2003). 'Working Children and International Labour Law: A critical analysis', *International Journal of Children's Rights*, 11 (1), 73–146.

Harriss-White, B. (2010). 'Work and Wellbeing in Informal Economies: The regulative roles of institutions of identity and the State', *World Development*, 38 (2), 170–83.

Heady, C. (2003). 'The Effect of Child Labor on Learning Achievement', *World Development*, 31 (2), 385–98.

Hesketh, T., Gamlin J., and Woodhead, M. (2006). 'Policy in Child Labour', *Archives of Disease in Childhood*, 91 (9), 721–3.

Hindman, H. (2009). *The World of Child Labor: An historical and regional survey.* ME: Sharpe Inc.

Hinton, R. (2008). 'Children's Participation and Good Governance: Limitations of the theoretical literature. International development: attending to the political', *International Journal of Children's Rights*, 16 (3), 285–300.

ICAC (2008). 'Literature Review and Research Evaluation Relating to Social Impacts of Global Cotton Production for ICAC Expert Panel on Social, Environmental and Economic Performance of Cotton (SEEP)'. Prepared by Ergon for The International Cotton Advisory Committee, July 2008.

ILO (2002). *A Future Without Child Labour. Global report under the follow-up to the ILO Declaration on Fundamental Principles and Rights at Work 2002*. Geneva: ILO.

ILO (2005). *A Global Alliance Against Forced Labour*. Geneva: ILO.

ILO (2006). *Tackling Hazardous Child Labour In Agriculture: Guidance on Policy and Practice.* Geneva: ILO IPEC.

ILO (2007). *Consolidated Good Practices in Education and Child Labour.* (Nick Grisewood), Geneva: ILO.

ILO (2010). *Accelerating Action Against Child Labour. Global report under the follow-up to the ILO Declaration on Fundamental Principles and Rights at Work.* Geneva: ILO.

ILO (2011). *Children in Hazardous Work: What we know, what we need to do.* Geneva: ILO.

ILO-IPEC (2005). *Training Resource Pack on The Elimination of Hazardous Child Labour in Agriculture.* (Peter Hurst), Geneva: ILO.

Jensen, R. (2001). *Mainstreaming Gender into the International Program on Child Labor.* Geneva: ILO/IPEC.

Jones, G. (2005). 'Children and Development: Rights, globalisation and poverty', *Progress in Development Studies*, 5 (4), 336–42.

Jones, N., Vargas, R., and Villar, E. (2007). 'Conditional Cash Transfers in Peru: Tackling the multidimensionality of childhood poverty and vulnerability'. In A. Minujin (ed.), *Social Protection Initiatives for Families, Women and Children: An Analysis of Recent Experiences.* New York: New School and UNICEF.

Kambhampati, U., and Rajan, R. (2006). 'Economic Growth: A Panacea for Child Labour?' *World Development*, 34 (3), 426–45.

Kane, J. (2004). *Helping Hand or Shackled Lives? Understanding child domestic labour and responses to it.* Geneva: ILO-IPEC.

Kolomiyets, T. (2004). *Global Child Labour Data Review: A gender perspective.* Geneva: ILO-IPEC.

Levison, D. (1996). *Is Child Labour Really Necessary in India's Carpet Industry?* Employment Department, Geneva: International Labour Office.

Levy, V. (1985). 'Cropping Pattern, Mechanization, Child Labor, and Fertility Behavior in a Farming Economy: Rural Egypt', *Economic Development and Cultural Change*, 33 (4), 777–91.

Liebel, M. (2003). 'Working Children as Social Subjects: The Contribution of Working Children's Organizations to Social Transformations', *Childhood*, 10 (3), 265–85.

Manzo, K. (2005). 'Exploiting West Africa's Children: Trafficking, slavery and uneven development', *Area*, 37 (4), 393–401.

Masum, M. (2002). 'Eradication of Hazardous Child Labour in Bangladesh: The need for an integrated strategy', *International Journal of Children's Rights*, 10 (2), 233–68.

Mathews, R., Reis, C., and Lacopino, V. (2003). 'Child Labor: A matter of health and human rights', *The Journal of Ambulatory Care Management*, 26 (2), 181–2.

McKechnie, J., and Hobbs, S. (1999). 'Child Labour: The View from the North', *Childhood*, 6 (1), 89–100.

Murray, U. (2003). *Gender Mainstreaming in Actions Against Child Labour: Good practices*. Geneva: ILO.

Myers, W. (1999b). 'Child Workers in Asia', *CWA newsletter*, 15 (3).

Myers, W. (2001b). 'The Right Rights? Child Labor in a Globalizing World', *The Annals of the American Academy of Political and Social Science*, 575, 38–55.

Myers, W. (2001a). 'Focus on Human Rights Organisations. Child workers in Asia', *Asia-Pacific Journal on Human Rights and the Law*, 2 (2), 149–54.

Noguchi, Y. (2002). 'ILO Convention No. 182 on the Worst Forms of Child Labour and the Convention on the Rights of the Child', *International Journal of Children's Rights*, 10 (4), 355–69.

OHCHR (1989). *United Nations Convention on the Rights of the Child* (1989). <http://www2.ohchr.org/english/law/crc.htm> accessed 20 October 2012.

Salmon, C. (2005). 'Child Labor in Bangladesh: Are children the last economic resources of the household?', *Journal of Developing Societies*, 21 (1–2), 33–54.

Sharma, S., Basnyat, B., and Ganesh, G. (2001). *Nepal Bonded Labour Among Child Workers of the Kamaiya System: A rapid assessment*. National Labour Academy – Nepal, Geneva: ILO-IPEC.

Steinberg, S., and Kincheloe, J. (2004). *Kinderculture: The corporate construction of childhood*. Boulder CO: Westview Press Inc.

Swaminathan, M. (1998). 'Economic Growth and the Persistence of Child Labor: Evidence from an Indian city', *World Development*, 26 (8), 1513–28.

Tabassum, F., and Baig, L. (2002). 'Child Labour a Reality: Results from a study of a squatter settlement of Karachi', *The Journal of the Pakistan Medical Association*, 52 (11), 507–10.

Tabatabai, H. (2003). Mainstreaming Action against Child Labour in Development and Poverty Reduction Strategies. TBP-MAP (Paper 4–01). Geneva: ILO.

UNESCO (2009). *Overcoming Inequality: Why governance matters. Education For All Global Monitoring Report*. Oxford and Paris: UNESCO Publishing and Oxford University Press.

UNICEF (2007). *Making UNGEI Work. Lessons from four African countries*. United Nations Girls' Education Initiative (UNGEI) (Fay Chung), Nairobi: UNICEF Eastern and Southern Africa Regional Office, Educational Section: Nairobi.

UNICEF (2008). *The State of the World's Children 2008*. United Nations Children's Fund.

White, B. (1994). 'Children, Work and Child Labour: Changing responses to the employment of children', *Development and Change*, 25 (4), 849–78.

Woldehanna, T., Jones, N., and Tefera, B. (2008). 'The Invisibility of Children's Paid and Unpaid Work', *Childhood*, 15 (2), 177–201.
Woodhead, M. (1999). 'Combating Child Labour: Listen to what the children say', *Childhood*, 6 (1), 27–49.

SAMUEL OKYERE

4 An Assessment of the Impact of Hazardous Work on Children's Educational Attainment

Introduction

Education is deemed indispensable to development and this is in part why it is today presented as an alternative to children's work. The linkage between education and children's work was actually made centuries ago (Weiner 1990). Those favouring the regulation of children's work in factories, coal mines and other places in nineteenth-century Britain realized that existing control measures were rendered useless unless children were compelled to attend school. Indeed, as Weiner (1990) himself reflects, 'no country has successfully ended child labour without first making education compulsory. As long as children need not attend school, they will enter the labour force' (quoted in Bhat et al. 2010: 326).

It is perhaps in view of the above that education was cited as the desired outcome of the ILO's child labour elimination programmes when the organization was created by the 1919 Treaty of Versailles. As seen in Article 427 of the Treaty, one of the founding principles of the ILO is to seek 'the abolition of child labour and the imposition of such limitations on the labour of young persons as shall permit the continuation of their education and assure their proper physical development' (Treaty of Versailles 1919, Article 427). A significant step towards this ambition was ILO Convention Number 138 on the minimum age for admission to employment and work (Convention No. 138) in 1973.

The Convention aimed to harmonize the minimum age of employment with that of schooling (see Article 2, section 3). As such, it called for the exclusion of all children below age fifteen from paid work, asking that they attend school instead. However, this demand has been criticized due to its potentially adverse consequences for many children worldwide (Myers 2001; White 2002). On education specifically, Bourdillon et al. (2010) note the irony that when the Convention was created in 1973, educational institutions were non-existent, unaffordable and inaccessible to many of the children who were most affected; a situation which prevails even today. The Convention's potential implication for such children is therefore a no work no school situation.

Another outcome of Convention 138 and subsequent policy directives on children's work has been the creation of a perception that prohibited forms of work are necessarily antithetical to children's educational access. The ILO (2008) itself acknowledges the fact that many children have to work in order to be able to attend school. However, this point is either not stated clearly enough, or it is lost on many commentators. This is because, on the basis of the ILO's conventions and initiatives, there is widespread support for the view that as long as children are engaged in prohibited work, their educational attainment will at best suffer, or at worst be denied them entirely.

I aim to subject this assumption to critical scrutiny in this chapter. I concede that participation in prohibited work, and any other type of work perhaps, can have negative consequences for children's educational access. Nonetheless, drawing on the accounts of children working in artisanal gold mining, I trouble the conventional assumption. I highlight the fact that even occupations such as artisanal gold mining can have positive implications for children's educational attainment and their access to development opportunities. At the end, the chapter reiterates the argument that children's work is complex and therefore requires a case by case analysis when attempting to address it (Boyden et al. 1998, Panelli et al. 2007).

The chapter sets out its case by first reviewing the existing literature on the correlation between children's work and their educational attainment. The next section discusses the research which informs the chapter's arguments. I then present the children's accounts of their participation in artisanal gold mining work, and go on to show how this impacts on their access to education and other developmental opportunities. The final section discusses the presented evidence in connection with the conventional assumption and concludes the chapter.

Use of child or children in this section implies a person under the age of eighteen. The chapter uses child labour or child work interchangeably to refer to any form of work undertaken by a child. While it would be more convenient to do so, I do not distinguish between the two, as I share White's (2009: 11) disquiet about the binary of 'harmless "child work" and harmful "child labour"'. It is actually a contributory factor to the issue which this chapter sets out to problematize.

A review of the existing literature

Hindman (2009) notes that a fundamental argument against children's participation in prohibited engagements is that it robs them of their dignity, their childhood and their development. Partly underlying the notion of developmental deprivation is the view that their educational access is also blocked by their work (Anu 2000; Allais and Hageman 2008). In reality, many children actually rely on prohibited occupations to fund their education, as the ILO (2009) has acknowledged. Yet, this has done little to change the perception that education is absent from the lives of children in prohibited employments (Tzannatos 2003). Indeed, this belief is central to the idea of a child labour poverty trap which implies that because children from poor homes go out to work, they are unable to attend school or access other developmental opportunities (Emerson and Souza 2003).

As a consequence of the above, such children are said to grow up as uneducated and unskilled adults who have little or no prospects of employment and are thus trapped in poverty (Barham et al. 1995; Emerson and Shawn 2007). This point is forcefully reiterated by Harvey and Lauren (1994: ii) with their argument that 'child labour recycles poverty and hopelessness by turning today's generation of child labourers into tomorrow's sick, unemployed, uneducated and unproductive adults who are tragic in their own lives and a burdensome weight on their countries' hopes'. Thus, for Baland and Robinson (2003), child labour is clearly inefficient and its abolition will lead to economic benefits for the society due to the creation of a more educated, skilled and productive workforce.

Evidently, there exists consensus that deprivation of educational access or skills and qualifications are the main possible outcomes for children involved in prohibited work (Ray 2000; Dammert 2008). This is said to be especially true for those working in occupations such as artisanal gold mining (ILO 2011). Children in such occupations have 'no educational or future perspective' (ILO 2009: 12), as such, they are condemned to a harrowing present and hopeless future (UNICEF 2001: 11). There are of course other considerations which inform these assessments. These include health and safety concerns (Jennings 1999; Human Rights Watch 2011). For artisanal gold mining, in particular, there is also fear for children's morals because prostitution, drug abuse and lawlessness may be present at the sites where work takes place (ILO 2005).

Nevertheless, in Fyfe's (2005) work it remains clear that a significant part of the opposition to children's participation in prohibited work is based on concern for their educational attainment. It is certainly out of such concern that the World Bank, UNICEF, UNESCO, the ILO and other organizations have adopted a concerted approach to child labour abolition, the Millennium Development Goals on Education and the Education for All Campaign in recent times (ILO 2008).

In the view of Heady (2003), and Guarcello et al. (2008), these concerns are not without merit. Research carried out by the ILO (2003) with child miners in the Philippines established that almost a third of the children involved either quit school or had not attended at all because of their work. Drawing on evidence from Bangladesh, Ahmed (2011) has also shown that children's school attendance rates drop when they take up work. Likewise, Psacharopoulos' study (1997) in Latin America shows that children's entry into the labour market often led to a cessation of their schooling. The Latin America finding is also confirmed by Sedlacek et al. (2005) who argue in their own work that child labour impacts negatively on children's educational enrolment and their final outcomes.

In spite of the above, however, Fan (2004) has also provided evidence to show that the converse is also possible. Canagarajah and Coulombe's (1997) work is another alternative example. They firstly found that over a third of the working children they surveyed were actually attending school. They equally established that even in cases where working children eventually quit school, this was not necessarily due to their work. Rather, there were also on-going household issues such as economic distress at play. Cockburn's (2000) conclusion in his own study also suggests a similar occurrence for the phenomenon whereby children fail to continue with their education and remain in work.

The above also fit with a study by Cardoso and Verner (2006) who found that in urban areas in Brazil, extreme poverty, rather than work, accounted for the cessation of education among working children. Essentially, there are numerous other factors which need to be taken into account in attempts to explore the correlation between children's work and their education (Quayes et al. 2004). These include the quality or standard of education they are receiving, proximity of educational facilities, health considerations and shocks in the household such as the bereavement of parents and guardians.

The research context

The chapter is based on research conducted in 2010 for my PhD fieldwork. The ethnographic fieldwork aimed to seek and use the views of working children themselves to contribute to child labour discourses. The research setting was an artisanal gold mining site at Kenyasi, a rural district in the Ghana. Ethical approval for the study was provided by the University of Nottingham, where I did my PhD, and all ethical principles were adhered to. At all times during the study, I recognized that I had a duty of care to my research participants and that success of the study was ultimately going to rely on building a relationship of trust, honesty and respect with all involved.

I lived within the mining community for ninety days, walking to and from the mining site to the main town daily with workers. On several occasions, I slept on the mining site itself at night. A total of fifty-seven children generously provided information about their lives. All core child participants of the study were aged between fourteen and seventeen. Thirty of them were girls and twenty-seven boys. Twenty-four participants were from the local area, but the remaining participants had travelled independently from other parts of the country, particularly the North, to work at the mining site. This issue of children's independent migration is another topical issue which has been examined in detail by Hashim (2005) as well as Kwankye et al. (2007).

Data was collected primarily though unstructured interviews using Twi, a local dialect. These were later translated into the English language for analysis. Observation was also conducted as the children went about their work and other activities. Photo-elicitation was equally employed at various stages of the fieldwork. At the end, I met with each participant to confirm that they agreed with my understanding of the information they had given me and to seek clarification where gaps existed. Before leaving the site, I thanked the participants for their assistance by providing them with personal safety items, stationery and story books.

Children's work at the artisanal gold mining site

There were no third party recruiters or middle men involved in the recruitment of children into work at the artisanal gold mining site. This point is underlined below in the account of Ayesha (15), one of the participants:

> [W]e turn up in the morning and go door knocking [...] we move from one spot to the other to find out the sorts of work available and who the owner is. If we are interested, we ask the owner if they want to work with us for the day. When we finish, he pays us and we go our way. (24 August 2010)

Alternatively, in a manner similar to spot markets for labour, others congregate at places where people with work go to seek helping hands.

It is worth pointing out that the site was not operated by a company or individual. Its creation, the subject of a forthcoming paper by the author, was the result of a series of events which imposed poverty and destitution on those living in the area. The resulting artisanal gold mining site is, therefore, an economy of makeshifts; men, women and children who are all hustling to provide for themselves (Brace 2004). For waged labour particularly, the relationship between owners of work and those selling their labour power was certainly not that of employer and employee. Their situation was more comparable to a pre-capitalist mode of production.

Waged labour begins at eight in the morning and ends at four or five in the evening with a one-hour break usually at mid-day. Several similarities and contrasts were established between the work of children at the artisanal gold mining site and that of others discussed within the dominant literature. In some settings, it is said that children work underground digging mining tunnels and shafts or mining gold ore to be hauled to the surface (Jennings 1999; Groves 2005; Human Rights Watch 2011). There is also evidence to suggest that girls either work as prostitutes at some artisanal mining sites or are exposed to sexual abuse and attacks while they work (Gueye 2001; Hinton et al. 2004).

The above were non-existent at the place where this study was carried out. What was found to be true, however, was the highly gendered organization of work at artisanal mining sites (Heemskerk 2000; Chakravorty 2001; Yakovleva 2007). In view of this, girls' work opportunities were mostly confined to those that have traditionally been considered to be females' roles in the house or farm. These comprise carrying sand, stones and water from one location to the other. They also work as hawkers, parading around the site with food, water and a plethora of items on their heads. Some girls were also assistants at the various shops and restaurants at the site. On the whole, due to the gendered work divide and discrimination precisely, females' work opportunities were quite limited.

In contrast, boys and males had access to the full spectrum of jobs that were available at the site. One of the boys' engagements is the cracking of gold ore into smaller pieces to prepare them for grinding. Others also assist in the operation of milling machines which crush and grind the broken up rocks into fine dust. Many others were also general labourers who could be hired to perform a variety of tasks such as running errands, helping with the milling process, turning the ground sand into a slurry or mud, heaping the mud on wooden planks to be washed and so on.

Besides entering into work at the site of their own volition, the children were not bound by any contracts or measures to remain in work with anyone there. At the end of each day, they are paid their wages and their partnership with the work owner is done. In view of some of the claims which have been made about the remuneration of children working at such places (see ILO 2011 for instance) findings about children's pay at the site was quite surprising. As long as they did the same jobs, both adults and children received equal pay. Despite the belief that children are cheated at such places due to their ages, in reality, due to gender discrimination, boys actually earned more than women at this mining site.

One of the most worrying parts of work and life at the site was in connection with safety. Very few wore any protective items such as safety boots, respirators and goggles, and so all workers, both young and old, were exposed to numerous hazards in the course of their work. Consequently, some complained of bodily pains while others suffered from cuts and abrasions. Others, particularly adults who had worked at the site for a long time, were afflicted with persistent coughs and catarrh, signs of more sinister diseases, according to Bose-O'Reilly et al. (2008). To alleviate their pains and tiredness, and partly because they were unable to access health facilities, many relied on self-medication. These issues have stayed with me since the fieldwork was carried out, and in numerous respects it is clear to see why some clamour for the immediate cessation of children's participation.

Yet, in reflecting on their circumstances, the children themselves were of a different opinion. They did not like working in artisanal gold mining, as Sakara pointed out in a conversation: '[W]hen we are coming here to work everybody's eyes are red. Nobody likes it, but if you have plans, then you must come' (Conversation extract, 14 August 2010). However, in terms of their overall participation, they were very positive of their experiences of work at the mining site. As discussed in the next section, their positive views were premised mainly on the impact their work had on their access to education and other opportunities.

Exploring the linkages between the participants' work and their educational attainment

A most surprising finding by this research was that the overwhelming majority of children working at the site were in fulltime education. Indeed, only seven of those who participated in the study were not in school. Two of these had never attended at all, but the other five, such as Kojo (17), had completed secondary school and were working at the site to save money to pay for apprenticeships:

> [W]hen the JHS results came, I had passed and so I thought about going to SHS. In the end, it was not possible for me to go because the money for that was just too much. I was left at home while others went and so my father asked me what I wanted to do. I told him I wanted to learn a job though I was not sure which one. While I was at home deciding, I started coming to the site so I can start saving some money for when I make up my mind. (12 July 2010)

This reliance of children on prohibited work to fund access to apprenticeships and other training opportunities is also explored in the literature (Punch 2002). On the issue of educational access itself, forty-two of the fifty school-going research participants were unequivocal in their assertion that their continued educational access was hinged on access to income earning opportunities at the site. The interview extracts below buttress this point:

> I am now in JS 2 and to be honest if I did not do this work, then by now I will have joined those boys who are no longer going to school. (Hamza, 15)

> If you ask your mother and she does not have the money, what do you do? I don't want to stay at home because of this. When I come here to work, I can buy my own books, school dress, and other things. (Akua, 16)

> When you watch the TV or listen to the radio, they always tell you that education is the future. I believe that one and that is why I come here to work. If I did not want to go to school then I don't have to come here and work at all. (James, 17)

Local children worked at the site after school or on days when they were not in school. However, the majority worked there during school vacations. One of the main reasons for the choice of artisanal gold mining work over other supposedly easier or safer forms of work was that it offered the chance to make money quicker. This was particularly true for independent migrant children who were in a real scramble to save as much money as possible for the new school term within the six week vacation.

The entry of children into prohibited occupations is mostly attributed to poverty (Fallon and Tzannatos 1998; Udry 2003), though there are some disagreements with this position (Bhalotra and Heady 2003). The poverty argument was not conclusive in this research because there were other equally significant factors such as how the work itself was not viewed entirely pathologically by the children. Nonetheless, poverty did play a crucial role in the circumstances behind their reliance on work for their education.

Also worthy of mention is the fact that the positive linkages they made between their education and work was not without some concerns, as evident in Yao's case:

> The work helps me a lot, but sometimes I think differently. I am getting to seventeen and I am the oldest in my class. Because I often leave school to work to save money when things become hard, my classmates leave me behind and I have to repeat JS1 twice. (Yao, 16)

These considerations aside, examination of the education-child labour nexus on the basis of the children's accounts does trouble the dominant assumption. The evidence undermines claims that prohibited engagements such as artisanal gold mining necessarily deprive children of their education. The converse was actually found to be true. This does not idealize children's participation, or that of adults, in work which can potentially harm them. Rather, as discussed in the concluding section, the circumstances surrounding children's work, and the outcomes of their work, differ, as such; a similar approach could prove more useful in attempts to address it.

Discussion and conclusion

Efforts to reduce the number of children in prohibited employments have been married with educational attainment initiatives because the two issues are seen to be related. It has been shown earlier that an outcome of the joint venture has been the creation of an assumption that education is incompatible with those occupations which have been prohibited by the ILO. However, this chapter has drawn on the accounts of children working in artisanal gold mining to show that even occupations of this kind can be complementary to children's educational attainment rather than leading to its denial. Indeed, the evidence highlights the fact that children are in school because of artisanal gold mining work, not in spite of it.

The chapter sought to achieve two main objectives. Firstly, it aimed to highlight how working children themselves evaluate their work, and contrast it with how it is being evaluated within the dominant literature. More importantly, the chapter shows that even beyond the education-child labour nexus, there are other aspects about children's work which differ from one place to the other. It is of course true, as some have found, that children's education is traded off with their work. The same hypothesis has, however, been proven to be false in this research and others. A critical point which emerges, therefore, is that children's work is set in different circumstances and has different outcomes.

The ILO's goal of withdrawing children from prohibited work through improvements in educational access is laudable. However, I urge caution against what has thus far been the prohibition of children's work on the basis of generalized evidence and assumptions. Education can be an effective tool in the promotion of children's development. Where children's work is the main means by which they can access educational and other developmental opportunities then, contrary to the conventional assumption, such work is not antithetical to children's development. Acknowledgement of this possibility could foster a better understanding of the place of work in children's lives and bring about innovative ways of addressing children's participation in occupations which they themselves may not actually like.

References

Ahmed, S. (2011). 'Trade-off between Child Labour and Schooling in Bangladesh: Role of parental education'. Monash University Department of Economics. *Discussion Paper* (21–11).

Allais, B. F., and Hagemann, F. (2008). *Child Labour and Education: Evidence from SIMPOC surveys*. Geneva: ILO.

Anu, R. (2000). 'Interaction of Child Labour and Schooling in Developing Countries: A theoretical perspective', *Journal of Economic Development*, 25 (2), 85–99.

Baland, J. M., and Robinson, J. A. (2000). 'Is Child Labour Efficient'? *Journal of Political Economy*, 108 (4), 663–79.

Barham, V., Robin B., Maurice M., and Pierre P. (1995). 'Education and the Poverty Trap', *European Economic Review*, 39 (7), 1257–75.

Beegle, K., Rakeev, D., and Roberta, G. (2004). 'Why Should we Care about Child Labor? The education, labour market, and health consequences of child labour'. *NBER Working Paper*, No. 10980.

Bhalotra, S., and Heady, C. (2003). 'Child Labor and Development: Child farm labor: The wealth paradox', *World Bank Economic Review*, 17 (2), 197–227.

Bhat, B. A. (2010). 'Gender, Education, and Child Labour: A sociological perspective', *Educational Research and Reviews*, 5 (6), 323–8.

Bose-O'Reilly, S., Lettmeier, B., Gothe, R. M., Beinhoff, C., Siebert, U., and Drasch, G. (2008). 'Mercury as a Serious Health Hazard for Children in Gold Mining Areas', *Environmental Research*, 107 (1), 89–97.

Boyden, J., Ling, B., and Myers, W. (1998). *What Works for Working Children*. Stockholm: Radda Barnen and UNICEF.

Brace, L. (2004). *The Politics of Property: Labour, freedom and belonging*. Edinburgh: University Press.

Canagarajah, S., and Coulombe, H. (1997). 'Child Labor and Schooling in Ghana', *World Bank Policy Research Working Paper*, No. 1844.

Cardoso, A. R., and Verner, D. (2006). 'School Drop-out and Push-out Factors in Brazil: The role of early parenthood, child labor, and poverty', *IZA Discussion Paper*, No. 2515.

Chakravorty, S. L. (2001). 'Artisanal and Small-scale Mining in India'. <http://goo.gl/AudtS> accessed 31 December 2011.

Cockburn, J., and Dostie, B. (2007). 'Child Work and Schooling: The role of household asset profiles and poverty in rural Ethiopia', *Journal of African Economies*, 16 (4), 519–63.

Dammert, A. C. (2008). 'Child Labor and Schooling Response to Changes in Coca Production in Rural Peru', *Journal of Development Economics*, 86 (1), 164–80.

de Lange, A. (2007). *Deprived Children and Education in Ghana*. Amsterdam: IREWOC.

Emerson, P., and Souza, A. (2003). 'Is There a Child Labor Trap? Intergenerational persistence of child labor in Brazil', *Economic Development and Cultural Change*, 51 (2), 375–98.

Emerson, P. M., and Shawn, D. K. (2007). 'Fiscal Policy, Expectation Traps, and Child Labour', *Economic Inquiry*, 45 (3), 453–69.

Fallon, P., and Tzannatos, C. (1998). *Child Labor: Issues and directions for the World Bank*. Washington, DC: World Bank.

Fan, C. S. (2004). 'Child Labour and the Interaction between the Quantity and Quality of Children', *Southern Economic Journal*, 71 (1), 21–35.

Groves, L. (2005). 'Implementing ILO Child Labour Convention 182: Lessons from the gold mining sector in Burkina Faso', *Development in Practice*, 15 (1), 49–59.

Guarcello, L., Lyon, S., and Rosati, F. (2008). 'Child Labour and Education for All: An issue paper', *Journal of the History of Childhood and Youth*, 1 (2), 254–66.

Gueye, D. (2001a). 'Small-Scale Mining in Burkina Faso, Mining, Minerals and Sustainable Development'. Working Paper 73. London: International Institute for Environment and Development.

Harvey, P., and Lauren R. (1994). *Trading away the Future: Child Labour in India's export industries*, Washington DC: International Labour Rights and Education Research Fund.

Hashim, I. M. (2004). *Working With Working Children: Child labour and the barriers to education in rural north-eastern Ghana*. D. Phil, Brighton: University of Sussex.

Hashim, I. M. (2005). 'Exploring the Linkages between Children's Independent Migration and Education: Evidence from Ghana', *Migration DRC Working Paper*, WP-T12.

Heady, C. (2003). 'The Effect of Child Labor on Learning Achievement', *World Development*, 31 (3), 385–98.

Heemskerk, M. (2005). 'Collecting Data in Artisanal and Small-Scale Mining Communities: Measuring progress towards more sustainable livelihoods', *Natural Resources Forum*, 29 (1), 82–7.

Hilson, G. (2009). *Challenges with Eradicating Child Labour in the Artisanal Mining Sector: A case study of the Talensi-Nabdam district, upper East Region of Ghana*. <http://www.yorku.ca/cerlac/EI/papers/Hilson.pdf> accessed 5 June 2012.

Hinton, J. J., Veiga, M. M., and Beinhoff, C. (2003). 'Women and Artisanal Mining: Gender roles and the road ahead'. In G. Hilson (ed.), *The Socio-Economic Impacts of Artisanal and Small-scale Mining in Developing Countries*, pp. 161–302. London: Taylor and Francis Publications.

Hindman, H. D. (2009). *The World of Child Labor: An historical and regional survey.* London and New York: M. E. Sharpe.

Human Rights Watch (2011). *A Poisonous Mix: Child labor, mercury, and artisanal gold mining in Mali.* <http://goo.gl/LY9Tx> accessed 12 March 2012.

ILO (2002). *A Future Without Child Labour.* Geneva: ILO.

ILO (2003). *Facts on Child Labour in Small-scale Mining.* Geneva: ILO.

ILO (2005). *A Load too Heavy: Children in mining and quarrying.* Geneva: ILO.

ILO (2006a). *Child Labour in Gold Mining.* Geneva: I. L. O.

ILO (2006b). *Attitudes to Child Labour and Education on Indonesia.* Geneva: ILO.

ILO (2007). *Girls in Mining: Research findings from Ghana, Niger, Peru and the United Republic of Tanzania.* Geneva: ILO.

ILO (2008). *Ghana Child Labour Data: Country Brief.* Geneva: ILO.

ILO (2009). *Overview of Selected International Initiatives: Child labour in artisanal and small-scale mining.* 9th CASM Annual Conference. <http://goo.gl/XTJFA> accessed 1 January 2012.

ILO (2011). *Children in Hazardous Work: What we know, what we need to do.* Geneva: ILO.

Iversen, V. (2002). 'Autonomy in Child Labour Migrants', *World Development*, 30 (5), 817–34.

Jennings, N. S. (1999). *Small-scale Gold Mining: Examples from Bolivia, Philippines and Zimbabwe.* Sectoral Activities Programme Working Paper, SAP 2.76/WP.130, Geneva: ILO.

Kwankye, S. O., Anarfi, J. K., Tagoe, C. A., and Castaldo, A. (2007). 'Coping Strategies of Independent Child Migrants from Northern Ghana to Southern Cities', *Migration DRC Working Paper*, WP-T23.

Myers, E. W. (2001). 'The Right Rights? Child Labour in a Globalizing World', *Annals of the American Academy of Political and Social Science*, 575 (1), 38–55.

Panelli, R., Punch, S., and Robson, E. (2007). *Global Perspectives on Rural Childhood and Youth: Young rural lives.* New York: Routledge.

Post, D. (2001). *Children's Work, Schooling and Welfare in Latin America.* Colorado: Westview Press.

Psacharopoulos, G. (1997). 'Child Labor versus Educational Attainment: Some evidence from Latin America', *Journal of Population Economics*, 10 (4), 377–86.

Punch, S. (2003). 'Childhoods in the Majority World: Miniature adults or tribal children?' *Sociology*, 37 (2), 277–95.

Quayes, S., Amin, S. M., and Rives, J. M. (2004). 'Poverty and other Determinants of Child Labour in Bangladesh', *Southern Economic Journal*, 70 (4), 876–92.

Ravallion, M., and Wodon, Q. (2000). 'Does child Labour Displace Schooling? Evidence on behavioural responses to an enrolment subsidy', *Economic Journal*, 110 (462), 158–75.
Ray, R. (2000). 'Child Labor, Child Schooling, and their Interaction with Adult Labor: Empirical evidence for Peru and Pakistan', *World Bank Economic Review*, 14 (2), 347–67.
Sedlacek, G., Suzanne, D., Nadeem, I., and Masaru, S. (2005). 'Child Labor, Schooling, and Poverty in Latin America', World Bank Social Protection Discussion Paper, No. 0511.
Udry, C. (2003). *Child Labour*. Centre discussion Paper No. 856. Economic Growth Centre: Yale University.
UNESCO (2007). *Education for All by 2015: Will we make it?* EFA global monitoring report 2008. Paris: UNESCO.
UNICEF (2001). *Beyond Child Labour, Affirming Rights*. New York: UNICEF.
White, B. (2009). 'Social science views on working children'. In H. Hindman (ed.), *The World of Child Labor: An Historical and Regional Survey* (pp. 10–17). Armonk NY and London: M. E. Sharpe.
Yakovleva, N. (2007). 'Perspective on Female Participation in Artisanal and Small-Scale Mining: A case study of Birim North District of Ghana', *Resources Policy*, 32 (1–2), 29–41.

SECTION 2

Early Years Policy and Practice

HELEN PENN

5 Does International Aid Work? The Example of Early Childhood

The extent of inequality

Live Aid and other similar popular events drew mass attention to the extreme gaps between the resources consumed every day in rich countries and the resources available on a daily basis in low income countries. Across the world there is intolerable inequality between the haves and the have-nots. There are, of course, poor people in rich countries and rich people in poor countries. But overall, the degree of global inequality between high income and low income countries is insufferable, and at the extremes of wealth and poverty they are obscene.

The chief research economist of the World Bank, Branco Milanovic (2011), has made a special study of the measurement of global inequality. He points out that 1 per cent of the world's population own 40 per cent of the global assets. The richest 2 per cent of the world's population own more than 51 per cent of the global assets; the richest 10 per cent own 85 per cent of the global assets. By contrast, Save the Children UK has claimed between 9 and 10 million children under five die each year – approximately a cull of 27,000 children per day. The difference between 9 and 10 million deaths a year, the difference of a million or so in the figures, is because births and deaths of children in some places are such an insignificant event that they go unrecorded. Even in India, regarded as a superpower, there are approximately 2 million child deaths per year.

In addition to the high mortality rates, at present roughly 60 per cent of the world's children are denied basic rights to the facilities that are deemed necessary for ordinary, everyday life in the North (Gordon et al. 2003). They lack access to water, sanitation, food, healthcare, education and basic shelter.

Milanovic demonstrates very clearly that how you fare in life depends on the country in which you are born. If you are born in a poor country your chances of survival are precarious and your chances of improving your circumstances are slight; if you are born in a rich country your life chances will be greater in every respect.

International aid as a means of combating inequality

International aid giving is a reflection of this discomfort in rich countries about the unfairness of the world, an attempt to redress the balance and make the world easier to live in for the poorest people. But there is no easy consensus about how it should be done. There are some who argue, including Milanovic himself, that the biggest source of aid is through remittances, that is through the money sent back by immigrant workers to their relatives who remain behind. More immigration would be the most efficient way to increase the life chances of the poorest people and increase the flow of money from rich to poor countries without any need for government or charitable intervention. But such a radical solution is politically unacceptable to xenophobic Americans and Europeans (Milanovic 2011).

Another source of international aid is the many hundreds of thousands of small charities that concerned people set up, usually for a specific purpose in a specific country – for example to help the children of market traders in Kampala, or for street children in Thailand or Bosnian refugees. The work and impact of these small charities, often motivated by individual experiences, is impossible to track on a global basis and the contributions may be very important, or marginal, it is not clear. It would seem to be a very important task to try to scope such initiatives.

However, what is clear is that such aid is very fragmented, and reflects the desire of the founders 'to do good' about the problems they have personally encountered, rather than a concerted attempt to address the problems a country faces. In Mongolia for example, one of the world's poorest countries, before transition in 1990, around 25 per cent of the country's aid income came from one source, Russia, and went directly to the government to fund education, health and veterinary services. As a result, Mongolia had very high literacy rates and very good health outcomes, and healthy animal stock – essential for pastoralists. After transition, Russian aid was withdrawn, and the aid budget in Mongolia fell slightly, but instead of one major donor, aid was fragmented – made up of literally hundreds of aid organizations funding what they, as outsiders, thought was important – everything from projects for seed distribution to building projects using straw bales as insulation. The net result was that Mongolia's health and literacy rates have been falling ever since and are now at their lowest for fifty years. A charity free-for-all has pushed Mongolia backwards, even if a very few people now lead materially better lives as a result, and even if there is a less oppressive regime.[1] It is a common experience of anyone working in the field of development aid, that co-ordination of charities on the ground to avoid overlap and competition, is a major issue.

A large proportion of international aid is delivered mainly through bilateral aid – rich governments helping poorer governments – and through major international non-governmental organizations (INGOs) such as the World Bank, and United Nations organizations like UNICEF or UNDP. The Department for International Development (DfID) in the UK now has policies which have been very much influenced by the development economist Paul Collier – the priority is to aid countries in post-conflict situations, since these are the countries that are most damaged and where recovery is likely to be most problematic without assistance, particularly at the level of governance, civil society, and maintaining order – although helping dodgy and corrupt regimes presents huge challenges (Collier 2008). In DfID too, 'value for money' and 'evidence based policy' have become catchwords. But other government aid departments have different priorities,

1 Mineral wealth has been recently discovered in Mongolia, fuelling speculations that it will become very rich indeed. Such valuable mineral wealth sources are sometimes regarded as a curse rather than as an asset, leading to violence and increased inequality rather than to a raised standard of living for all (Fonseca Rendeiro 2010).

whether it is to promote trade as with the USA; or to maintain cultural influence, as with France; or for religious reasons like some of wealthy Arab states.

Almost all large-scale aid has complicated chains of funding. I have recently been involved in a household survey in Iraq. The original money came from Oz-aid, the Australian equivalent of Irish Aid. It was given to UNICEF in Iraq, who contracted out the tender to a refugee organization, the Council for Assisting Academic Refugees (CARA), based in London. CARA in turn subcontracted the work to the Institute of Education at London University, who in turn employed me and other academics to do part of the work. We reported back to Iraqi ministers and officials, but at each stage money was extracted by each set of subcontractors (UNICEF/CARA 2011).

Many aid projects are put straight out to tender. Almost all of the EU international development budget, for instance, goes in the first instance to private consultancy firms that have grown up, or changed their remit, from backgrounds as diverse as forestry, petrochemicals, engineering, or teacher education, in order to tender for the work. These firms sign on consultants, at very short notice, knowing nothing about them apart from CVs, in order to bid for the work. The terms of the tender are decided in advance and they are paramount; there is no flexibility about dates or terms of reference, even if, in the field, it becomes self-evident that the project will not work as originally conceived. Business confidentiality and intellectual property clauses, which all contractors are required to sign, means that it is rarely possible to be fully transparent about the tenders and how they have been undertaken. It is hard to find any criticism of the processes of procurement or tendering in the development literature, or any discussion of the short-termism and lack of long term commitment that the tendering process implies. Even comprehensive discussions on aid, such as Stern for the OECD (2008), do not consider the tendering process to be in any way problematic.[2]

2 My concern with tendering arises from projects I was directly involved with as a consultant on successful bids. See Penn (2008) for an account of one of these projects.

In the USA, it has been the practice of very rich families to set up foundations, to disperse some of their profits to charitable causes. The Bill and Melinda Gates Foundation is the latest in a long line of charitable foundations dating back to Andrew Carnegie and the Ford Foundation at the beginning of the twentieth century. This kind of philanthro-capitalism has been described as 'autocratic, ineffective and wilful, elitist, cloistered, arrogant and pampered' (*Economist* 2006). Fleischman (2009) provides a robust critique of American Foundations highlighting their lack of transparency and even their tax avoidance. Herz (2002) makes similar accusations. She has charted how private philanthropists are able to dominate and change aid agendas for their own self-interest and self-aggrandizement. The Bill and Melinda Gates Foundation has been heavily criticized for the way that it is funding high profile health and education projects in developing countries, bypassing traditional health and education systems and instead supporting private entrepreneurial solutions, and about raising money for the Fund from unethical investments which damage the very countries the Fund aims to help through its charitable endeavours (Fleischman 2007).

More recently, private equity firms and hedge funds are 'investing' in aid, using business contacts to raise money and business principles to initiate and control development projects, using a 'cost-effective' and 'sustainable' process of micro financial management which assesses projects by their business plans, their spread sheets and quarterly returns (Wolfenson Centre 2008). An example in the UK is the Children's Investment Fund Foundation (CIFF), which invests in children's projects including early childhood education. The CEO, Chris Cooper-Huhn, an ex-banker, who is also on the Foundation Board of Trustees, works with investment managers from Goldman Sachs, J. P. Morgan, and Ernst and Young to develop projects – with a sprinkling of senior aid professionals recruited to advise on policy. He says on CIFF's webpage that:

> CIFF recognizes that our approach is a substantial divergence from the norm of development funding. The truth is that implementing this strategy is proving exciting, challenging and, often, uncomfortable. We recognize many outside the organisation are sceptical that a donor can successfully marry the acumen and discipline of the private sector with the best thinking and evidence of what works in development. (<http://ciff.org/about-us/message-from-the-ceo.html>)

His wife, also a member of staff, and Chairperson of the Trustees of the Foundation, described the work in an interview as follows:

> The foundation is Chris's motivation – to work hard and get the returns. We started with $10m and reckoned that if he could produce 11 per cent returns, we'd be able to donate $10m a year going forward. When we started it all it suddenly gave him a huge motivation. He'd come back from working hard and say, 'Have you fed those children in Malawi yet? We've got to do it!'. (<http://www.telegraph.co.uk/finance/economics/2792014/The-couple-behind-the-466m-charity-donation.html>)

The CIFF office is based in Mayfair, a very wealthy part of London. The company directs financial enquirers to Companies House and the Charity Commission, and its annual financial report is brief. It is unclear how much directors get paid, or what proportion of costs are 'administrative'. The annual report, in the form of a press release says: 'We are an independent, non-profit, philanthropic organisation formally linked to an investment fund, which contributes a portion of its management fees and profits to the Foundation'. The Fund appears to have spent only £175 million in total on aid projects over three years out of its investment fund of £2,072 million, but at the same time appears to be gaining considerable kudos for its contribution (<http://ciff.org/assets/financial/CIFF_FY2011_financial_statements_beyond_final.pdf>).

As Herz (2002) comments, these simplistic approaches to charitable aid giving, negate the importance of governmental policy in recipient countries, and often serve as a cloak for lucrative self-employment, and for self-congratulation. Pogge (2010) has also commented on the way in which the rich have captured the regulatory processes in unequal countries like the USA, and skew the law in their favour, whilst appearing to be neutral or even beneficial.

A further problem with all aid giving is that EU tenders, bilateral programmes, foundations and charities almost invariably peg their payment rates of experts to American or European standards of remuneration rates. The costs of INGO staff and consultants are usually pegged to the dollar or euro, so that there is always a huge disparity between the pay and conditions of those who are employed by international organizations or aid agencies, and those who are in-country local staff, who receive local rates. Hancock, in a memorable phrase, has described such experts as 'Lords of Poverty' (1989).

Failure as a norm

It is a matter of widespread concern that international aid projects frequently fail to achieve all their original objectives despite claims to the contrary. This is partly because charities have to sell their products and talk up their successes in competition with one another for donations. It is also because there are fashions in international aid giving and priorities and justifications shift. But in the long term, failure is the norm. Projects in poor countries generally turn out to be unsustainable, that is even if they make a short-term difference, in the long term they do not survive without continued funding. There are undoubtedly some successful projects judged by practical outputs – for example the Kuru art project for the San people or Bushmen, which has produced some spectacular painting; and the nomadic weaving project in Arbil in Kurdish Iraq which has attempted to revive the carpet weaving traditions amongst the tribes dispersed and killed by Saddam Hussain – but they come at high personal cost to those concerned, both those who are giving and those who are recipients of the aid; both sides must bridge huge cultural divides across a hurtful past and very uncertain present; such projects require huge ongoing commitment.[3]

These aid failures have led some long term activists to suggest that aid projects should be avoided altogether, and the best use of the money would be to give it directly to the poor through cash transfers, i.e. by guaranteeing men and women a minimum income through various benefit systems. The development group at Manchester University led by David Hulme, have brought out a series of publications which have been tracking the impact of these cash transfers in a number of countries, and they conclude that they are a more effective means of poverty reduction than project based approaches (Hulme 2010; Lawson et al. 2010).

Edwards (2011) has argued that many organizations working in the field of development aid are faced with 'thick' problems that are complex, politicized and unpredictable, but their response is to provide 'thin'

3 These projects have not been written up and I am basing my comments on my personal knowledge of both projects.

solutions, which are focused on single issues (e.g. feeding the children in Malawi) and based on narrow criteria for success.

The liberal newspaper, *The Guardian*, attempted to track publicly, over a three-year period, a project in war racked Northern Uganda based in a district called Katine, to make the aid process as visible and transparent as possible. Through local NGOs, it attempted to sponsor a three-year community wide integrated health, education and farming programme, and to document it on the web and in the *Guardian* newspaper on a regular basis. This anatomy of an aid project is very interesting and very accessible, and it makes for illuminating reading. But the lessons of this three-year project were regrettably familiar:

Context is vital – in this case the project failed to recognize the bitterness in the community about the loss of their cattle herds in the war, and their wish to regain their previous way of life. The project did not engage sufficiently with people's memories and hopes and ambitions. 'While NGOs raise funds on the claim that they do something new and different, part of the truth is that each individual project connects to a much longer and more complicated history'.

Poverty is all encompassing – although the aid project was generous by international standards – £1.5 million over three years, it was a drop in the ocean to meet the needs of many thousands of people who had been victims of war and conflict. International aid does not redress global inequality on any significant scale.

Government backing is essential to sustainability, yet in a poor country with high levels of corruption, and a tax revenue base in local government which is far less than the aid money, government help is not likely to be forthcoming.

Empowerment relies on a lot of voluntary participation, and there is a practical limit to the extent that people will volunteer. NGOs frequently expect too much of people's time and willingness to contribute.

Three years – the average life of a project – is nowhere near enough time to bring about lasting change, especially if the wider context is difficult or hostile.

Although there were undoubtedly some gains in the Katine project – for example, villagers had better access to water – the project very clearly illuminated the overwhelming complexities of the aid process (Jones 2010).

International aid in early childhood

Bearing in mind these complexities and difficulties, I now want to explore a very particular case, that of aid in the field of early childhood development. I have been involved with contributing to and evaluating various aid projects in Central Asia and Southern Africa for the last fifteen years, and I have become increasingly uneasy about the process.

Here I am going to discuss four areas which seem to me very problematic in thinking about support for international aid for early childhood projects:

Definitional problems – what does early childhood encompass?
An absence of data on which to base policies.
A failure to consider gender dimensions.
Over-reliance on 'human capital' arguments involving future projections.

i) Definitions

Early childhood care and education is variously referred to in the literature as Early Childhood Care and Education (ECCE e.g. by UNESCO), Early Child Development (ECD e.g. by the World Bank) and Early Childhood Education and Care (ECEC e.g. by the EU and OECD). In the social policy literature it is also known by the shorthand of care or childcare. This confusion over nomenclature reflects a deeper confusion over what kind of interventions or services might be most appropriate for young children and in what circumstances; whether they should focus primarily on education and preparation for schooling; or on health and welfare interventions for the very poor geared towards child survival; or on childcare for working mothers. Latterly, interventions have been viewed as an aspect of development economics; as a human capital investment bringing long term returns in productivity (IFS 2012).

It is commonly accepted in the Global North that some kind of non-familial supports should be provided for young children, whether education, childcare or welfare based. These non-familial supports draw on a variety of rationales and assumptions about young children (EU/NESSE 2010). By contrast, development programmes by INGOs and others draw on a broadly shared underpinning view of young children's development and how it might be enhanced, derived from the discipline of psychology. These interventions assume that there is an optimal process of growth and development which follows universally accepted milestones, and which can be measured in standard ways largely irrespective of context (Fernald et al. 2009).

In poorer countries the definition promoted by the World Bank is frequently used: Early Childhood Development or ECD. This is paradoxically a more ambitious definition than that used in Europe – it refers to a child's overall health and state of development. For example, in South Africa, as in many other African countries, ECD is defined by the government in the legislation as: 'The processes by which children from birth to nine years grow and thrive, physically, mentally, emotionally, morally, socially'.

This goal of total concern with child wellbeing is both very ambitious and at the same time rather vague. It is a medically derived, welfarist definition, rather than an educationally based one, and it makes target setting very difficult. It expresses no view about what kind of services should be available for young children and their families; on the other hand it implies that governments should adopt a holistic approach to supporting ECD, and that it is possible to work horizontally across departments as well as vertically between national, and tiers of local government, to realize such an ill-defined goal.

The reality is that provision is rarely holistically delivered – except possibly the ex-communist countries where such vigilance about child wellbeing once existed (Bronfenbrenner 1965). The only country which can now claim with some justice to have achieved this goal is Cuba. It has a universalistic and theory driven approach to ECEC and has produced the best outcomes for children by far in Latin America, or indeed for any low income country (Carnoy 2007).

But most countries flounder with such an open-ended definition in resource poor contexts, and it is never clear what is meant, other than health and nutrition should be part of any ECD programme. Most often it is taken to mean encouraging mothers, and sometimes fathers, to adopt strategies for bringing up their children that experts – schooled in Euro-American ways of child upbringing – deem appropriate for mental and emotional wellbeing (Walker et al. 2011). This is explored further below in the section on gender.

ii) Poor data

The question of definitions leads onto the question of data. The Open Society Foundation published a booklet about Roma children entitled *No Data – No Progress* (2010). It illustrated the difficulties in obtaining the most basic data about the Roma populations in Eastern Europe – no accurate data about family size or composition, infant mortality rates, migratory patterns, school take-up, housing conditions and so on. As the booklet points out, accurate information is a priority. Without such data there can be no coherent plans for social inclusion, or any other realistic planning. Good monitoring data is necessary to plan ahead and to provide information about the efficacy of services.

Accurate data is problematic in poor countries (UNESCO 2007). Education statistics may be widely inaccurate, or in the case of many ex-communist countries, simply falsified (Steiner-Khamsi and Stolpe 2006). Improvements to education management information systems are now routinely included in major education aid programmes. Increasingly, there is good household survey data to give information at the level of the family or the household. On a project level it is possible to systematically collect relevant data, but this kind of focus on statistical, aggregated information, instead of being seen as complementing qualitative data, is often regarded as antithetical to it. This point is discussed further below. Definitional and data problems mean that it is not easy to get a clear picture of who wants services, and for what sorts of reasons. Questions such as who supplies services, on what basis and how should information be collected about children's progress, and about the services they and their families use, are conspicuous by their absence in ECD programmes in poor countries.

iii) Gender

A recent special edition of the development journal *Development and Change* (2011) explored the way in which families, and especially mothers, are supported in bringing up and caring for young children, and the likely consequences if this support is not forthcoming. The articles explore recent trends in 'the feminization of responsibility' whereby 'women with young children are having to assume an increasing share of the responsibility for meeting household needs with little or no support from the fathers of their children' (875) and the implications of these trends for social planning. Women are increasingly participating in the formal or informal economy, often in harsh and low-wage working conditions with few if any related job benefits.

In the absence of any government support in caring for their children, they make do with a variety of coping strategies – frequently partial internal or even external migration, often leaving children at home in rural areas with relatives (e.g. South Africa, China, the Philippines). In China, for example, there are an estimated 23 million internal immigrants, mostly working in factories producing cheap consumer goods for export to rich countries (Cook and Dong 2011).

Heymann (2003, 2006) has also shown how mothers in poor townships or in other vulnerable circumstances, most often migrants, make inadequate and risky arrangements for their children at the place of work or at home. She shows that urbanization and migration have meant that many millions of women with small children have ended up living on their own without minimal family networks in slums or favelas or squatter townships. They work, mainly in the informal sector as market traders or domestic servants. Often there is no childcare or very poor childcare. In one study, in Botswana, she showed that 29 per cent of women in the townships left their young children unattended or in the care of slightly older children; and, as a result, found that accident rates were horrific.

Childcare, where it exists in such circumstances, is mainly provided by small entrepreneurs trying themselves to make a profit and earn a living, sometimes in very grim circumstances. There is widespread use of unregulated private-for-profit childcare in most conurbations. Since quality is directly related to price, the poorer the mother the poorer the quality of the provision her child is likely to receive. Inequality is inevitably perpetuated in private childcare markets (Woodhead et al. 2009; Penn 2013).

Able bodied women with young children who work in many countries face acute problems of caring. Yet many major ECD projects led by international organizations, some of them quite widely cited, ignore this issue of working women altogether. Instead, a majority of projects favour a more 'cost-effective' approach, teaching mothers of young children how to respond to their children, in terms of 'appropriate stimulation' and 'better nutrition', irrespective of context (Walker et al. 2011). In many of the programmes cited by Walker and her colleagues in *The Lancet*, and in a recent conference on development economics convened by the Institute of Fiscal Studies (IFS) and the Development Economics Department at University College London, almost all the early years projects focus on 'cost-effective' interventions with home-visiting and nutrition programmes, whereby locally trained women on a minimum wage or no wage, are trained to give standard advice on bringing up children to other local women (IFS 2012).

Razavi (2011: 881) argues that 'needs are always interpreted through existing forms of power distribution so that those who are the most marginal are least likely to have their needs recognized' and that 'elites can satisfy their care needs by hiring others (domestic workers, nannies)' and in doing so fail to see or understand the overwhelming care needs of those they hire, or of other women living in marginal conditions. She argues that care-related social policies which recognize gender inequality are not only necessary but possible in the global South and to an extent have been introduced by governments, especially in South America.

A review of the websites of major INGOs who have initiated, or who run, early childhood programmes suggest gender equity and childcare

are barely mentioned as a rationale for intervention (Penn 2011). Yet by contrast they are increasingly a preoccupation of OECD and EU policy analysis. The OECD now publishes a series of comparative tables in its family database, showing how the impact of economic policies on households can be measured. One key aspect of these indicators is the range of ECCE (ECEC) services provided by governments and how they impact on poverty and equality. Very broadly, universal public services alleviate poverty and promote equality more efficiently than services which are targeted only to the poor. This has led Richardson (2012), writing about ECCE in developed countries for the UN Family Division, to suggest that:

> Countries should review options for progressive universalism/cascaded service delivery to improve efficiency without leaving families or children behind. Systems of family service delivery that provide universal services with more intensive delivery to targeted populations (to maximize coverage by ensuring take-up in low income populations for instance), enhance social fairness and social integration of all the children, in the most cost-effective manner. (Richardson 2012: 11)

iv) Human capital arguments

The human capital or returns on investment arguments are very popular amongst those advocating for ECD (Penn 2011). James Heckman, a Nobel prizewinner for economics, argues that investment in early childhood interventions brings greater returns – profits – than investment in any other stage of education (Cunha and Heckman 2007). In his view, it is economically worth investing in early childhood services for the most disadvantaged children. In development economics early childhood is a topic of increasing interest, and there are now a tranche of studies which try to calculate the return on investment for early childhood programmes – in particular nutrition and of motherhood training of the sort discussed by Walker et al. in *The Lancet*.

The 'returns on investment' argument focuses on the economic productivity of individuals and the situations in which it might be maximized. The emphasis is on a neo-liberal approach of enabling *individual* success and striving in an unequal world, rather than any kind of vision of a welfare partnership between individuals and the state. The poorest children can be manipulated, through certain kinds of interventions, to be more productive citizens; they can learn how to compete better against others and to earn more for themselves. It is hardly an argument for social justice or gender equality.

Heckman's work has become iconic in the field of early childhood. Even though his argument originated in a USA context and is most relevant to that context, it is assumed it is applicable everywhere. It is a centrepiece in the World Bank early childhood development lending policy in education – as might be expected of a bank concerned with investment returns on loans. But the same argument is extrapolated from the USA without caveats to apply to Africa and other regions (Garcia, Pence and Evans 2008). The World Bank has even funded the development of an 'early childhood calculator' to enable countries to calculate the profits of investment in programmes per 1,000 children (World Bank 2011).

Heckman's work is augmented by arguments about brain development (Young and Mustard 2008). The reasoning is that nutritional status is known – in very general terms – to affect brain development, and nutritional supplements are standard practice in aid programmes directed at very young children. By analogy, the stimulation of the brain through 'appropriate' care giving (that is by the carer talking, singing and reading to very young children) is said to develop neural networks and promote brain growth. This implies that intimate ideas about child rearing can be shifted from one continent to another.

There are very rarely any references in the INGO literature to detailed anthropological studies of childhood, such as those documented by LeVine and New (2008). Anthropology is almost never referred to or used as a helpful discipline in documenting indigenous practices. Core cultural concepts like children, family, work, play or even learning are rarely explored (Jones and Vilar 2008). It is assumed that standard psychological milestones and growth indicators, and developmentally appropriate practice for young children, developed for Euro-American populations, can be more or less unproblematically applied (Fernald et al. 2009).

One further aspect of the human capital approach is in the use, especially by development economists, of empirical large-scale data, randomized controlled trials (RCTs) of interventions and systematic reviews – what is sometimes known as 'evidence-based policy' (Boller, Ross and Paulsell 2011). On the one hand it is important that data is collected meticulously for project outcomes; that empirical work is undertaken to test out assumptions; and that evidence is reviewed very carefully and systematically. But as Boller, Ross and Paulsell have demonstrated, even where researchers claim significantly important findings for aid interventions in early childhood, measurements of outcomes may be very limited and non-comparable across studies, and context (e.g. migration, women's economic and domestic circumstances, local demography etc.) is invariably ignored. Yet a major article in the prestigious medical journal, *The Lancet*, reports many hundreds of findings as empirical evidence for early childhood interventions, especially nutrition and/or caregiving interventions for very young children, with little or no attention paid to context (Walker et al. 2011).

'Evidence-based policy' is increasingly a mantra for researchers, governments, and business organizations like CIFF, cited above. Research stringency is important, but unless the concept of evidence itself is broadened to include household, local, regional and national contexts, the evidence produced will be narrow and misleading. One model project that has managed to avoid these pitfalls is the DfID *Young Lives* project, which is longitudinal rather than a randomized controlled trial, based on successive interviews on a sample of 15,000 children across four countries. It is worth stressing again that the OECD *Family Database* acknowledges the complexity and variability of household circumstances and the difference to households made by various kinds of health, education, and ECEC provision. This kind of analysis is readily understood and applied in rich nations, but is not viewed as relevant for poor countries.

Discussion

If international aid is problematic, often wasteful, and always complex, then it matters a great deal that those involved in early childhood programmes should also understand the complexities of aid, the macro and micro issues involved, and the overwhelming situation of inequality within which all aid interventions take place. Instead, INGO and charitable discourses about early childhood very often draw on ideas and knowledge from the Global North, in particular from North America. They assume that ideas and knowledge constitute universal precepts which are applicable everywhere. They tend to minimize contextual issues, in particular the adverse effects of inequality, and hold few expectations of government intervention (Penn 2011).

Early childhood aid projects are increasingly based – in theory at least – on a concept of child rights, and children's rights to basic services. But often projects reflect the needs and beliefs of the funder rather than the needs and beliefs of local women and children. Such aid is often missionary in its intent; it wants to see change in a particular direction, and it wants to see change overnight.

Instead there are always many problems to address – regional, national and international policies and circumstances that have brought the aid agencies in; the relevance and reliability of local data; and the local context and language. The position of women is often overlooked, and aid agencies may inadvertently exploit women, or make careless assumptions about their time and availability. All aid projects, given their precariousness, require rigorous evaluative criteria built in at the beginning, which participants in the programme can agree and use.

It is easy to criticize, and in the process of deconstruction, to appear nihilistic – nothing works very well so it is better to do very little. This is very far from what I wish to say. Instead I want to end this chapter on an upbeat note by citing two rather extraordinary campaigners for a better world. The first is the Archbishop of Canterbury, who I heard speak in person at the opening of Canterbury University Childhood Research Centre.[4] He put forward three tentative principles for research and advocacy. The first was that just as we have become more environmentally aware about the consequences our actions may have for environmental degradation, so we should also think in terms of human ecology, the ways in which our decisions and actions, individually and collectively, advertently or inadvertently, might degrade the lives of others, especially children. The second principle was empathy, the techniques of listening very carefully to others, especially to children who are often ignored. The third principle was empowerment, by which he meant a kind of solidarity with others, an affirmation of their worth and endeavours, a view that no individual is ever beyond the pale.

The second person I want to cite is an American, Paul Farmer, whose book *Partner to the Poor* is also inspirational (ed. Sassy 2010). Farmer is Professor of Medical Anthropology at Harvard, and has worked for many years in Haiti, with HIV/AIDS sufferers, and latterly in Russian prisons with tuberculosis sufferers and in Rwanda on health systems. He argues for free medical care everywhere, for the benefits of science to be made universally free and available. By international standards this is extraordinarily radical. He suggests that no person anywhere in the world should ever be refused good medical care – a human good – on any grounds, especially not ability to pay. He considers that such care is transformative. But, crucially, he also argues that analysis and documentation are essential to demonstrate the benefits of medicine or indeed any intervention; that we are also obliged to be accurate and meticulous witnesses to people's suffering.

So, very briefly, my conclusion is that it is a worthwhile task to try to make policies appropriate and systems work better to improve the lives of young children, even if the task is full of pitfalls, and the effort often seems uphill.

4 University of Canterbury, Official Opening of the Childhood Research Centre, 1 April 2011.

References

Boller, K., Ross, C., and Paulsell, D. (2011). *Supporting a Culture of Evidence Based Practice and Continuous Program Involvement: A Staged approach to implementing and studying early childhood development programs*. University of Chicago Human Capital and Economic Working Group, Economic Research Centre. Working Paper, No 2011–040. <http://humcap.uchicago.edu/RePEc/hka/wpaper/Boller_Ross_Paulsell_2009_Supporting-culture-evidence.pdf> accessed 15 October 2011.

Bronfenbrenner, U. (1965). *Two Worlds of Childhood*. London: Penguin Books.

Carnoy, M. (2007). *Cuba's Academic Advantage: Why students in Cuba do better in schools*. California: Stanford University Press.

Collier, P. (2008). *The Bottom Billion*. London: Oxford University Press.

Cook, S., and Dong, X. Y. (2011). 'Harsh Choices: Chinese women's paid work and unpaid care under economic reform', *Development and Change*, 42 (4), 947–65.

Cunha, F., and Heckman, J. (2007). *Investing in Our Young People*. <http://jenni.uchicago.edu/human-inequality/papers/inv-young-rep_all_2007-01-31b_mms.pdf> accessed 15 October 2011.

Development and Change Special Issue (2011). 'Seen, Heard and Counted: Rethinking care in a development context', *Development and Change*, 42 (4).

The Economist (2006). 'The Birth of Philanthrocapitalism', *The Economist*, 23 (2), 23 February 2006. <http://www.economist.com/node/5517656?story_id=5517656> accessed 15 October 2011.

Edwards, M. (2011). 'Thick Problems and Thin Solutions: How NGOs can bridge the gap', *Future Calling – Think Piece*, Hivos. <http://www.hivos.nl/eng/Hivos-Knowledge-Programme/Themes/Future-Calling/News/Thick-Problems> accessed 15 October 2011.

EU/NESSE (2009). *Early Childhood Education and Care: Key lessons from research for policy makers*. Brussels: NESSE network of experts. <http://www.nesse.fr/nesse/nesse_top/tasks> accessed 15 October 2011.

Fernald, L., Kariger, P., Engle, P., and Raikes, A. (2009). *Examining Early Child Development in Low-Income Countries: A toolkit for the assessment of children in the first five years of life*. Washington: World Bank.

Fleischman, J. (2009). *The Foundation: A great American secret: How private wealth is changing the world*. New York: Public Affairs.

Fonseca Rendeiro, M. (2010). *Mongolia's Mining Wealth is Cause for Concern*. <http://www.guardian.co.uk/commentisfree/2010/may/15/mongolia-mining-wealth-concern> accessed 15 October 2011.

Garcia, M., Pence A., and Evans J. (eds) (2008). *Africa's Future, Africa's Challenge: Early childhood care and development in sub-Saharan Africa*. Washington, DC: World Bank.

Gordon, D., Nandy, S., Pantazis, C., Pemberton, S., and Townsend, P. (2003). *Child Poverty in the Developing World*. Bristol: Policy Press.

Hancock, G. (1989). *Lords of Poverty: The power, prestige and corruption of the international aid business*. New York: Atlantic Monthly Press.

Herz, N. (2002). *The Silent Takeover: Global capitalism and the death of democracy*. London: Arrow Books.

Heymann, J. (2003). *The Role of ECCE in Ensuring Equal Opportunity*. Policy brief No. 18. Paris: UNESCO.

Heymann, J. (2006). *Forgotten Families: Ending the growing crisis confronting children and working parents in the global economy*. Oxford: Oxford University Press.

Hulme, D. (2010). *Global Poverty*. London and New York: Routledge.

Institute of Fiscal Studies (IFS) (2012). *Early Child Development in Developing Countries*. Conference held at University College London, 25–26 June.

Jones, B. (2010). 'Katine: An academic review'. *The Guardian*, 30 October. <http://www.guardian.co.uk/katine/interactive/2010/oct/30/ben-jones-academic-review> accessed 15 October 2011.

Jones, N., and Vilar, E. (2008). 'Situating Children in International Development Policy: Challenges involved in successful evidence-informed policy making', *Evidence and Policy*, 4 (1), 31–51.

Lawson, D., Hulme, D., Matin, I., and Moore, I. (2010). *What Works for the Poorest?* Rugby: Practical Action Publishing.

LeVine, R., and New, R. (eds) (2008). *Anthropology and Child Development: A cross cultural reader*. London: Blackwell.

Milanovic, B. (2010). *The Haves and the Have Nots*. New York: Basic Books.

Penn, H. (2011). 'Travelling Policies and Global Buzzwords: How international non-governmental organizations and charities spread the word about early childhood in the global South', *Childhood*, 18 (1), 94–113.

Penn, H. (2013). 'Childcare Markets: Implications for equity and quality'. In A. Raikes (ed.), *UNESCO Handbook of Early Childhood Care and Education*. Paris: UNESCO. Forthcoming.

Pogge, T. (2010). *Politics as Usual*. Cambridge. Polity Press.

Razavi, S. (2011). 'Rethinking Care in a Development Context: Introduction', *Development and Change*, 42 (4), 873–90.

Richardson, D. (2012). 'Good Practices in Anti-Poverty Family Friendly Policies and Programmes in Developed Countries', Paper given at a UN Expert Group meeting on the family, May. <http://social.un.org/index/LinkClick.aspx?fileticket=kCKuIJ-jCTo%3D&tabid=1748> accessed 15 October 2012.

Sassy, H. (ed.) (2010). *Partner to the Poor: A Paul Farmer reader*. California: University of California Press.

Steiner-Khamsi, G. and Stolpe, I. (2006). *Educational Import: Local encounters with global forces in Mongolia.* London: Palgrave Macmillan.

Stern, E. (2008). *Thematic Study on the Paris Declaration: Aid effectiveness and development effectiveness.* Paris: OECD.

UNESCO (2007). *Education for All Global Monitoring Report 2007*. Paris: UNESCO.

UNICEF/CARA (2011). *A Study of the Education of Children with Disabilities and Early Childhood Development in Iraq*. Baghdad: UNICEF IRAQ.

Walker, S. P., Wachs, T. D., Grantham-McGregor, S., Black, M. M., Nelson, C. A., Huffman, S. L., Baker-Henningham, H., Chang, S. M., Hamadani, J. D., Lozoff, B., Meeks Gardner, J. M., Powell, C. A, Rahman, A., and Richter L. (2011). 'Inequality in Early Childhood: Risk and protective factors for early child development', *The Lancet*, 378 (9799), 1325–38.

Wolfensohn Center for Development and the Committee for Economic Development (2008). *Business Champions for Early Child Development.* <http://www.brookings.edu/events/2008/12/~/media/Events/2008/12/04%20early%20child%20development/20081204_early_child_development_summary.PDF> accessed 15 October 2012.

Woodhead, M., Ames, P., Vennam, U., Abebe, W., and Streuli, N. (2009). 'Equity and Quality? Challenges for early childhood and primary education in Ethiopia, India and Peru', Working Paper No 55, *Studies in Early Childhood Transitions*. The Hague, The Netherlands: Bernard van Leer Foundation.

World Bank (2011). ECD Calculator. <http://web.worldbank.org/WBSITE/EXTERNAL/TOPICS/EXTCY/EXTECD/0,,contentMDK:20259116~menuPK:527329~pagePK:210058~piPK:210062~theSitePK:344939,00.htm> accessed 15 October 2012.

Young, M. E., and Mustard, F. (2008). 'Brain Development and ECD: A Case for Investment'. In M. Garcia A. Pence and J. Evans (eds), *Africa's Future, Africa's Challenge: Early childhood care and development in sub-Saharan Africa*, pp. 71–88. Washington DC: World Bank.

Young Lives Project. London: DFID. <http://www.dfid.gov.uk/r4d/SearchResearchDatabase.asp?ProjectID=60637> accessed 15 October 2012.

JOHANNA DAVIS

6 Values in Early Childhood Development: A Venture into the Field of Childhood Aid

Introduction

This chapter deals with programmes which are set up by aid agencies or charities with the aim of relieving poverty or assisting development in poor countries. Often, these countries are referred to as developing countries, a term which defines them by the economic, cultural and social status assigned to them by the self-declared developed world. These labels contain a value judgement, which presumes that all countries must develop in the same direction, towards the industrialized, economically oriented society of materialist modernity. To avoid this judgement, I prefer to label countries in the less biased terms of their geographical positioning within the Global South or Global North (Russell 2009), or in terms of the size of their population, in which case southern countries are referred to as the Majority World and northern countries as the Minority World (Pence and Marfo 2008).

This venture into the field of childhood aid relies on a recent research project with the title 'Values in Early Childhood Development Aid' in which I explored the experiences and perceptions of thirteen Irish-based development practitioners. My interest in the topic was rooted in my academic background in Early Childhood Care and Education (ECCE) in combination with my own experiences in 2003 of working with disadvantaged children in a charitable project in Argentina. It was my search for the meeting point of these two fields, development aid and ECCE, which led me towards ECD and my venture into the field of early childhood aid.

It was my personal volunteering experience which first caused me to assume a critical point of view. While I personally witnessed the profound effect which a development project can have on the community in which it is situated, some of the problems encountered in the delivery also made me realize that the experience was somewhat selfish – very much contrary to my intent. In a sense, I used these children to satisfy my need to 'do good' without verifying my assumption that they were needy, and needy for the kind of good which I had to give.

My critical thoughts were confirmed once I began to engage with the literature, which showed ECD to be quite two-faced and somewhat difficult to make out. On the one hand, everything is extremely simple: 34,000 children die every day of poverty (Riddell 2007: 121) and early childhood interventions have been shown to directly improve the lives of participating children. They have also proven to have a long term positive effect on the economic and social situation of a country in general (Nores and Barnett 2009). On the other hand, however, everything is extremely complicated: the proof for early childhood intervention is often based on insecure data from Minority World countries, which is so specific that it can certainly not be generalized to all communities of the Majority World (Stacey 1996; Samoff 1999: 252); some people who say they have the best interests of children and of the poor in mind strive, in fact, only for their own personal gain (Shrestha 2000; Penn 2002; Riddell 2007); those who give of their time and money selflessly sometimes achieve no improvements or even do harm with their gifts without ever realizing it (Shrestha 1995); and some of those who go to great lengths to advocate for children fall prey to the dominant western view of childhood which, in its over-simplification, is almost as far from reality in the rich countries of the North as it is in the poor countries of the South (Burr 2002; Pence and Nsamenang 2008; Penn 2008).

In taking a critical standpoint, I do not wish to doubt the good intentions of individuals who give of their time and resources to help those in need. I am, however, concerned with the tension between the positive outcomes or intentions versus the criticisms and dangers of Early Childhood Development. To represent the three stages of my venture, this introduction will be followed by three sections. Section one is the largest and deals with the academic debate surrounding ECD and development aid more generally. The second part of the chapter presents the main findings of my study. By showing ECD from these two different angles, I hope to give a voice both to those who research and write about ECD and those who are actively involved in ECD practice. The final section of the chapter will bring the research journey to a close by bringing the two voices together and drawing conclusions on what has been learnt.

Voices from the academic field of ECD

A venture into the field of ECD cannot begin without firstly situating Early Childhood Development within the debates surrounding development aid more generally. While the following can be no more than a snapshot of the greater aid discourse, I wish to present some of the more pertinent critical voices in aid, which I encountered during my venture, as well as some current thoughts on best practice before dealing with the area of Early Childhood Development.

In a teaching resource for children called 'What is Aid?' Oxfam explains to its young readership that 'richer countries give poorer countries aid to help them to make a better future for themselves'. This includes 'giving people the tools and skills they need to fix their own problems' and 'persuading people to drop unfair debts' (Oxfam 2008: 1). If explained in these simple few words, the idea of aid seems easy enough to understand and most people would probably agree that these are indeed some of the main ingredients of aid. But why, then, is aid so heavily criticized at times? The following story, passed on by Russell (2009) at the Sustainable Global Development Conference at the University of Limerick, may be useful in highlighting why doing good is not always helpful. The Lion of the Village, a former village leader in a remote desert village in Africa, was asked to tell of a time when his village was strong. The time he recalls is a time before the arrival of foreign aid, when the people of his village had neither a word for poverty nor any concept of it. Since then, the population has been 'enabled' to understand how poor they are and leadership has changed from those who knew the strengths of the group, to those who understand its weaknesses and needs and can relate these to foreign donors. While the intervening forty years of aid succeeded in convincing the inhabitants that their former way of life was 'poor', it did not succeed in helping the population out of this poverty.

There are many other stories such as Russell's, which tell of the failures of aid. Some of the more common criticisms are that 'poor countries are still poor' and that, therefore, aid doesn't work, that income inequalities are perpetuated or increased, that aid causes a dependency of poor countries on the richer donor countries and that, since recipients are failing to make developmental progress, aid is a waste of money (Crosswell 1999: 1). Crosswell, from his position as an economist with the USA Agency for International Development (USAID), is keen to prove these arguments wrong. He cites a data record several pages long of ninety countries who have received US aid in the three decades between 1960 and 1990. This data shows that fifty-seven of the ninety countries have achieved significant economic growth and that economic growth almost always resulted in a decline in the percentage of people living in poverty. Crosswell's records also show an improvement of social wellbeing in terms of lower infant mortality, higher life expectancy, literacy and other social indicators. However, the problem with such impressive quantities of statistical data is that the same data can often serve as proof for opposite sides of an argument. Steer (2006: 12), for example, sees a real sign of hope in the fact that overall incomes in Africa are 'now growing at a faster rate than in rich countries for the first time since the 1960s'. In combination with Crosswell's data, however, Steer's comment gives away the fact that while poor countries may have experienced statistically significant growth, at least in African countries, this was still lower than the growth experienced by rich countries during the same period.

It is, therefore, not necessarily out of ignorance of statistical evidence that critics voice their concerns. On the contrary, their disapproval is often based on equally convincing sets of data in addition to long term observations and an objection to the underlying world-view of the development discourse. For De Sousa Santos (1999), for example, the development concept is related to the Age of Enlightenment and Europe's mission to bring modernity to the world. In his article in *Critical Development Theory* (Munck and O'Hearn 1999: 30), he points out that in the nineties, textile and electronic workers in the Majority World earned twenty-two times less than workers in Europe or North America who did the same jobs with the same productivity. He also mentions that more people died of hunger in the twentieth century than in any of the preceding centuries and that the gap between rich and poor countries, at the time of writing, was still widening. He sees a gross inequality in the fact that poor countries in debt were paying rich countries an average of $30 billion a year more than they received in new loans. Also of concern to De Sousa Santos is the statistic that the eighteenth century witnessed the deaths of 4.4 million people in sixty-eight wars, while in the twentieth century 99 million people died in 237 wars. These and other statistics proved to De Sousa Santos that modernity did not fulfil its promises for equality, liberty, peace and the dominion over nature. A decade later, De Sousa Santo's data could be considered outdated and his recommendation to think of alternatives to the development concept declared as invalid. However, the fact that an estimated 7 million children die unnecessarily each year (Jubilee 2000 Coalition, in Penn 2002) would suggest that certainly the promise of equality still remains unfulfilled today. And even more so if we consider that those who survive have limited access to education or health services and are often forced into child labour – producing goods which are consumed thoughtlessly and unknowingly every day by children and adults in the westernized world (Penn 2002).

The theoretical background of many of the hardest aid criticisms lies in the discipline of post-colonial studies. Pioneered by the Palestinian intellectual Edward Said with his influential book *Orientalism* (1978), post-colonialism tries to break down the residual effects of colonization on cultures. Said criticizes the binary opposition of the East and the West and identifies the need to deconstruct the underlying racist and imperialist assumptions with which colonizing powers have defined their colonized subjects. Said follows in the footsteps of post-structuralist Foucault in recognizing the inseparable link between knowledge and power (Haralambos and Holborn 2004: 581–5). It is the construction of a scientific picture of the Orient as uncivilized, irrational, mysterious and generally 'Other', which allows the West to take economic and political control from its self-defined position of civilized, rational and progressive superiority (Viruru 2005: 8).

Post-colonialism has had a profound influence on a whole generation of cultural and sociological studies and it is from these disciplines of critical thought – which show up the fundamental weaknesses underlying the concept of development – that aid receives its strongest criticisms.

While the doubts of the above cited De Sousa Santos are grounded in the unfulfilled hopes of Enlightenment Europe, Sachs (1993) aims his disapproval at the ambitions of the Truman era in the USA. To Sachs, those who have driven development since Truman's time, conceive of the world as an economic arena, and see it as the duty of the lead runners to help all nations to participate in the race for development. Traditional modes of living which are not built around a frenzy of accumulation are usually at odds with this economic ethos. The ideals, rules of governance, modes of knowing and patterns of work that are the fabric of the world's different cultures are, therefore, seen as obstacles to development. To bring nations into the arena and remove barriers to growth, all kinds of institutions such as schools, work and the law had to be revamped in the name of productivity. The problem is, however, that this economic race-track has been leading in the wrong direction all along. As we know now, Planet Earth cannot sustain the kind of development which helped today's leading nations to their life-style. Sachs suggests that the capacity of six planets would be necessary if we were to offer all nations the exploitation and dumping resources needed to catch up in the race. Unfortunately, according to Sachs, the economic world-view has already infiltrated societies around the world and, as a result, has undermined their capacity to retain any independence in securing their own wellbeing.

An example of such infiltration is given by Shrestha's (1995) poignant account of development in his native Nepal since he was a boy. 'Poor and hungry', he writes, 'I certainly was. But underdeveloped? I never thought – nor did anybody else – that being poor meant being "underdeveloped" and lacking human dignity' (ibid: 268). But then, in the 1950s, the Nepalese word *bikas* (development) began to gain currency and society was restructured and re-categorized into those who were backward or uncivilized (and usually poor) and those who strove for the new culture of materialism with its awe of modern science, technology and westernized education. The new society wanted to be part of the fancy buildings, new roads, airplanes and other symbols associated with bikas projects and foreign aid. The people began to scorn the old way of life, the hard labour and traditions which had been a part of it, in the hope of replacing it with the life of luxury associated with the sophisticated, white, civilized Westerners. Western-style development was seen as the only way out of poverty. In this process, Nepalese society freely accorded Westerners a dominant superior position, never realizing that only the former elite benefited from the changes as they assumed positions in the bureaucracy and development enterprise. Poverty was increasingly seen as self-inflicted, through resistance to bikas, and what formerly allowed families to eke out their meagre existence was now judged as uncivilized. Thus the gap between rich and poor widened, the life of the poor outside of the glistening American school became harder and where there had once been pride in self-reliance and cooperation, they were replaced by despondency and dependency. Let someone else come and fix the problem!

In light of Shrestha's experience, it is not surprising that he calls development a social Darwinian project, an eloquent rhetoric which engenders tantalizing hopes for the poor and serves to heighten the class control and power of the rich (Shrestha 2000: 154–5). And he is not alone with his disenchantment. There are many voices that suspect issues of power and underlying motives of self-interest in development aid (Boone 1995: 26). Tucker (1999), in his passionate article 'The Myth of Development', emphasizes the cultural universality with which development is applied. He defines development as 'the process whereby other peoples are dominated and their destinies are shaped according to an essentially Western way of conceiving and perceiving the world' (ibid: 1). A case in point is the Jonglei Canal Project in Sudan, which was resisted by Sudanese indigenous peoples because it would destroy their nomadic way of life. In answer to this cultural conflict of interests, the then Vice-President commented: 'We will drive them to paradise with a stick if necessary' (ibid: 11), thereby aptly summing up the struggle which indigenous peoples face in having a say in the shaping of their futures.

However, not all criticisms are as fundamental or as radical as the above and there is a general acceptance, even from supporters of development aid, that there are types of aid which are less successful in reducing poverty than others. Steer (2006), the Country Director of the World Bank in Indonesia, admits that the overall progress which is made by some poor countries in terms of their GDP, 'is little comfort to a mother of six living on $1 per day in Mali' (ibid: 12). Steer gives a summary of the kind of aid that fails. This includes: assistance given for political or commercial reasons, assistance which is tied to the products or people of the donor country, assistance which is driven by foreign expertise, or which is unsustainable in the long term. Failed aid projects around the world in the form of incomplete, rusting water systems or half-built hospitals, are the most visible proof – though not the worst of the effects – of the failures of aid (Fletcher School 1999: 5).

Current thoughts on best practice

The dire situation in which today's poor still find themselves in spite of the past decades of aid, have prompted policy makers, investors and practitioners to search for ways in which aid can better achieve its aims. Some of the criticisms mentioned above have been influential in broadening the aid concept to incorporate not only the economic situation of a country or community, but also social and cultural factors, human rights and environmental concerns. The Human Development Index (HDI), for example, was developed in 1990 to shift the centre of attention from national income economics towards a more people-centred development policy (Haq 1995). The HDI tries to measure development in terms of life expectancy, education and standard of living. The aid focus has also moved from a more short-sighted, immediate approach towards sustainability into the future. Sustainable development, in the much cited words of the Brundtland Report (1987, cited for example in Pramling-Samuelsson and Kaga 2008:

10), is defined as 'development that meets the need of the present without compromising the ability of future generations to meet their own needs'. The question then, is how can aid achieve its goals? If rich countries do not wish to turn their backs on those who are less well off, how should they react to the worldwide state of unequal distribution, human suffering and conflict?

Ellerman (2007) examines what he considers to be the fundamental conundrum of development assistance, the concept of helping people to help themselves, and identifies two kinds of unhelpful help. In Ellerman's terms aid donors are called 'helpers' and aid recipients 'doers', which already discloses aspects of what he considers to be a more successful approach to aid. On the one hand, helpers can override the self-help capacity of doers by supplying both detailed instructions and the motivation to do what helpers demand from their position of supposed insight or expertise. This approach presumes that aid recipients lack either the motivation or the capacity to help themselves out of their poverty. On the other hand, the helpers may undercut the doers' capacity for self-help. This happens, for example, in long term benevolent aid which causes learned helplessness as the benefits to being in a needy, passive recipient role erodes the doers' motivation for being independent and autonomous actors. As a solution, Ellerman proposes what he calls indirect aid, which is most easily summed up in Schumacher's (1964: 374) slogan: 'Find out what the people are trying to do and help them to do it better'. This includes starting from where the doers are, seeing the world through their eyes and respecting their autonomy throughout the process of helping. What Ellerman's idea of indirect aid does not include is providing motivation of any kind, including financial support or providing the answers or solutions. It means merely facilitating self-directed learning of whatever kind, in whatever manner, and helping to remove obstacles to transferring this learning into policies and actions on the ground.

Similarly to Ellerman, Russell (2009) examines the discourse and identifies helpful and unhelpful strategies in development. Some of the approaches currently employed to improve the outcomes of development assistance, are the World Bank's (1996) 'participatory rural appraisal' or the United Nations Development Programme's 'sustainable livelihoods approach' (Chambers and Conway 1992). Russell welcomes the elements of these approaches which move on from doing development to, for or with the people, to enabling communities to proactively drive their own development. He points out how the needs-based attitude to development, which is still most frequently employed by policy makers and non-governmental organizations (NGOs), makes communities dependent on outside intervention and, therefore, more vulnerable than before. The solution proposed by Russell (2009) is McKnight's (1995) Asset-Based Community Development (ABCD), which radically changes the focus from deficiencies to assets and the approach from powerless reception of development 'cures', to citizen-driven societal change from the inside.

What Ellerman and Russell have in common is that they see local citizens as the doers of development, who should have ownership over the process of change. The concept of local ownership is based on the observation that interventions tend to be more effective if the local population is involved in their conception and execution and has a sense that the project is their project and the improvement is their achievement (Greany and Elliott 2001; Mathie and Cunningham 2003; Ellerman 2007; Russell 2009). Most charities and organizations today subscribe to this mind-set, as can be seen from the numerous references to 'helping people to help themselves' (Oxfam Ireland website 2010), 'helping people to build a better future for themselves' (Hope Foundation website 2010) and 'supporting community-based long term solutions' (Chernobyl International website 2010). The same understanding evidently informed the Oxfam teaching resource which was mentioned at the beginning of this chapter, explaining to children that aid helps poorer countries to 'make a better future for themselves'. It can be summed up in the words of the government *White Paper on Irish Aid* (2006: 6): '[W]e believe that development can only occur with countries themselves as owners and leaders of their own development'.

Following this snapshot of critical voices on aid and current thoughts on best practice, we will now turn our attention to ECD.

What is ECD?

Early Childhood Development is a concept which is used very broadly in the literature to refer to programmes for children before school-going age. These could be centre-based or home-based, regulated or unregulated and they might be not-for-profit, private or state-funded. Most often, such programmes are intended to educate children or prepare them for school, to free mothers for work, to support children's development, health or nutrition and to improve parenting practices (Penn 2004: 2; Nores and Barnett 2009). Collingwood (2008: 4) uses a broad and holistic definition of ECD as 'strengthening families and households to reduce the vulnerability of children'.

While ECD in the Global North usually extends to little more than the education and care of children before school-going age, ECD provision in the South is much broader and can include interventions for pregnant mothers, nutritional programmes, health clinics, immunization programmes and parental supports which are aimed at promoting a healthy and sustainable home life for children (Penn 2008).

From an optimistic point of view the case is very simple: ECD is scientifically proven to be beneficial for children, families, communities and societies. This claim is based on a quantity of research and data and can be argued from a number of different points of view. Neuro-scientific evidence, for example, proves the significance of early childhood learning for the development of the mind (Lindsay 1998). From the point of view of social justice it can be argued that it is necessary to counteract early disadvantages in order to give children a level playing field from which to reach their potential (Siraj-Blatchford and Woodhead 2009: 4). There is also a substantial research body which supports the view that early childhood is the most effective time to build social capital, since early childhood experiences are considered as particularly effective in laying the foundations for positive social networks which prepare children for active citizenship and sustainable living (Evans and Myers 2000; Vandenbroeck and Bie 2006; Pramling-Samuelsson and Kaga 2008; Siraj-Blatchford and

Woodhead 2009). The UN Convention on the Rights of the Child is the most significant influence on global policy for young children (ibid) and serves as a foundation for many interventions in the early years (Burr 2002; Nsamenang 2008; Pence and Nsamenang 2008). According to the UN Committee on the Rights of the Child (2006: 10) ensuring personal development from birth, especially for the most vulnerable groups is, therefore, merely a human right. However, the most forceful and most frequently cited case for early childhood supports and education is the economic case, which argues that investment in early childhood pays off. Especially vulnerable children who attend high quality early childhood provision consistently appear to show benefits compared to their peers, who did not attend provision. Benefits in later life include higher educational attainment, higher employment status and lower rates of delinquency and addiction. The economic return to society quoted in the literature reaches from \$3 to \$16.14 for every dollar invested in early childhood provision (Schweinhart and Weikart 1997; Sylva et al. 2003; Siraj-Blatchford and Woodhead 2009).

Problems of ECD

While proof of the benefit of ECD has no doubt helped to bring early childhood onto policy agendas around the world, ECD is not without problems or criticisms. And while it seems far-fetched at first to criticize something as universally accepted and positive as helping children by way of early childhood supports and services, there are concerns which surface repeatedly in the literature. The problem is that multiple readings can be made of development projects for young children. Where one observer sees successful interventions which help children to be ready for school and improve their employment chances in later life (Anderson et al. 2003), another sees a spread of the dominant ideology on how children grow and develop, like a new form of colonialism which is imposed unhesitatingly and 'for their own good' upon peoples around the world (Viruru 2005: 16).

The most common of the criticisms refer to the overgeneralization of USA-based findings regarding the effectiveness and economic savings of early childhood interventions (Penn 2002: 124; Nores and Barnett 2009); the exportation of culturally specific education models – such as the American Developmentally Appropriate Practice (DAP) – as universally valid in any cultural or social context (Viruru 2005; Pence and Nsamengang 2008; Pence and Marfo 2008; Penn 2002, 2008; Moss 2009); the application of models which demand a high input of training, salaries and resources in a context which is underpaid, under-resourced and untrained (Penn 2002: 127; King 2009: 176); and an over-reliance on one universal Western notion of childhood – which misrepresents almost as many children in the Global North as in the South (Stacey 1996; Penn 2002) – rather than the acceptance of diverse childhood experiences from diverse contexts and cultures (Penn 2002; Viruru 2005; Pence and Nsamengang 2008; Pence and Hix-Small 2009).

Those advocating childhood education for development need to be aware that the dominant approach to childhood is a culturally specific discourse based on the western democratic notion of an individualist market society. As this discourse became more popular it universalized its subjective claims and came to be seen as an objective truth which applies to all contexts (Moss 2009: 2). However, where ECD claims to have not only universal validity for all other contexts but self-evident superiority over all rival approaches it is an example of a 'regime of truth' (Foucault 1988) or 'hegemonic globalisation' (De Sousa Santos 2004). This phenomenon caused Sardar (1999: 44) to conclude that 'the real power of the west resides in the power to define'. One of the side effects of this power is today's 'culture of consultancy' (Stirrat 2000: 31), where experts in the Western discourse survey the situation in a Majority World country, make a diagnosis and prescribe a remedy (Samoff 1999: 253). This custom is partly based on a deficit attitude towards Majority World countries, which assumes that Africa can be 'fixed' with just a little more sophisticated analysis, more expertise and more funding (Penn 2002: 119; Quarles van Ufford and Giri 2003: 5). It erroneously claims to be based on scientific research (Burr 2002; Penn 2002: 125) which 'proves' that the African education sector is in crisis (Samoff 1999: 250) and that the West possesses educational expertise which is 'systematically' shown to solve such problems (Bredekamp and Copple 1997).

The above is a short summary of the different problems and criticisms encountered by ECD. And these problems by no means appear only in discussion forums, but refer to the real lives of real children who can at times receive no benefits or even be harmed by unhelpful approaches to ECD. However, the field is beginning to acknowledge this and new approaches to ECD will help to strengthen the positive impact and safeguard against the problems.

As a specialized field within the greater aid debate, ECD is naturally not only subject to general criticisms but any suggestions on how to improve the effectiveness of development assistance apply equally to early childhood development. It is, therefore, important for aid donors to stand back and allow the local population to take ownership over the process of change and become the drivers of their own development. Sustainability, autonomy, a focus on assets rather than needs and the absence of imposed aims and strategies from the outside are all associated with successful development projects. However, suggestions for improvement of ECD in particular can also be found in the literature. Greany and Elliott, for example, suggest the use of appreciative inquiry (AI) as a means of improving the outcomes of ECD. AI emphasizes that the world looks very different from different points of view and, therefore, approaches any context from the point of view of those who feel most at home in it. AI always begins by appreciating the possibilities, valuable attempts and partial achievements, rather than seeing deficiencies, unsolved problems and failures. In terms of ECD this means discovering the strategies already in place to bring up children, the child rearing practices valued by the community, and the coping mechanisms developed.

Following this insight into some of the arguments surrounding aid and ECD, we shall now hear about ideas of those who are involved in the practical application of ECD.

Voices from the practical field of ECD

With my study of values in ECD, I aimed to get a deeper insight into the complexities of giving development aid to young children. I wanted to learn from those who work for an Irish organization and have practical, organizational or academic expertise in the area of ECD. The following research question and embedded questions built the basis for my study.

Research question

How do Irish-based development practitioners value aid interventions for young children, based on their perceptions and experiences in the field of Early Childhood Development (ECD)?

Embedded Questions

1 How are participants motivated to become and stay involved in the field?
2 What are the perceptions of aid on which participants base their work in ECD?
3 How do participants reflect on the experiences gained through their work in ECD?
4 What are the challenges faced by participants in their field of work?

The findings generated during my interviews with thirteen Irish-based development practitioners can be summarized as follows (the issues are presented here in order of their importance during the interviews):

1. How do participants reflect on their experiences from the field? It appears from the data that the most significant experience in the field

relates to cultural differences and similarities between donors and recipients. These caused participants to speak very admiringly and appreciatively of their recipients, to put much effort into being culturally sensitive and appropriate in their work, but also to judge many practices of the recipient cultures as negative or inappropriate. The data also shows that participants witnessed significant impacts from aid, both in terms of saving or changing thousands of lives and in terms of making a little difference at a time to the lives of individual recipients.

2. What are the perceptions of aid on which participants base their work? The data shows that participants have a very strong concept of best practice, evidenced by their perceptions on how aid should best be given. Issues of empowerment and local ownership were emphasized most strongly, for example, through close collaboration with families, communities and governments.

3. What are the challenges faced by participants in their work? The third most important factor in the perceptions of study participants relates to the living conditions of aid recipients. Some of the severe poverty, health problems and educational under-resourcing witnessed by participants seem to illustrate with real-life stories, some of the statistics of inequality and human suffering which regularly make for shocking media headlines and which are part of the reason why the work of participants is extremely challenging at times.

4. How are participants motivated to become and stay involved in the field? This was not a subject of great significance during the interviews. However, the data suggests that both issues of benevolence and a thirst for adventure have a role to play and that the significant personal benefits experienced through the work are an important, if unexpected, motivator.

5. More generally it should be said that not many participants valued ECD as a separate entity within aid. In fact, a number of the participants, who were by definition involved in ECD, were unfamiliar with the term which may explain why specific comments to ECD were rare throughout the interviews.

6. Aid criticisms were also of comparatively small significance and, where they did surface, were largely unrelated to the post-colonial and other categorical criticisms offered in the literature.

7. The low levels of data for both criticisms and for the ECD sector, would suggest that there is a gap between the theory and practice of ECD.

8. Finally, it should be emphasized that the manner in which participants told their stories and the considerable challenges which they overcame on a daily basis revealed a great deal of passion for their work and compassion for the people with whom they work.

Conclusion

This study set out to explore values in ECD through the experiences and perceptions of Irish-based development practitioners. On the basis of the literature review and the data gathered from my interview participants, I have drawn the following six main conclusions:

1. The critical questioning of ECD in terms of its underlying assumptions, historical or social power relations and cultural dynamics, which formed the starting point for this project, are very much present and debated in the literature. It is not, however, a value of great significance to practitioners. While cultural influences did indeed play a very important role for participants, their comments related mostly to personal interactions and observations of the recipient cultures, which caused participants to admire, aim to respect, or disagree with aspects of the customs and habits experienced on the ground.

2. Participants' strong feelings regarding best practice in aid showed them as critical observers who reflect on their practice and use strategies, which were developed in response to previous, less successful approaches. The interview responses showed, for example, that Western expert-driven assistance has gradually made way for ideas of locally driven change towards locally developed goals. Their ideas on best practice, however, failed to extend to a broad understanding of the absolutist assumptions of aid and the potential for politically and socially self-interested motivations, which have caused aid to be unsuccessful or even harmful in the past. Most participants also made comments which suggest that the empowerment value

found elsewhere in the interviews, on charity websites and in the literature may not yet fully permeate every programme and every interaction of participants in the field. It is difficult to judge whether these slips of the tongue were proof only of the difficulty of always using the correct and currently accepted terminology, or whether they betrayed participants' real values, which were not entirely harmonious with the current popular rhetoric.

3. ECD may be one of those topics to which few people who come in close contact with it can assume an attitude of indifference. Maybe it is the association with children, with vulnerability and suffering, with good and evil forces which stirs a deep-rooted reaction of compassion, responsibility and guilt in people and gives ECD its force. An overview of the literature seems to reveal that some authors engage in hot debates with each other over how very wrong the allegations of the critics are, or how very damaging indeed the wrong kinds of aid can be. Where the interview participants were concerned, it was their way of speaking which revealed their passion, the way in which they overcame considerable challenges every day, working in conditions of abject poverty, illness, desperate under-resourcing and, at times, desolation in order to make a difference in someone's life. In any case, it does not take the keenest observer to notice that writers and interview participants alike were emotionally involved in the subject, and I think this thesis may have proven that I, myself, did not stay immune to this influence.

4. Through this project I discovered within me a strong postmodernist tendency, which began to object whenever I came across a universal claim or reliance on an absolute truth. This poses a conflict, however, as virtually all participants were motivated by a belief in an ultimate truth relating to what all children deserve to have, or what no child should have to endure. Even if we accept that certain rights are universal, as agreed by almost every country in the world in the case of the UN Convention on the Rights of the Child, where does the universality end and cultural or personal interpretation begin: with a child's right to life or a child's right not to live in certain conditions? With the right to be safe from harm or the right not to be exposed to certain types of behaviour management? With the right to develop, or the right to a certain standard of good education? The fine line between universal rights and cultural judgments on how to implement these rights remains, as yet, unresolved.

5. Different perceptions of aid could be located on a continuum which, on the one side, interprets development as an orchestrated reform driven by investors towards their own financial benefits and, on the other, as a natural process directed by social forces similar to the process of evolution. It was the experience of this project that critical writers in ECD were inclined towards the former interpretation, suspecting a conspiracy by those in power, while ECD practitioners tended towards the latter side, taking the circumstances in which they found their recipients as a given and thereby accepting them like the natural forces of a societal evolution. As so often where there are two opposing views, it is likely that the truth lies somewhere in between and never in the same place for different communities or at different points in time.

6. Early childhood has experienced an unprecedented worldwide surge of policy attention in recent decades. This is evidenced, for example, in the emergence of the field of ECD, where funding is increasingly made available for the world's youngest citizens as a measure to improve economic, social and cultural development. This global attention could contain a unique opportunity to firmly anchor the value of childhood in our social structures and political agendas. However, it should not cause the globalization of one universal notion of childhood, which subsumes the world's many customs of child rearing, which may deprive children and their communities of what is locally appropriate and, therefore, possibly do more harm than good. In order to achieve a global appreciation and celebration of local childhoods, much remains to be learned about how childhood is valued by the different cultures and peoples of the world.

Recommendations and implications

As with any field of study, it is desirable to work towards an increased understanding between the theory and practice of ECD. As this is a comparatively young discipline, one of the most important ingredients may be time and further development of the field of thought. Ideally, this development should happen through practitioners of ECD who take up writing, and through writers of ECD who also have experience of the practice. It may be useful to give practitioners an incentive to take a more active role in shaping the academic field through their own reflections. Writers on the other hand, in the interest of their discipline, might aim to give a voice to those who practice ECD, and disseminate their findings in order to facilitate an exchange of thought and knowledge between writers and practitioners.

In order to avoid the globalization of one universalized concept of childhood it is necessary to learn about alternative ways of bringing up children. Considering that practitioners showed a keen interest in making cultural observations, they may be interested in turning their attention to traditional education and making their findings available to the field. Also their direct involvement with countless communities across the globe means that they are ideally positioned to promote local forms of upbringing, collect indigenous viewpoints and help to bring light to this issue.

The UN Convention on the Rights of the Child has no doubt had an enormous impact on early childhood since its adoption in 1989 and it is used by many charities which practice ECD as a basis for their interventions. As this document was signed in record time by almost every country in the world, let us presume for a moment that all communities and cultures within those countries do indeed agree with its content. However, what we cannot presume to know without careful inquiry into the local culture is how these communities understand and interpret the Convention and how they consider it correctly implemented. If we accept the postmodernist premise that truth is temporary, context dependent and ever-changing, we must be careful to continuously question our own assumptions in aid, even if we rely on something as universally accepted as the UN Convention on the Rights of the Child.

In concluding this chapter, it remains to be said that my venture into the field of ECD has been a rich and exciting journey which opened my eyes not only to issues of early childhood and global development. It gave insights, also, into sociological, historical, medicinal and interpersonal aspects which made this project a truly enriching, multi-disciplinary experience. I hope to have contributed a tiny fleck of new understanding to the field, but it is likely that many years of further study, of further ECD practice and interpretation will be necessary before we can fully understand the greater part of this complex form of aid.

References

Boone, P. (1995). *Politics and the Effectiveness of Foreign Aid.* London: Centre for Economic Performance; London School of Economics and Political Science.

Bredekamp, S., and Copple, C. (eds) (1997). *Developmentally Appropriate Practice in Early Childhood Programs.* Washington, DC: National Association for the Education of Young Children.

Burr, R. (2002). 'Global and Local Approaches to Children's Rights in Vietnam', *Childhood*, 9 (1), 49–61.

Chambers, R., and Conway, G. (1992). *Sustainable Rural Livelihoods: Practical concepts for the 21st century.* Brighton: Institute of Development Studies.

Collingwood, C. (2008). *Urban Children at Risk Project. Final Evaluation Report*, Cape Town: PMU Interlife.

Crosswell, M. (1999). 'The Development Record and the Effectiveness of Foreign Aid', *Praxis: The Fletcher Journal of Development Studies*, 15, 1–11.

de Sousa Santos, B. (1999). 'On Oppositional Postmodernism'. In R. Munck and D. O'Hearn (eds), *Critical Development Theory: Contributions to a New Paradigm*, pp. 29–43. London: Zed Books.

Ellerman, D. (2007). 'Helping Self-help: The fundamental conundrum of development assistance', *The Journal of Socio-Economics*, 36 (4), 561–77.

Evans, J., and Myers, R. (2000). *Early Childhood Counts: A Programming guide on early childhood care for development.* Washington DC: The World Bank.

Fletcher School (1999). 'Does Development Really Work: The Praxis interviews' *Praxis: The Fletcher Journal of Development Studies*, 15, 1–13.

Foucault, M. (1988) in L. Kritzman (ed.), *Politics, Philosophy, Culture: Interviews and other writings 1977–1984.* New York: Routledge.

Government White Paper on Irish Aid 2006. Dublin: Government Publications.

Greany, C., and Elliott, C. (2001). 'Enabling Communities to Practice the Best in Early Childhood Development: Using appreciative inquiry in ECD', *Notes for a UNICEF workshop*, Masaka, 12–30 March 2001: University of Cambridge.

Haq, M. (1995). *Reflections on Human Development.* New York: Oxford University Press.

Haralambos, M., and Holborn, M. (2004). *Sociology: Themes and Perspectives*, 6th ed., London: Collins.

King, K. (2009). 'Education, Skills, Sustainability and Growth: Complex relations', *International Journal of Education Development*, 29, 175–81.

Mathie, A., and Cunningham, G. (2003). 'From Clients to Citizens: Asset-based community development as a strategy for community-driven development', *Development in Practice*, 13 (5), 474–86.

McKnight, J. L. (1995). *The Careless Society: Community and its counterfeits*. New York: Basic Books.

Moss, P. (ed.) (2009). *There are Alternatives! Markets and democratic experimentalism in early childhood education and care*, Working Papers in Early Childhood Development Nr 53 ed., The Hague, The Netherlands: Bernard van Leer Foundation and Bertelsmann Stiftung.

Munck, R., and O'Hearn, D. (1999). *Critical Development Theory: Contributions to a new paradigm*. London: Zed Books.

Nores, M., and Barnett, S. (2009). 'Benefits of Early Childhood Interventions Across the World: (Under) Investing in the very young', *Economics of Education Review*, 29 (2), 271–82.

Nsamenang, B. (2008). 'Agency in Early Childhood Learning and Development in Cameroon', *Contemporary Issues in Early Childhood*, 9 (3), 211–23.

Oxfam Ireland (2008). 'What is Aid'. <http://www.oxfam.org.uk/coolplanet/kidsweb/oxfam/campaigns/downloads/What_is_Aid.pdf> accessed 3 March 2010.

Pence, A., and Hix-Small, H. (2009). 'Global Children in the Shadow of the Global Child', *International Critical Childhood Policy Studies*, 2 (1), 75–91.

Pence, A., and Marfo, K. (2008). 'Early Childhood Development in Africa: Interrogating constraints of prevailing knowledge bases', *International Journal of Psychology*, 43 (2), 78–87.

Pence, A., and Nsamenang, B. (2008). 'A Case for Early Childhood Development in Sub-Saharan Africa', *Working Papers in Early Childhood Development*, No. 51. The Hague: Bernard van Leer Foundation.

Penn, H. (2002). 'The World Bank's View of Early Childhood', *Childhood*, 9 (1), 118–32.

Penn, H. (2004). 'Childcare and Early Childhood Development Programmes and Policies: Their relationship to eradicating child poverty', *Childcare and Early Childhood Development Programmes and Policies*, Chip Report No. 8.

Penn, H. (2008). 'Working on the Impossible: Early childhood policies in Namibia', *Childhood*, 15 (3), 37–395.

Pramling-Samuelsson, I., and Kaga, Y. (eds) (2008). *The Contribution of Early Childhood Education to a Sustainable Society*. Paris: UNESCO.

Quarles van Ufford, P., and Giri, A. (2003). *A Moral Critique of Development: In Search of global responsibilities*. London: EIDOS/Routledge.

Riddell, R. (2007). *Does Foreign Aid Really Work?* Oxford: Oxford University Press.

Russell, C. (2009). 'From Needs to Assets: Charting a sustainable path towards development in sub-Saharan African countries'. Paper presented at the *Sustainable Global Development Conference*, University of Limerick, September.

Sachs, W. (1993). *Global Ecology*. London: Zed Books.

Said, E. (1978). *Orientalism*. New York: Vintage Books.

Samoff, J. (1999). 'Education Sector Analysis in Africa: Limited national control and even less national ownership', *International Journal of Education Development*, 19 (4–5), 249–72.

Sardar, Z. (1999). 'Development and the Locations of Eurocentrism'. In R. Munck and D. O'Hearn (eds), *Critical Development Theory: Contributions to a new paradigm*, pp. 44–62. London: Zed Books.

Schumacher, E. F. (1964). 'A Humanistic Guide to Foreign Aid'. In D. Novack and R. Lekachman (eds), *Development and Society*, pp. 364–74. New York: St Martin's Press.

Schweinhart, L., and Weikart, D. (1997). *Lasting Differences: The High/Scope preschool curriculum comparison study through age 23*. Ypsilanti, MI: High/Scope Press.

Shrestha, N. (1995). 'Becoming a Development Category'. In J. Crush (ed.), *The Power of Development*, pp. 266–77. London: Routledge.

Shrestha, N. (2000). 'Book Review: Nepal's Failed Development: Reflections on the mission and the maladies. Devendra Raj Panday', *Comparative Studies of South Asia, Africa and the Middle East*, 20 (1), 154–5. <http://muse.jhu.edu/journals/comparative_studies_of_south_asia_africa_and_the_middle_east/v020/20.1shrestha.html> accessed 8 September 2009.

Siraj-Blatchford, I., and Woodhead, M. (2009). *Effective Early Childhood Programmes – Early Childhood in Focus 4*. Milton Keynes: Open University Child and Youth Studies Group.

Stacey, J. (1996). *In the Name of the Family: Rethinking family values in the postmodern age*. Boston, Mass: Beacon Press.

Steer, A. (2006). 'Does Development Work? An encouraging assessment', *Encounters Mission Enzine*, 14, 12–17.

Stirrat, R. (2000). 'Cultures of Consultancy', *Critique of Anthropology*, 20 (1), 31–46.

Tucker, V. (1999). 'The Myth of Development: A Critique of a Eurocentric discourse'. In R. Munck and D. O'Hearn (eds), *Critical Development Theory: Contributions to a new paradigm*, pp. 1–26. London: Zed Books.

UNHCHR (United Nations High Commissioner for Human Rights) (1990). *United Nations Convention on the Rights of the Child*, Geneva: Office of the United Nations High Commissioner for Human Rights.

Vandenbroeck, M., and Bie, M. B. (2006). 'Children's Agency and Educational Norms: A tensed negotiation', *Childhood*, 13 (1), 127–43.

Viruru, R. (2005). 'The Impact of Postcolonial Theory on Early Childhood Education', *Journal of Education*, 35, 7–29.

World Bank (1996). *The World Bank Participation Source Book, Environmentally Sustainable Development*. Washington DC: World Bank.

ROSARII GRIFFIN AND JACQUI O'RIORDAN

7 Early Childhood and Primary Education in Sub-Saharan Africa: The Impact of HIV and AIDS on Education in Lesotho

Introduction

The idea that education is considered one of the most important pillars of development has long been established (Sinclair 2001; Brock 2011). Education has long been recognized as a critical part of the development agenda; it is seen as an enabling right, critical to achieving other rights (Annan 1999). The promotion of education has long been associated with the growth and promotion of democratic institutions and the general and international acceptance of universal human rights, as well as the promotion of social cohesion and economic growth at both the micro and macro level (World Bank 1999). The promotion of literacy through education is also associated with higher income generation, and, for women, better health and lower infant mortality rates. The notion of education as a humanitarian response is particularly important in the context of countries at war or in conflict. It is thought that education can promote stability, harmony and tolerance. Most importantly, education brings hope: hope for a brighter, more promising future (Paulson 2011).

The international context

At the turn of the millennium, a heightened awareness was created amongst the world community at the levels of extreme poverty that still existed, predominantly in the Global South, and how the gap between rich and poor countries was ever widening. The world community was mobilized and committed itself to addressing the causes of extreme poverty in a quest to eliminate such poverty forever.

One of the main challenges sub-Saharan Africa faces for the twenty-first century is that of 'basic education development' (Verspoor 2008: 13). As aforementioned, educational attainment has been widely recognized as one of the most important founding blocks of social and economic development. As a result of the World Education Forum in 2000, the international community came together in Dakar, the capital of Senegal on the most Westerly port of Africa, to highlight the critical importance of education in the global developing economy. At this conference, the 'Dakar Framework for Education' was developed setting out an 'Education for All' roadmap for low income countries to follow, and for the international community to support, so that low income countries might become self-sufficient and competitive within a global economy. Soon after, as a result of this mass mobilization of the global community, the Dakar 'Education for All' (EFA) goals were formulated. However, these were soon to be overtaken by, and morphed into, the 'Millennium Development Goals' (MDGs). These were eight target goals, identifying areas of social deprivation that needed to be tackled in order to eliminate extreme poverty as well as to encourage sustainable development. They became universally endorsed by the international community, in the form of the UN and UNESCO, as well as other multilateral donors and countries.

The eight MDGs included the right to: universal primary education; gender and equality of opportunity for girls and women; access to proper maternal healthcare; access to clean water; tackle the incidence of killer diseases such as TB, Malaria and HIV and AIDS; address and tackle the root causes of poverty, and to form international cooperative relationships for sustainable development. The only difficulty was that, in some ways, the MDGs eclipsed the Dakar Goals and the drive towards educational attainment and achievement was diluted in favour of a single educational goal – the achievement of universal primary education (UPE) – when the initial Dakar 'Education for All' objectives were far broader that this singular goal. Many argue that the UPE essentialist goals short-changed the many educational settings (especially non-formal and informal) in which education occurs, and that need to be developed. UPE focused almost singularly on the formal sector of primary education, initially, virtually to the exclusion of adolescent education, adult education, early childhood education and the educational provision for those with disability (Urwick et al. 2012). Similarly, the focus became almost entirely on increasing enrolment figures and ensuring universal and free primary education for all children, irrespective of how this was to occur, or of its quality.

In the course of concentrating on school-going numbers, enrolment figures (or 'bums on seats'), it quickly became apparent that the quality of education being taught, the quality of educational provision, and the quality of teacher education to match requirements, were sorely lacking. As Verspoor points out, 'the quest for quality is not just an issue of educational policy, but is a key development challenge' (2008: 13). However, it is also true to say that in the absence of international donor aid directed towards UPE, many more children would be 'out of school and, or, sitting in even more overcrowded classrooms, without books or desks' (UNESCO 2009: 206).

Financing Universal Primary Education (UPE)

Overall, since 2000, there has been very little increase in the share of overall aid allocated to education, including basic education to what are termed the least developed countries (UNESCO 2007: 212). The least developed countries or LDC is the UN designated name given to countries that are the poorest globally in terms of human development indices, socio-economic growth and conditions, as well as human development indices including, but not exclusive of, education, water, security, health and food security. Currently, there are forty-eight recognized LDC and there is a commitment by the UN to assist these countries to rise above this status in the short term. However, since the 1960s, only three countries have moved out of this status, from the lowest tier of poverty, and up into a 'developing country' status. The only African country to do so was Botswana in 1994.

In 2007, the *EFA Global Monitoring Report* estimated that an annual US$ 11 billion of aid was required for low income countries to achieve UPE, that significant gains were made in reducing adult literacy and in the expansion of early childhood programmes (2007: 208). However, aid in support of basic education in low income countries was just one-third of the estimated requirement (UNESCO 2007: 204). France, Germany and Japan had shown a relative neglect of basic education funding to low income countries while The Netherlands, the UK and the IDA were responsible for 60 per cent of all aid for basic education. However, a recent commitment by the French government to work with the UK to ensure the education of 15 million children living in sub-Saharan Africa by 2015 has been welcomed (UNESCO 2007: 217).

Education and HIV and AIDS in sub-Saharan Africa

As is well documented, HIV and AIDS is a major killer in Africa, affecting upwards of 45 million people (UNAIDS 2010). Its impact spans all areas of life and livelihood and it can be argued that any attempt to address poverty reduction will be adversely affected, should it not be cognizant of the prevalence of HIV and AIDS as well as having a familiarity and appreciation of local knowledge of and attitudes to it (Griffin and O'Riordan 2012). There is no doubt but that the HIV and AIDS pandemic is sabotaging the fabric of sub-Saharan society. Nowhere is this felt more than in the area of education. The supply and demand for the quality of education and the 'supply chain' of educators, school managers, education policy makers and school going children are impacted daily, as more and more people are sick or dying. This directly and indirectly affects and reduces the supply, demand and quality of education. The relationship between education and HIV and AIDS is complex, dynamic and cumulative (Coombe 2002). For example, when HIV prevalence increases, it affects the education sector negatively in the sense that institutions, educators and learners are affected and suffer. Overall, the HIV and AIDS pandemic impacts the whole education system negatively. In sub-Saharan Africa, education systems, learners and educators and the quality of teaching and learning have all been affected by the HIV and AIDS pandemic, to varying degrees (Coombe 2002; Bennell 2005; Bhana et al. 2006). It is clear that if educators are sick or absent from school, or leaving the education profession, the national education system and its impact on society and the economy stands to lose.

According to Carr-Hill, Katabaro, Katahoire and Oulai (2002), in their report *The Impact of HIV/AIDS on Education and Institutionalizing Preventive Education: Education in the context of HIV/AIDS*, the education systems of most countries in sub-Saharan Africa, including Lesotho, are on the brink of disaster, due to the HIV and AIDS pandemic. This is also supported by the work of Coombe (2002) and Badcock-Walters, Kelly and Görgens (2004). For example, school enrolments are shrinking in most African countries; AIDS is undermining the ability of education systems to perform their basic social mandates, as more teachers and administrative staff are lost to the disease. The education sector can barely cope with the additional costs associated with training and replacing teachers (Bennell 2005, Moon and Wolfdenden 2012).

Education, HIV and AIDS in Lesotho

Lesotho has the third highest HIV and AIDS prevalence in the world, with just under one in four people in the country living with HIV. The *UN Development Programme Action Plan (2008–2012)* for Lesotho identifies HIV and AIDS as mainstream issues across all of its elements (UNDP 2008). Without a doubt, HIV and AIDS impacts on every facet of life in

Lesotho, leading the King of Lesotho, King Letsie III, to declare it a national disaster in 2003 (National Aids Commission 2003). Some years later, the Chief Executive of the National AIDS Commission in Lesotho, Kekesto Sefeane, suggested that if the pandemic was not tackled urgently, the entire Basotho nation could conceivably be wiped out (Kaiser Foundation 2007). The *Kingdom of Lesotho Education Sector Strategic Plan 2005–2015*, published by the Ministry of Education and Training (MoET) in 2005, also acknowledged the significance of the HIV and AIDS pandemic in Lesoho.

The *WHO (2005) Lesotho: Summary Country Profile for HIV/AIDS Treatment Scale-Up* reported that one quarter of its people aged between fifteen and forty-nine are HIV positive and that there is no sign that the epidemic is stabilizing. Particularly disturbing also is the ratio of infection for those aged between twenty-five and twenty-nine, at 39 per cent, mostly female, while overall adult prevalence is estimated at 28.9 per cent. Especially noticeable are very high rates of infection in those with TB (over 50 per cent) or those with STIs (over 60 per cent) and for children born with HIV AIDS. In 2003, the *HIV Sentinel Survey Report* (MOHSW) estimated that 100,000 under-fifteens in ten districts had lost one or both parents to AIDS. The USAID *Health Profile Lesotho* states categorically that 'AIDS constitutes an alarming threat to Lesotho and its people' (2008: 8) as can be seen by the figures below in Table 1.

Table 1 Lesotho's HIV and AIDS statistics (UNAIDS 2008)

Indicator	2005	2007	% Variation
Adult prevalence rate	23.2%	23.2%	0
HIV infected people	266,000	270,000	1.5%
Adult HIV incidence rate	2.9%	2.35%	(19%)
Number of new infections	26,000	21,558	(17%)
AIDS mortality	24,000	18,000	(25%)
AIDS related OVCs	97,000	108,700	12%
Projection of ART needs	42,640	81,270	91%

The *Report* states that HIV and AIDS is not the only barrier to Lesotho's economic development, but adds that capacity depletion and economic decline 'are major obstacles to short and long term responses to humanitarian and development needs' (2008: 1).

In 2009 there were around 23,000 new HIV infections and approximately 14,000 people died from AIDS. Over half of the 260,000 adults living with HIV in Lesotho are women. Pregnant women and mothers living with HIV and their infants need to be treated throughout pregnancy and breastfeeding in order to stop the transmission of the virus. Persistent and pervasive barriers to treatment include: lack of medication, high cost of antenatal care and delivery, long waits in clinics, lack of transport to healthcare facilities and HIV related stigma and discrimination. There are also significant differences between HIV prevalence rates in urban (28 per cent) and rural (21 per cent) areas. Unofficial figures are reportedly much higher, especially in the rural areas.

In Lesotho, the education system has begun to experience the loss of inspectors, education officers and education planning and management personnel to the HIV and AIDS pandemic. It is also becoming increasingly difficult to attract experienced managers. It must be pointed out also that up to now, many school principals have not received sufficient support and training on educational management. It is important to note that supply and quality issues are inter-related. The supply of education has to do with educators being available to teach effectively. In order for quality learning to take place, educators must be available and in a position to offer quality education (Coombe 2002).

Primary education and early childhood education in Lesotho

In spite of the HIV and Aids pandemic that has afflicted Lesotho, nonetheless, it has been shown to have made 'impressive quantitative progress' since the turn of the century in relation to the educational Millennium

Development Goals as well as in terms of gender parity (Urwick et al. 2012: 74). Free primary education has been introduced year on year since 2000 (until 2006) as tuition fees were removed. The *Global Monitoring Report* of 2009, which monitors progress towards achieving 'Universal Primary Education' attainment targets, as well as identifying barriers to achieving these goals, shows that the net enrolment rate (NER) in Lesotho increased from 57 per cent to 72 per cent (UNESCO 2008: 307, cited in Griffin 2012: 74) during this period. This was only surpassed by Tanzania in sub-Saharan Africa. Similarly, gender parity is being achieved for Basotho boys, as traditionally in Lesotho, more girls attend school than boys, as boys are traditionally retained from schooling due to their herding duties. However, with the onset of universal free primary education, and a new compulsory requirement that all children attend school, the gender disparity is shifting slowly. However, the jump in attendance of primary education has also been bolstered by the fact that schools have reinstated a free school meals scheme, which encouraged children to attend school especially in the lowlands (World Bank 2005).

Yet, in spite of these advances, there are significant regional disparities even within Lesotho, with those living in more rural areas experiencing greater disadvantage due to access difficulties and the unavailability of qualified teachers to teach in more remote areas (Moon and Wolfenden 2012). Urwick and Elliott (2010) illustrate this disparity very well in respect of the regional disparities in quality and outcomes within Lesotho. However, children with disabilities in Lesotho remain the most disadvantaged of all, with very poor access, little or no specialized provision, and poorly qualified teachers working in this domain (O'Riordan et al. 2012). Often, those with disabilities are left behind, and for physical, mental or social reasons, do not attend school. Even if they do, the school experience provides little more than a social experience for those with disability. As Urwick et al. (2012: 75) point out, 'Lesotho's most serious problems lie not so much in the areas of the educational MDGs, as in those of the EFA goals, that are not explicitly supported by the MDGs'.

Urwick et al. (2012) also point out that early childhood education is another area of neglect within the Lesotho educational landscape. However, Lesotho is not unique in this respect, this being a common feature of most sub-Saharan African countries. Little emphasis, or investment is placed on early year intervention and education. Within Lesotho, until recently, this has not been perceived as a priority by either the household or the state, despite the fact that an administrative unit was established for early childhood care and development within Lesotho's Ministry of Education and Training (MoET) as early as 1985. In line with international practice, this unit has since been renamed as 'integrated early childhood care and education development' (IECCED) implying a more holistic approach to what traditionally was just ECCD (Urwick et al. 2012).

Due to an increase in female employment in the textile industry of recent years, demand has increased for either formal or informal care of children. Informal ordinarily consists of a local person 'minding' the child in the absence of the parent or extended family member; formal often, in practice, means that the child is enrolled in reception classes attached to primary schools. These reception classes constitute a preparatory year for children aged five to six, prior to their enrolment in primary school. There is also pre-school/crèche provision at community, home-based or private pre-schools or crèches. Quality, however, varies considerably and teachers/carers typically have low levels of qualifications.

In spite of the daunting situation that the government of Lesotho faces, slow and steady progress has been made on the ground. For instance, in Lesotho, the government of Lesotho enacted landmark legislation on 11 May 2010 when it enacted the Education Act 2010, which legalized the right to free and compulsory education for all children (UNICEF 2010). Although free primary education (FPE) was introduced in 2000, it took ten years for this major strategy officially to become a milestone in the fight to eliminate extreme poverty. The Act itself is the outcome of a widely consultative process that aimed to review and replace the 1995 Education Act. It is said that the Ministry of Education and Training (MoET) was also driven by the need to improve the quality of education as well as make it 'more responsive to the impact of HIV, AIDS and poverty' (Barbadoro 2010: np). Education, it is hoped, will make some inroads into tackling the root causes and myths that prevail around the high incidence of HIV and AIDS in Lesotho. In spite of the fact that Lesotho has one of the highest proportions of orphans in the world (12 per cent), and the third highest prevalence of HIV and AIDS, Dr Magan (UNICEF Lesotho representative), believes that this educational reform will ensure that children 'are fully equipped with the means to make healthy and informed decisions that will improve the quality of their lives' (UNICEF 2010: np).

Conclusion

Multinational donors and educational partnerships are currently working together to translate the Education Act into systems and structures that will make the provision of education immediately accessible to all Basotho children. Nevertheless, the issue of the quality of education still remains a key development priority, and one that still needs urgent support and attention, and especially investment. Only with the proper financing can education – including teacher education and training (Griffin 2012) and classroom resources and provisions (including the continuation of free nourishing school meals) – improve the quality of education on the ground and directly impact on children. This, in turn, will promote sustainable development of the Basotho people and their society.

It is imperative, therefore, that the international community stand behind the Basotho efforts to assist themselves, to ensure the future viability of their younger generations and social and community development. For this reason, the international community cannot afford to take their attention away from one of the world's poorest and least developed countries, and let yet another generation of children become lost victims of the HIV and AIDS pandemic that currently is threatening the very fabric of Basotho life and nationhood. Let's hope and work towards ensuring that the next ten years will give the children of Lesotho the chance they deserve to lead full and healthy lives through the provision of a full and proper quality education system and experience.

References

Annan, K. (1999). 'Foreword'. In C. Bellemy, *The State of the World's Children 1999* (Executive Director of United Nations Children's Fund). New York: UNICEF.

Badcock-Walters, P., Kelly, M. and Görgens, M. (2004). 'Does Knowledge Equal Change? HIV/AIDS education and behaviour change', Background Paper for *EFA Global Monitoring Report 2005*. <http://unesdoc.unesco.org/images/0013/001373/137333e.pdf> accessed 30 October 2010.

Barbadoro, C. (2010). 'Free Education becomes Legally Compulsory in Lesotho', UNICEF, Lesotho. <http://www.unicef.org/media/media_53653.html> accessed 18 October 2012.

Bennell, P. (2005). 'The Impact of the AIDS Epidemic on Teachers in Sub-Saharan Africa', *Journal of Development Studies*, 41 (3), 440–66.

Bhana, D., Morrell, R., Epstein, D., and Moletsane, R. (2006). 'The Hidden Work of Caring: Teachers and the maturing AIDS epidemic in diverse secondary schools in Durban', *Journal of Education*, 38, 5–24. London: Taylor and Francis.

Brock, C. (2011). *Education as a Global Concern*. London: Continuum.

Carr-Hill, R., Katabaro, K. J., Katahoire, A. R., and Oulai, D. (2002). *The Impact of HIV/AIDS on Education and Institutionalizing Preventive Education. Education in the context of HIV/AIDS*. Paris: International Institute for Educational Planning [IIEP]/*United Nations Educational, Scientific and Cultural Organization* (UNESCO].

Coombe, C. (2002). 'HIV/AIDS and Education', *Perspectives in Education*, 20 (2), vii–x.

Griffin, R. (ed.) (2012). *Teacher Education in Sub-Saharan Africa: Closer perspectives*. Oxford: Symposium Books.

Griffin, R., and O'Riordan, J. (2012). 'Saving Lives through Capacity Building – Implementing a Peer Education Life Skills Programme through Action Research: Lesotho and the HIV and AIDS pandemic'. Proposal submitted to Irish Aid/HEA PSC Programme 2011–2016. Outline of proposal published in 'Annual Report: Centre for Global Development 2012', p. 28. UCC: Cork Snap Printers (in house publication in process).

Kaiser Foundation (2007). 'HIV/AIDS Could "Wipe Out" Lesotho, Official Says', Kaiser Health News. <www.kaiserheathnews.org/daily-report/2007/august/22/dr00047035.aspx > accessed 12 October 2012.

Moon, B., and Wolfenden, B. (2012). 'Teacher Education in Sub-Saharan Africa: Issues and challenges around teacher resources and practices.' In R. Griffin (ed.), *Teacher Education in Sub-Saharan Africa: Closer perspectives*, pp. 27–55. Oxford: Symposium Books.

National Aids Commission (2011). <www.nas.org.ls/hivaids/ > accessed 22 May 2011.

O'Riordan, J., Urwick, J., Long, S., and Campbell, M. (2012). 'Towards a Holistic Understanding of Special Educational Needs'. In R. Griffin (ed.), *Teacher Education in Sub-Saharan Africa: Closer perspectives*, pp. 129–47. Oxford: Symposium Books.

Paulson, J. (ed.) (2011). *Education, Conflict and Development*. Oxford: Symposium Books.

Sinclair, M. (2001). *Education in Situations of Emergency*. Paris: UNESCO.

UNAIDS (2000). *Report on the Global HIV/AIDS Epidemic: June 2000*. Geneva: UNAIDS. <http://www.unaids.org/en/dataanalysis/knowyourepidemic/epi demiologypublications/2008reportontheglobalaidsepidemic/> accessed 10 October 2012.

UNDP (2008). *United Nations Development Programme Lesotho, Country Programme Action Plan: 2008–2012*. New York: UN. <http://www.undp.org.ls/practice/CPAP%20-%202008%20to%202012.pdf> accessed 14 October 2012.

UNESCO (2007). *Education for All (EFA) Global Monitoring Report: Strong foundations – early childhood care and education*. Oxford: Oxford University Press.

UNESCO (2009). *Education for All (EFA) Global Monitoring Report: Overcoming inequality: Why governance matters*. Oxford: Oxford University Press.

UNICEF (2010). <http://www.unicef.org/media/media_53653.html> accessed 18 October 2012.

Urwick, J., and Elliott, J. (2010). 'International Orthodoxy versus National Realities: Inclusive schooling and the education of children with disabilities in Lesotho', *Comparative Education*, 46 (2), 137–50.

Urwick, J., Griffin, R., Opendi, V., and Khatleli, M. (2012). 'What Hope for the Dakar Goals? The Lower levels of education in Lesotho and Uganda since 2000'. In R. Griffin (ed.), *Teacher Education in Sub-Saharan Africa: Closer perspectives*. pp. 71–90. Oxford: Symposium Books.

Verspoor, A. M. (2008). 'The Challenge of Learning: Improving the quality of basic education in sub-Saharan Africa'. In D. Johnson (ed.), *The Changing Landscape of Education in Africa: Quality, equality and democracy*, pp. 13–43. Oxford: Symposium Books.

World Bank (2005). 'Working for a World Free of Poverty – Lesotho'. <http://data.worldbank.org/country/lesotho> accessed 3 October 2012.

World Bank (1999). <http://web.worldbank.org/WBSITE/EXTERNAL/EXTDEC/EXTRESEARCH/EXTWDRS/0,,contentMDK:22295143~pagePK:478093~piPK:477627~theSitePK:477624,00.html#fulltext> accessed 10 October 2012.

JACQUI O'RIORDAN, JAMES URWICK, MATEMOHO KHATLELI, STELLA LONG, GRACE NTAOTE, FLORENCE NYAKUDYA AND NTHABELENG MAKETELA

8 Identification of Disabilities in Young Children in Lesotho: The Role of the Early Childhood Sector

Introduction

This chapter draws on research carried out in Lesotho in 2009 that sought to identify key capacities and challenges in developing a framework for inclusion of children with disabilities in education in Lesotho. Lesotho is a small mountainous country located in southern Africa, bordered by South Africa. It is ranked 156th on the Human Development Index (UNDP 2009) and has a population of over 1.8 million people (Bureau of Statistics 2010). The research included formal educational institutions, as well as government ministries, medical units, households, communities and pre-schools. This chapter focuses on the capacities and challenges found within the early years sector in Lesotho in identifying and including children with disabilities in education. It outlines the development of the IECCD sector in Lesotho and examines the context of children with disabilities in the country, highlighting the potentially important role that the sector has to play in the early identification of children's needs.[1] It is argued that such identification can contribute towards the development of a needs-based inclusion of children with disabilities/SEN. Such an approach has the potential to improve the quality of their educational experiences and contribute towards their holistic, and meaningful, inclusion in education.

1 Integrated Early Childhood Care and Development (IECCD), the approved term in Lesotho.

In 2006, questions on disability were asked for the first time in the Population and Housing Census and, from data produced, it is estimated that 3.7 per cent of the population have a disability of some sort, 2.1 per cent being male and 1.6% female (Bureau of Statistics 2009). Reported figures of 1,385 in the 0–4 age group, and 3,218 in the 5–9 age group, suggest that there may be a high degree of failure to identify disabilities in the younger group. The IECCD sector has the potential to increase early identification and possible interventions, with investment in resources and training of teachers/practitioners. Given the structure of IECCD in Lesotho, which is both centre- and home-based, the exploitation of this potential could have profound impacts on access to education for children with disabilities, appropriate interventions, and quality of life more generally. While it is notable that current policy recognizes the importance of early intervention and seeks the integration of children with disabilities in education, in practice a number of limitations remain that present obstacles to its fulfilment.

A brief overview of the IECCD sector in Lesotho

In Lesotho, IECCD provision comprises community centres, those centres attached to primary schools, privately-run centres and home-based resource persons. The inclusion of home-based provision in Lesotho's IECCD sector has been noted as an example of good practice in a study of early childhood care and education in selected sub-Saharan African countries. Its strengths are said to include (i) its targeting of 'children from poor families and other disadvantaged backgrounds' and (ii) its working 'according to parents' expectations in terms of its impact on the children, their parents and the community' (UNESCO-ICCBA 2010: 28–9). Furthermore, its location and contextualization within the community, with parents taking active roles as educators/carers, has been particularly noted as positive. These home-based centres are also the only type of early years provision available in Lesotho to which, in principle, fees do not apply, as they comprise groups of parents who co-operate in providing pre-school care and education for their children.

The IECCD sector in Lesotho has grown and developed since the early 1970s and while its development is uneven, the presence of IECCD centres is now evident throughout the country. Estimates of the gross enrolment ratio for children aged three to five in 2006 vary from 18 per cent (UNESCO 2008: Table 3b) to 33 per cent (UNESCO-ICCBA 2010) and in any event participation is less likely for children living in rural and highland areas and those from poorer families (UNESCO 2007). It is also noted that both IECCD trainers and teachers, while often having an amount of experience working in the sector, generally have few formal qualifications (UNESCO-ICCBA 2010; Sebatane and Lefoka 2011). Problems also arise regarding low and delayed pay for teachers and the quality of the centre structures (Sebatane and Lefoka 2011).

The development of the sector originated through a range of interest groups, initially including the Lesotho Council of Women and the Lesotho Day Care and Community Centre. Later, in the mid-1980s, the Lesotho Pre-school and Day Care Centre was formed as an umbrella group for a range of early years services, including crèches, pre-schools, and kindergartens. In 1995, all early years centres came under the remit of the IECCD unit at the Ministry of Education and Training (MoET). The Unit has responsibility for monitoring and inspecting all early years centres and is involved in training and support for the sector. Additionally, the sector is overseen by the IECCD National Council, and IECCD District Councils, with committees operating at local levels. This structure is consistent with Lesotho's commitments as a signatory to the UN Convention on the Rights of the Child (UN 1989) and the Dakar Agreement on Education for All (UNESCO 2000), in which early childhood education and inclusion of children with disabilities are identified as important goals.

UNESCO, in its assessment of IECCD in Lesotho, remarked that the continuing development of the sub-sector *should* be in accordance with '[i]ts constitutional duty to protect the rights of young children and to provide them with security, nutrition, health and education as a matter of right' (UNESCO-ICCBA 2010: 20). But actual progress in this direction has been hampered by lack of public funding and by the priority given to primary schools. As Urwick and Griffin point out (2011: 76–7), MoET has focused on attaching reception classes (for children aged five to six) to a limited number of primary schools and has provided no subsidies to IECCD centres. In-service training at this level has depended on workshops funded by UNICEF and on a network of volunteer resource teachers at the district level.

According to its draft policy document, prepared in 2000, the IECCD Unit's stated goal is that all children aged from 0–6, and not yet in primary school, have access to IECCD 'in order to facilitate [a] child's survival, growth, development and learning. Priorities are to be given to those populations identified as being at risk' (MoET 2000: 10). Incorporated into its definition of care is 'the early detection of disabilities and early intervention' (9). The policy also recognizes the importance of integration of children with special educational needs at an early stage, as is clear from the following statement:

> In accordance with the Ministry of Education and Training (MoET) – Special Education policy on integration, the integration exercise should start from early childhood education through primary, secondary, right up to tertiary and vocational level. (MoET 2000: 1–2)

Having stated the above, however, the document goes on to highlight a lack of personnel and special educational needs (SEN) specialisms within the IECCD sector: limitations that it views as very serious, given the potential of early intervention to identify and possibly remedy emerging barriers that may present – a potential that it states is not practised.

Teacher training for IECCD and for SEN in Lesotho

One positive development in this context was the launching in 2007 of a Certificate in Early Childhood Education (CECE) programme at the Lesotho College of Education (LCE). This in-service programme, in which practitioners are taught and supervised by specialists of LCE and MoET over a two-year period, is 'designed for the education and training of teachers and caregivers who are or will be responsible for children aged three to six' (LCE 2007: 2). It includes a short module on Child and Parent Counselling and Special Educational Needs. The UNESCO-IICBA report (2010: 17) notes that the development of this certificate marked the beginning of professional development of IECCD teachers in the country.

For special educational needs (SEN), LCE has a compulsory course (i.e. module) within its initial teacher training (diploma) programmes for primary and secondary education. The college also offers an Advanced Diploma in Special Education (ADSE). This is a one-year, full-time programme, aimed at teachers with responsibilities for SEN in primary, secondary and special schools who already hold a Diploma in Education. However, very few early years practitioners could qualify for participation on the SEN Advanced Diploma: a large proportion of them have only a primary education and the CECE programme trains mainly those who hold a Junior Certificate (which represents just three years of secondary education). A case can, therefore, be made for the LCE Department of Special Education to offer an additional programme of training in SEN for the benefit of early years practitioners. In the selection of trainees, priority could be given initially to IECCD officials and volunteer resource teachers (known as district teacher trainers) at the district level. The latter would then be in a better position to assist the IECCD centres in their districts, especially on issues of recognition of disabilities, referral for screening and teaching strategies for SEN.

Currently, a review of IECCD policy is underway in Lesotho and, although it is not yet finalized, commitment to the sector has recently been reiterated, with particular reference to its role in supporting children with disabilities/special needs (Makhele 2010). The IECCD Unit's information officer recently indicated that the revised policy 'will ensure vulnerable children receive early childhood intervention services [...] especially for children in difficult circumstances' (2011: 4). A consultation process that was undertaken to inform the review supports the evidence from earlier studies that many children with special needs are currently not accessing services and that their parents are often unsure where to go for information and assistance. Indeed, the recent CGDE report on SEN in Lesotho (to which most of the authors of this chapter contributed) recommended that, in addressing this issue, a network of school-based SEN co-ordinators should link with IECCD centres as well as schools in their areas (CGDE 2010). It should also be noted that across neighbouring countries in sub-Saharan Africa difficulties in accessing information and services for people with disabilities are also reported to be commonplace (Kotze 2012).

Children with disabilities in Lesotho

According to the 2006 Population and Housing Census, the first census in Lesotho to obtain data on disability, it is estimated that 3.7 per cent of the population of Lesotho, or 68,926 people, have disabilities of some form (Bureau of Statistics 2009).[2] It must be noted that this rate is well below that which would be expected, if looking at international figures, where, generally, 10 per cent of the population are expected to have some form of disability (UN Enable 2006). Given this, it is worth considering whether the questions that were asked were broad enough to capture a full range of disabilities. Lesotho College of Education's consultancy report of 2007 questioned these categories and pointed out that they omit, for instance, autism, ADHD and DCD (LCE 2007). Common disabilities, as listed by the Bureau of Statistics (2009) include blindness (total/partial), deafness, amputations and lameness/paralysis. Even for the 0–4 age group, the most common disabilities recorded are lameness/paralysed limb, total/partial blindness, speech problems, amputation of foot/leg, deafness, and mental retardation. Notwithstanding the limitations of the data provided, the Population and Housing Census also indicates that estimates of disability increase with age, implying that people go on to acquire disabilities with age and/or that disabilities are identified more as people age, as mentioned

2 The 2001 Lesotho Demographic Survey was the first official survey in Lesotho to collect data on disability and the 2006 Housing and Population Census drew on the questions asked in 2001 in incorporating questions on disability into its questionnaire.

earlier. SINTEF's study on *Living Conditions among People with Disabilities in Lesotho* (Kamaleri and Eide 2010) suggests that 32.6 per cent of disabilities originated at birth/were congenital and 35.4 per cent arose as a result of illness/disease.

The Bureau of Statistics points out that the educational system has a special education programme that has facilitated enrolment of students with disabilities (2009). A question arises, however, regarding the quality of such education. Recent research has found that children with disabilities commonly repeat classes and are unlikely to have individual educational plans developed to cater for their special needs. Identification of special needs is often informal and resources available for identification and assessment are either rudimentary, in short supply and/or absent (LCE 2007; CGDE 2011). With regard to the outcomes of school attendance, Kotze (2012) reports that people with disabilities across southern Africa, including Lesotho, are likely to have low levels of education and low literacy rates. In Lesotho, according to the 2006 Housing and Population Census, rates of participation in education beyond primary level fell significantly below that of people with no disabilities, at 12.2 per cent as opposed to 28.1 per cent participation. Furthermore, it was found that there were a substantial number of people with disabilities who never accessed education at all.

For the educational needs of children with severe or moderate disabilities who cannot easily be included in regular schools, Lesotho has four special schools that focus on different kinds of disability. These include one under government management: the Resource Centre for the Blind, Maseru. Two, under Roman Catholic management, focus on the hearing impaired: St Paul's School for the Deaf, Hlotse and Kananelo Centre for the Deaf at Ha Buasono in Berea District. Thuso School, in Butha-Buthe, which is under private management, focuses on various disabilities but more on mental and behavioural ones. A fifth special school is Phelisanong School, located at Pitseng, which is under community management and less specialized.

All these schools, although they have residential facilities for students, have limitations with regard to qualified teaching staff and only enroll a small proportion of the eligible children. All are, in principle, primary level schools and not structured to meet the needs of younger children, aged below six. Thus, although these schools have the potential to become resource centres with an outreach function, they have done relatively little so far to help meet the need for early identification of SEN. Indeed, some of the children attending these special schools, who have multiple disabilities, have never received adequate assessment of their special needs.

The special schools have links with regular primary schools nearby and succeed in preparing some of their pupils for transfer to those schools. In addition, there are a few homes for children with physical disabilities that facilitate their attendance at co-operating regular schools. But those who reach the regular schools in these ways are in a sense the 'fortunate few' among those with disabilities, whose needs have received timely recognition and support.

Further insights are provided by Mokoena (2007), reporting on workshops of Skillshare International's Disability Project in Lesotho. She indicates that children with disabilities are often 'not given adequate education like other children and they do not progress well'. They are often 'humiliated and given names, including ones like *seqouala* or *sekooa*, which are very degrading'.[3] Worryingly, she also highlighted the vulnerability of children with disabilities, especially those with mental and speech impairments, to sexual abuse. She also reports a lack of training and understanding of carers and schools in handling children with disabilities, particularly those with speech and hearing problems, making it difficult for the children to have their needs understood.

SINTEF's study found that those people with disabilities were more likely to be socially and economically isolated and to live in higher dependency households than those without disabilities (Kamaleri and Eide 2010). They found that one in five people with disabilities were likely to be discriminated against by society, while just over 16 per cent experienced discrimination in their families and in accessing pubic services. A report

3 'Sekooa': the correct term is 'Seqhoala', beginning with 'se', refer to objects with disability. The preferred term of people with disabilities, 'Motho ea nang le bokooa', translates to 'people with disabilities'. 'Seqouala' refers to physical disability and is also a degrading term.

by Kotze (2012) suggests that people with disabilities in the region are routinely unaware of campaigns and services that might be of benefit to them, an issue that was specifically noted with regard to access to health services in Lesotho. The report states that in Lesotho, commonly, people with disabilities:

> Do not know about various services that are available for them to address their health needs. In addition, PWDs [people with disabilities] do not have access to appropriate health treatment and care. Health centres do not have suitable infrastructure, necessary expertise and equipment to cater for the health needs of various disabilities. (Kotze 2012: 29)

While the services in question here are specifically health related ones, lack of awareness of them and their poor infrastructure, expertise, and so forth, can have direct impacts on education, since access to appropriate health services might may well be a pre-cursor to meaningful participation in education. Given that educational services generally are located in every community, in a diversity of forms, from pre-school, to primary and secondary schools, this level of non-awareness is worrying.

Furthermore, traditionally, stigma was associated with disability in Lesotho, leading to social isolation of people with disabilities and their families. This ranges from attitudes and practices at local to government and policy levels and has contributed towards exclusion of persons with disabilities from full participation in society (Khatleli et al. 1995; Mokoena 2007; Kamaleri and Eide 2010). Mokoena (2007) also found that children without disabilities were often afraid of people with disabilities. In the mountain kingdom of Lesotho, such isolation can be compounded by an often inaccessible, physical terrain, particularly in the highland areas, where the road networks can be rudimentary, but also in urban centres, where gravel roads can also be difficult to traverse.

Notwithstanding this, such attitudes are being challenged more recently. People with disabilities in Lesotho have come together to challenge discrimination against them and are actively contributing to change. The Lesotho National Federation of Organisations for the Disabled (LNFOD) is the umbrella organization under which four other national specific issue-based organizations operate. Owing to campaigning by these and other

NGOs, the government of Lesotho ratified and signed the UN Convention on the Rights of Persons with Disabilities on 2 December 2008. This was followed, in 2011, by publication of a *National Disability and Rehabilitation Policy*, prepared by the Ministry of Health and Social Welfare (MoHSW). The policy aims to challenge traditional views on disability and to promote the full inclusion of persons with disability in society. It states that '[t]he purpose of this policy is to create an environment where PWDs [persons with disabilities] living and working in Lesotho would be able to realize their full potential' (MHSW 2011: viii). The key ways to achieving this are identified as: the removal of barriers, including attitudinal changes in accessing employment; promotion of equal opportunities; and promotion of good practice in private and civil society sectors.

It is noteworthy that the first priority area identified in this policy is 'prevention, early identification and intervention', while it is recognized that important elements of this priority area relate to acquired disabilities. The policy also highlights the key role that IECCD has to play in the prevention and early identification of disability among young children. The policy also recognizes the key role of education in promoting and supporting the empowerment of people with disabilities.

Institutional capacity in early childhood education

Within this context we now specifically turn our attention to findings arising from the mapping exercise undertaken in 2009 on the identification and assessment of children with disabilities (CGDE 2011). As mentioned, this study attempted to map the capacity of relevant organizations in Lesotho to contribute to a national system of identification, assessment and support for children with special educational needs, with a view to developing recommendations on strategies for the use of available personnel and resources in this regard. The methodology informing the research exercise was based on the premise that educational opportunities of children with special needs are influenced by a range of organizational and social units, both within and outside the public services. The units selected for study included: managerial and professional bodies at national and district levels, international agencies, national NGOs, representative schools of different kinds, households and local communities. While the focus was on capacity to contribute to identification, assessment and support for SEN, the approach was sensitive to the existing cultures of these units and to the ways in which they interact. The sampling was limited to four districts (Berea, Leribe, Maseru and Quthing), but targeted both rural and urban contexts within these districts. Special, post-primary, primary and early childhood schools were included in the study. Data was obtained through semi-structured interviews with key informants, using pre-prepared interview templates customized for each sector.

While the findings then spanned the full range of sectors included in the study, here, we draw particular attention to those issues arising for the pre-school child, through interviews held with representatives of a small number of early childhood institutions, one in Maseru and two in Leribe district. The first of these was a community pre-school run under the supervision of the District Education Office and located in the rural part of Leribe District, adjacent to Hlotse town, the district headquarters. The second was a church-owned pre-school, attached to a primary and a secondary school. The third, a privately owned pre-school, was located in Maseru, the principal urban centre of Lesotho.

When those interviewed were asked whether any of the children had disabilities, the immediate answer, generally, was that there were none. However, although there was no systematic approach to identifying children with disabilities evident, there was some evidence that principals would contact parents if they noticed anything unusual about a child. The principal of one centre had expressed concern about one boy, who had very low levels of activity. Furthermore, on two previous occasions in recent years, the same principal had noticed, and reported to parents, problems with a child's eyes. This had resulted in the child being treated in South Africa in both cases. In one case, a doctor had said that the child would have become blind if the problem had not been treated.

While there are no official statistics, the principal of another centre reported that the school had about four or five children each year who could be identified as having SEN. At the time of the study, there were no children with a physical disability in this school, which indeed could not easily accommodate such children. The emphasis in this centre was on outdoor activity. It had many steps and a number of different access levels that could render it inaccessible for children with physical disabilities.

It is worth noting that in all three institutions, once the principal noticed that there might be a problem, she brought it to the notice of the parents, usually *gently* suggesting to them that perhaps they might need to have their child assessed. This process could take a few meetings; sometimes parents were initially defensive. In two of the schools, once parents acknowledged that there might be a problem, the teachers usually recommended that the child be taken to South Africa, where identification of problems and appropriate interventions might be more immediate. A common theme running throughout was that it was thought that the necessary levels of support were not available in Lesotho. Typical problems that we encountered during the course of this element of the research included ADHD, eye problems and hearing problems; intellectual, emotional and sensory rather than physical disabilities.

There were no official mechanisms for assessment internal to the any of the pre-schools. Children's needs were identified informally and parents were approached in a gradual empathetic way and encouraged to seek medical intervention or advice. The process is one of recognition through experience and working with children.

Furthermore, we found that there was little formal training in identifying disabilities and children's needs available to pre-school teachers. However, two principals interviewed who had received Montessori training believed that this training had been very helpful for them in identifying special educational needs of children. Their view is relevant, since the Montessori tradition in education has its origins in children with disabilities. Additionally, in attempting to identify children's needs, the principal of the church pre-school indicated that workshops that she had attended, which focused on the physical and emotional development of children, were also helpful in that they trained teachers to observe children closely through specified activities.

It was indicated to us that further training, particularly with a focus on early intervention, at national, regional and local levels, and including support for children, would be very helpful in equipping teachers to support children at the pre-school level. While it is acknowledged that relevant training, for relatively small numbers, has been provided by MoET and MoHSW, there is a strong desire for training among many IECCD teachers and caregivers. Those interviewed even requested training to provide spiritual support to children and their families, so that, if families faced problems, they could then offer a more holistic support to them. It was suggested that, if possible, training should be provided flexibly, possibly during the school vacation time, as teachers have problems in travelling during term time. It was also suggested that a database of SEN services available in Lesotho would be very useful as a resource to them.

Conclusion

It is clear from the above discussion that in Lesotho there is a commitment to the development of the early years sector in a variety of forms, as well as the recognition of its value in identifying and meeting the needs of children with disabilities. This is very clearly stated in policy and is facilitated through the development of educational courses aimed specifically at early years teachers/practitioners. It is also evident that, while significant challenges are presented to meaningful inclusion of people with disabilities in education, some notable steps have been taken that go some way to addressing these challenges. Early intervention is recognized as an important contributor towards a holistic integration of children with disabilities in education, with long term implications for their opportunities.

The commitment to challenging barriers presented to people with disabilities is also evident, especially through the work of advocacy groups and the signing and ratifying of international agreements that promote the recognition and inclusion of people with disabilities in all aspects of society. It is also noteworthy that, in policy statements, the emphasis is on viewing disability more from a social than from a medical framework, while recognizing the important role of medical personnel and interventions in contributing towards full inclusion and integration.

It is important, in realizing the potential of the IECCD sub-sector in identifying and contributing to setting appropriate interventions in place, that teachers and caregivers be provided with opportunities to gain knowledge and skills in SEN. Identification, assessment and the provision of appropriate SEN interventions requires communication across the education, health and social work sectors and access to appropriate health and care services to meet specific needs.

References

Bureau of Statistics (2009). *2006 Lesotho Population and Housing and Census: Analytical Report, Volume IIIB, socio economic characteristics*. Maseru: Ministry of Finance and Development.

Centre for Global Development through Education (CGDE) (2011). *Identification, Assessment and Inclusion for Learners with Special Educational Needs: Towards a national system for Lesotho: Final Report of the Research Team*. Limerick: CGDE, Mary Immaculate College.

Kamaleri, Y., and Eide, A. H., (eds) (2010). *Living Conditions among People with Disabilities in Lesotho*. Oslo: SINTEF Technology and Society and Global Health and Welfare.

Khatleli, P., Mariga, L., Phachaka, L., and Stubbs, S. (1995). 'Schools for All: National planning in Lesotho'. In B. O'Toole and R. McConkey (eds), *Innovations in Developing Countries for People with Disabilities*. UK: Lisieux Hall, Italy: AIFO. <www.eenet.org.uk/resources/docs/inno_dev_coun.php> accessed 8 March 2012.

Kotze, H. (2012). *Status of Disability Rights in Southern Africa*, OSISA (Open Society Initiative for Southern Africa), OSF-SA, OSF, OSISA.

Lesotho College of Education (2007). *Education Policies, Programmes and Legislation Relating to Disadvantaged Children and Children with Disabilities: Final report*. Maseru: Ministry of Education and Training, Special Education Unit.

Makhele, M. (2011). 'IECCD Policy Reviewed', *Informative*, 10 October.

Ministry of Education and Training (MoET) (2000). 'Final Draft of the National Policy Document: Early childhood care and development', prepared by ECCD Task Force and Dr Martha Llanos. Maseru: MoET.

Ministry of Health and Social Welfare (MoHSW) (2006). *National Policy on Orphans and Vulnerable Children*. Maseru: MoSHW.

Ministry of Health and Social Welfare (MoHSW) (2011). *The National Disability and Rehabilitation Policy: Mainstreaming persons with disabilities into society*. Maseru: MoSHW.

Mokoena, N. (2007). 'International Report for Foundation', Report on the Lesotho Disability Project, October to December. Maseru: Skillshare International.

Sebatane, E. M., and Lefoka, P. J. (2011). 'Knowledge, Attitudes and Practices of Parents and Caregivers of Children aged 0 to 8 Years Regarding Early Childhood Care and Development (ECCD)', Report submitted to the Ministry of Education and Training. Institute of Education. Roma: National University of Lesotho.

UN Enable (nd). *Factsheet on Persons with Disabilities*. New York: UN Enable.

UNDP (2009). *Human Development Report*. New York: UNDP.

UNESCO (2008). *EFA Global Monitoring Report 2009. Statistical Tables 2009: Final Longer Version*. Paris: UNESCO.

UNESCO (2009). *The Inclusion of Children with Disabilities: The early childhood imperative*. UNESCO, Policy Brief on Early Childhood, 46, April–June.

UNESCO-IICBA (2010). *Country Case Studies on Early Childhood Care and Education (ECCE) in selected sub-Saharan African Countries 2007/2008: Some key teacher issues and policy recommendations. A Summary report*. UNESCO-IICBA: Addis Abba.

Urwick, J., and Griffin, R., with Opendi, V., and Khatleli, M. (2012). 'What Hope for the Dakar Goals? The lower levels of education in Lesotho and Uganda since 2000'. In R. Griffin (ed.), *Teacher Education in Sub-Saharan Africa: Closer perspectives*, pp. 71–90. Oxford: Symposium Books.

MAHIMA MITRA

9 The Take-Up of Government Early Childhood Education and Care Services in Developing Countries: Evidence from India and Theoretical Frameworks for Guiding Research

Introduction

Early childhood, defined most commonly as the period between 0–8 years of age (UNESCO 2010), has been established as a critical, or sensitive, period in the life cycle of an individual, with much discourse on the impact of early experiences on later development (e.g. see Lilienfeld and Pasamanick 1954; Sylva and Wiltshire 1993; Nelson 2000; Shonkoff and Phillips 2000; World Bank 2004; NCERT 2006). Early Childhood Education and Care (ECEC) services include pre-school programmes and children's care centres as well as informal, home-based care options and arrangements. Additionally, ECEC policy embraces not only provisions for young children but also some leave and benefits schemes for their working parents (OECD 2006).

ECEC continues to be a universal government priority backed by global movements supporting the rights and needs of children aged 0–6. Some of the significant milestones in the field include the 1959 Declaration on the Rights of the Child, the 1989 UN Convention on the Rights of the Child, the 1990 World Conference on Education for All and the 2000 World Education Forum in Dakar.

According to the OECD (2006: 12), governments invest in the early years' provisions to 'increase women's labour market participation [...] reconcile work and family responsibilities [...] confront the demographic challenges [and] address issues of child poverty and educational disadvantage'. Head Start has been in existence in the USA since 1965, primarily to reduce educational disadvantage and childhood poverty (e.g. see Kamerman and Kahn 1997). In the UK, a plethora of initiatives have been introduced to support (disadvantaged) families and enable early education and care including Sure Start (1997), Early Excellence Centres (late 1990s) and Children's Centres (2006) (e.g. see HM Treasury 2004; Sylva and Pugh 2005; Smith 2007).

Movements within the country as well as worldwide have lent support to the growth of ECEC programmes in India. Nonetheless, the picture remains bleak for young children and their working mothers. Child-specific allocations, *vis-à-vis* the total expenditure in the Union Budget, have always been low, and most of this is spent on *child education*[1] (72 per cent) rather than *child development*[2] (17 per cent) (MoWCD 2007). Educational statistics reveal that the Gross Enrolment Ratio for ECEC in India stood at 47.1 per cent in 2007 compared to 73.4 per cent for the UK and 61.1 per cent for the USA in the same year (World Bank 2010). Further, the percentage share of enrolment in pre-primary classes to total enrolment in schools stood at a meagre 8.69 per cent in 2008–9 (NUEPA 2010). According to Sharma et al. (2008), only about 21 per cent of all children aged 0–6 are covered by any kind of ECEC services in the country. This is a clear failure of the government policy process (World Bank 2004), especially given the large body of evidence demonstrating the longer-term benefits of investing in early years education (see NIPCCD 1992; NCERT 1993; UNESCO 1996).

The trend remains the same when it comes to government support for working women in the country. 90 per cent of India's working women are employed in the unorganized sector (World Bank 1999), and most of these are poor. Additionally, 2005 figures show that social security benefits[3] were *not available* to 965 of 1,000 female casual labourers across rural and urban India (NSS Round 61 2005), indicating the weak position of women workers in the informal sector of the economy.

1 That is, for the older, school-going age group.
2 That is, for the early years and pre-school age.
3 Including provident funds (a savings fund to which an employer and employee contribute, which is given to the employee as a lump sum on retirement), pensions, gratuities (a lump sum 'free' amount given on retirement and based on the number of years of service), health care and maternity benefits.

When it comes to India, there are four factors that have guided the development of ECEC services in the country (Pattnaik 1996: 12): the growing participation of women in the workforce; the disintegration of the extended family system; the recognition that ECEC rids the older sibling[4] of caretaking duties, enabling her to go to school; and the positive influence of such programmes on health, nutritional and educational outcomes of children (ibid; Sharma et al. 2008). What started off as voluntary initiatives for ECEC in the pre-independence era slowly grew into significant initiatives such as the setting up of the Central Social Welfare Board by the government of India in 1953, and the launch of the Integrated Child Development Services scheme in 1975. Since then a number of schemes and programmes have been launched by the government, although a dedicated ECEC policy is still lacking. More recently, the eighty-sixth constitutional amendment has made education for all children between six and fourteen years a fundamental right.[5] Nonetheless, the 0–6 age group has been left out and is not protected under any law or government mandate.[6]

ECEC provisions and programmes in India

In the Indian context, the goal of enabling optimal child development has always received primacy over the needs of working mothers.[7] The Indian government's flagship programme for child development (the ICDS) is, in

4 Usually female.

5 With the Right to Education Act enforced as of April 2010.

6 Recent developments in the field have led to efforts to draft a national ECCE policy following the exclusion of 0–6 year-olds from the National Policy on Education. The first publicly available draft of this policy, at the time of this publication, can be viewed on the Ministry of Women and Child Development's website, <http://www.wcd.nic.in>.

7 This is evident in the existence of an integrated Child Development programme since 1975 but the lack of well-formed maternity benefits or parental leave in the informal sector.

principle, an *integrated* system in that it offers pre-school education to the three- to six-year-olds and childcare for the under-threes. Nonetheless, in practice, it is far more focused on the former group, with a recent emphasis on the nutritional aspects of the same age group, i.e. the three- to six-year-olds. Infant care through childcare and maternity leave is a second model that exists in parallel with the integrated system, through maternity benefits for the formal sector employee and a set of poorly implemented labour mandates and benefits schemes for the informal sector mother. The following section discusses each of these in detail.

Maternity benefits and childcare provisions

Laws governing the provision of maternity benefits include the Employees' State Insurance Act, 1948 for the organized sector (Employees' State Insurance Corporation 2007) and the Maternity Benefits Act (Government of India 1961) for the unorganized sector (viz. factories, mines and plantations) and all those not covered by the ESI Act, 1948.[8] Under these, a woman is entitled to twelve weeks of paid maternity leave, six weeks of paid leave on miscarriage or termination of pregnancy, and four weeks paid leave for sickness arising out of pregnancy, confinement or premature birth. Nevertheless, impact is limited, especially in the informal industry (that caters to the majority of working women in India), due to lack of a 'well defined employer or employment' (Gupta et al. 2007: 54). This is also true for most developing countries where mothers don't usually qualify for benefits because of a lack of association with the formal sector (Kamerman 2006). This is cause for concern, because the burgeoning informal sector has as many ECEC needs (if not greater) as the organized.

8 More recently, an amendment to the Act i.e. the Maternity Benefit (Amendment) Bill, 2007, has also been passed in the Parliament (Fernandes 2007a).

In 2001, the National Maternity Benefits Scheme was launched as an initiative to provide nutritional support to all pregnant women living below the poverty line through a cash benefit eight to twelve weeks before delivery. The larger objective was to reduce the high Maternal Mortality Rate (MMR) of the country. In 2005, this scheme was merged with the JSY,[9] the National Government's safe motherhood initiative that incentivizes institutional deliveries by awarding cash to beneficiaries (Supreme Court Commissioners 2008).[10]

Besides maternity leave, another set of statutory provisions under different Labour Acts mandate for crèches and day-care facilities, based on criteria such as number of women employed, number of children eligible for day-care/crèches and size of establishment. At present, these pertain to factory, mine, plantation and construction workers (NCERT 2006; Sinha 2006a). While guidelines are provided by these Central Acts, it is up to the State Governments to devise appropriate rules for implementation (NCERT 2006).

Evidence, however, indicates that such labour legislation has met with very limited success (The Consultative Group Secretariat 1992; Sareen 2004). According to one estimate, '[t]he number of crèches under existing crèche schemes is about 23,000 whereas 800,000 crèches are needed to cater to approx. 220 million women working in the informal sector and in dire need of child care services' (Sareen 2004: 2).

Reasons quoted for the absence of such facilities in work establishments include 'problems of transporting children to workplaces, variations in working hours, and the dangerous environments characterising many work settings' (ibid: 15). Research also indicates that employers prefer not to bear the costs of running such centres and thus recruit more men than women. They do this to evade the regulation that mandates provision of such facilities once an establishment employs a set minimum number of eligible women workers (The Consultative Group Secretariat 1992).

9 'Janani Suraksha Yojana', which can be translated as 'Mothers' Security Scheme'.

10 More recently, The Unorganized Sector Workers' Social Security Bill, 2007 (Fernandes 2007b) has been passed, and this provides an enabling framework for social security schemes for these workers in India.

Integrated services for childcare and pre-school education

Sponsored by the Central Government, the Rajiv Gandhi National Crèche Scheme (RGNCS) for the children of working mothers (2006), provides crèche and day-care services for working or 'deserving'[11] (Government of India 2005: 5) women whose combined monthly family wages do not exceed INR 12,000.[12] Three implementing agencies[13] have been identified to disburse funds to NGOs for setting up crèches. At least 50 per cent of places are allocated to children from families that have incomes below the poverty line. Although the funding is managed by the Central Government, assistance is limited to 90 per cent, the remaining borne by the implementing organization. User charges of INR 20 per child per month are collected from families below the poverty line, and INR 60 from the others. Services are meant to provide sleeping facilities, health care, supplementary nutrition, immunization and pre-school education for about twenty-five children aged 0–6 per centre, for eight hours a day, from 9am to 5pm (Government of India 2005).

According to the Ministry of Finance (2008) there are only about 28,000 sanctioned crèches running throughout the country with about 0.7 million child beneficiaries. Further, the present scheme is reported to operate on inflexible patterns and norms, and is limited in availability to a set of working mothers who fulfil specific eligibility criteria (Sinha 2006b). Although there are a number of agencies monitoring the scheme,[14] evaluation reports are limited, especially those relating to take-up of services by

11 '[W]omen belonging to poor families, who require support and relief from childcare as they struggle to cope with burden of activities, within and outside the home' (Government of India 2005: 2).

12 Approximately 164 GBP.

13 The Central Social Welfare Board, Indian Council for Child Welfare and Bhartiya Adim Jati Sevak Sangh.

14 National Institute of Public Cooperation and Child Development (NIPCCD), State Women's Development Corporation, women's study centres in universities and schools of social work.

beneficiaries. In contrast to this limited empirical data, there is a growing (although piecemeal) body of anecdotal evidence that suggests that a greater number of parents are choosing private over public childcare services (e.g. Anantharaman 2005; George 2008), reflecting either a preference for private childcare (paid for by parents) over public (state funded/subsidized provision), or a lack of sufficient public care services.

The Integrated Child Development Services scheme (ICDS) is a national level, flagship scheme launched by the Government of India in 1975 and targeted at three groups: young children (0–6 year-olds), women in the reproductive age span (including pregnant and lactating women) and adolescent girls. The scheme broadly offers health and nutrition, and childcare and pre-school education services.

The ICDS scheme is broad in its scope. Although it reported initial gains in terms of child and maternal health and education, it has been facing problems with implementation, especially uneven and poor coverage (MoWCD and the World Bank 2006; Saxena and Mander 2007). Moreover, inadequate infrastructure, poor coordination at the project level and disrupted services have also been reported (NIPCCD 2006), with an (over)emphasis on the nutrition component at the expense of others (Ghosh 1997; MoWCD and the World Bank 2006). There are a few studies that document ICDS implementation and take-up across various Indian states. For example, a 2004 study carried out by the Centre for Equity Studies in India that compared state performances in ICDS across six states in India indicated that when it comes to the ICDS, the western state of Maharashtra is doing much better than some of the northern states of the country.[15] Mothers in Maharashtra reported that the centres open regularly, and considered the ICDS to be important for their children's wellbeing. In clear contrast, the northern states experienced problems related to lack of funds, understaffing, poor infrastructure etc. (cited in Thukral 2005; Drèze 2006a, 2006b).

15 Only compared to the southern state of Tamil Nadu.

Research potential

In summary, support for parents and children is available in India through a number of services and benefits. However, evaluations indicate poor implementation and take-up at the local level. Despite basic descriptive evidence of poor implementation and flaws therein, there has been little research exploring parents' perceptions of schemes and reasons behind non-take-up of support. Moreover, where existing, such research is piecemeal and in many cases, anecdotal and journalistic rather than empirical. Further, the entirety of parents' ECEC experiences has seldom been explored. Finally, there is limited insight into the policy-making process and how that ties in with implementation and take-up at the local level.

It is in light of such research gaps that an exploration of user perspectives' on early childhood schemes is proposed. The underlying rationale is that in addition to studying child outcomes as a measure of the success or failure of ECEC programmes (as is usually the case), studying the take-up of services is also an important step in mapping effectiveness of early years' services. Questions that could be framed to undertake such research include:

1. What is the extent of take-up of government schemes such as the ICDS and RGNCS by working mothers in Indian slums?
2. What are their experiences of usage of the above services offered by the government?
3. What are the factors, or combination of factors, underpinning take-up and non-take-up of the above services? For instance:
    a) Do individual user factors matter?
    b) Do service implementation factors matter?

The rest of this chapter examines theoretical frameworks that can be utilized to guide such research on parents' take-up and experiences of using ECEC services.

ECEC service quality: multiple stakeholders, multiple perspectives

According to Katz (1993), quality in early childhood programmes can be viewed from a number of perspectives, each contributing uniquely to overall programme performance. These are as follows:

- The *top-down perspective*, referring to the quality of programmes as viewed by adults;
- The *bottom-up perspective*, wherein quality is ascertained through the experiences of children enrolled for the programme;
- The *outside-inside perspective*, referring to the quality as viewed by the families whose children are part of the programme;
- The *inside perspective*, or the evaluation through the experiences of children's centre staff and workers.

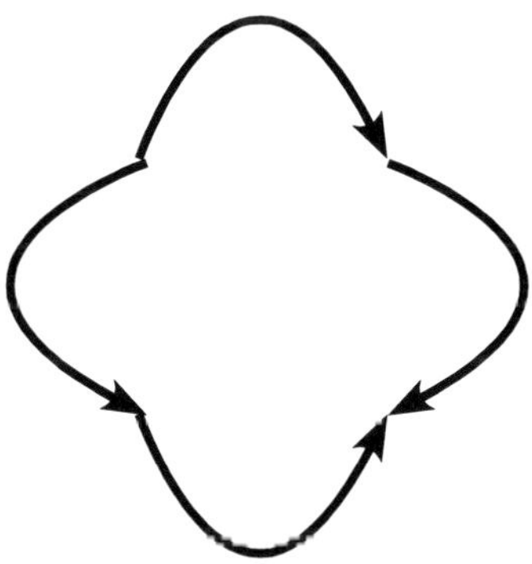

Figure 1 Perspectives on child care quality (Ceglowski and Bacigalupa 2002: 88)

Ceglowski and Bacigalupa (2002) discuss these in terms of the stakeholders involved i.e. researchers and professionals in the field, children, parents and childcare staff (see Figure 1), and are of the view that out of all four perspectives, evaluations centre mostly on researcher/professional perspectives, modestly on parental views and least on staff and children's perspectives. According to the authors, 'researchers have only begun to ask parents, teachers and children – the people who participate most directly in child care – how they define quality child care' (2002: 89). Nonetheless, they are of the view that accounting for each of these unexplored perspectives (including those of children and staff) is crucial in delivering services that meet local needs. In the context of the present chapter, then, a study of parental take-up, expectations and experiences reveals much in terms of the *outside-inside perspective* – a relatively under-researched area in the field of early years' policy.

What drives parental perceptions of ECEC?

According to James Walker:

> The lack of perfect information is the most striking difference between the child care market and the idealized perfect market [...] Information is obtained informally and consumers must actively search to find a provider [further], consumers do not know the quality of care offered by providers once identified. (1991: 65)

The first and foremost factor that affects parental perceptions and their experiences of take-up and use is the nature and amount of information on ECEC in general and a potential childcare service in specific. Among other factors impacting parents' perceptions of ECEC are demographic characteristics such as education and income (e.g. Browne Miller 1990; Cryer and Burchinal 1997; Noble 2007) – on which less is known at present but which is nevertheless an emerging domain requiring further study.

There is also evidence that culture impacts parental perceptions, for example, differences in perceptions of middle class versus ethnic minority and lower class parents (Powell 1994), and Native Americans versus others (Williams 1994). Culture also includes the values, beliefs and needs of parents as a group. These factors also impact how parents perceive early childhood education and care, as well as their experiences with related services (Moss 1994; Dahlberg, Moss and Pence 1999; Bernhard and Gonzalez-Mena 2000).

Finally, features of the ECEC system operating within a country/community may also impact how parents perceive and take up services. Carlson and Stenmalm-Sjöblom (1989) compare Sweden and the United States and conclude that the philosophies and societal characteristics related to children and childcare impact parents' perceptions of early childhood services in their country. Cryer, Tietze and Wessels (2002: 261) detail these as the 'costs of services, accessibility and the traditions influencing the services'. Framing research findings in terms of the above factors can be a useful means of theorizing about parents' experiences of ECEC and take-up of government services.

Barriers to take-up

When exploring the 'ifs and whethers' of provision take-up, it becomes imperative to indulge the 'whys' behind non-take-up. Of significance to any social programme that targets its services to a select section of the population is literature on barriers that prevent beneficiaries from utilizing the services appropriately. Such literature can serve to frame the findings of research in terms of the factors impacting take-up and non-take-up of early childhood services.

Hernanz et al. (2004: 18) present a taxonomy of factors that impact scheme take-up in OECD countries as follows:

Pecuniary determinants i.e. level of benefits and expected duration;
Information costs or the effort involved in procuring and understanding application procedures;

Administrative costs, understood as the delays and uncertainty of application outcome;
Social and psychological costs that relate to cultural attitudes and associated social stigma.

According to Currie (2006), although social stigma associated with means testing and lack of information about schemes are important factors, take-up of social programmes in the USA is low because of administrative barriers and transaction costs involved in accessing benefits. The theory of transaction or compliance costs particularly receives much support in literature (e.g. Currie 2000; Currie and Grogger 2001; Bitler et al. 2003). Bennett et al. define these as internal costs:

> incurred by individual benefit […] recipients […] which include time spent complying with obligations (both learning what the requirements are and fulfilling them), money costs (phone calls, postage, travel, etc.) and psychological costs (stigma, stress or frustration, for example). (2009: 8)

The time and effort involved in getting benefits especially makes a difference (Davies and Ritchie 1988; Stafford 2003). Other factors include low valuation of benefits because of which participants drop out or do not participate in social schemes (Bitler et al. 2003). The above factors, in various combinations, thus operate among a range of social benefits programmes across a number of countries in impacting the take-up of schemes by targeted beneficiaries (e.g. see Oorschot 1991; Kayser and Frick 2000; Riphahn 2001; Gibson and Weisner 2002; Bansak and Raphael 2006).

Conclusion: the implications of undertaking research with users on take-up of government ECEC services

This chapter has attempted to fill some of the existing methodological gaps in the field of Early Childhood Education and Care policy by proposing studies that document the voices of parents as potential beneficiaries of government ECEC services. Exploring the take-up, expectations and experiences of users is expected to contribute to an additional significant but under-researched domain in the multiple perspectives theory proposed by Katz (1993) and extended by Ceglowski and Bacigalupa (2002). Additional theoretical approaches that can guide such research include work on barriers to take-up and factors driving parents' perceptions of social programmes.

Finally, undertaking the proposed research is expected to contribute to, and extend, existing work in the field of ECEC policy in developing countries by:

Understanding the relationship between awareness of and significance given to Early Childhood Education and Care by primary stakeholders and the take-up of services by the target population;

Suggesting programme and implementation related reforms for effective policy delivery based on user feedback – for example, through greater dissemination of information on schemes among potential beneficiaries, or greater clarity on applicant enrolment procedures;

Identifying the driving factors for effective policy implementation – for example, demands for accountability, increased knowledge and political participation by citizens;

Understanding the role played by external actors such as NGOs in implementation of programmes and awareness among beneficiaries;

Understanding the relationship between political will and priority given to the early childhood period, and effective policy formation and implementation.

References

Anantharaman, A. (2005). 'Nightmare in Daycare', *Deccan Herald*. <http://www.deccanherald.com/archives/jun32005/she104545200562.asp> accessed 22 April 2009.

Bansak, C., and Raphael, S. (2006). 'The Effects of State Policy Design Features on Take-up and Crowd-out Rates for the State Children's Health Insurance Program', *Journal of Policy Analysis and Management*, 26 (1), 149–75.

Bennett, F., Brewer, M., and Shaw, J. (2009). *Understanding the Compliance Costs of Benefits and Tax Credits*. London: Institute for Fiscal Studies.

Bernhard, J., and Gonzales-Mena, J. (2000). 'The Cultural Context of Infant/Toddler Care'. In D. Cryer and T. Harms (eds), *Infants and Toddlers in Out-of-Home Care*, pp. 237–67. Baltimore: Paul H. Brookes.

Bitler, M., Currie, J., and Scholz, J. K. (2003). 'WIC Participation and Eligibility', *Journal of Human Resources*, 38, 1139–79.

Browne Miller, A. (1990). *The Day Care Dilemma: Critical concerns for American families*. New York: Plenum.

Carlson, H. L., and Stenmalm-Sjöblom, L. (1989). 'A Cross-Cultural Study of Parents' Perceptions of Early Childhood Programs', *Early Childhood Research Quarterly*, 4 (4), 505–22.

Ceglowski, D., and Bacigalupa, C. (2002). 'Four Perspectives on Child Care Quality', *Early Childhood Education Journal*, 30 (2), 87–92.

Cryer, D., and Burchinal, M. (1997). 'Parents as Child Care Consumers', *Early Childhood Research Quarterly*, 12 (1), 35–58.

Cryer, D., Tietze, W., and Wessels, H. (2002). 'Parents' Perceptions of their Children's Child Care: A Cross-national comparison', *Early Childhood Research Quarterly*, 17 (2), 259–77.

Currie, J. (2000). 'Do Children of Immigrants Make Differential Use of Public Health Insurance?', In G. Borjas (ed.), *Issues in the Economics of Immigration*, pp. 271–308. Chicago: University of Chicago Press and National Bureau of Economic Research.

Currie, J. (2006). 'The Take-Up of Social Benefits'. In A. J. Auerbach, D. Card, and J. M. Quigley (eds), *Public Policy and the Income Distribution*, pp. 80–148. New York: Russell Sage Foundation.

Currie, J., and Grogger, J. (2001). 'Explaining Recent Declines in Food Stamp Programme Participation', *Brookings-Wharton Papers on Urban Affairs*, pp. 203–44. Washington, D. C.: Brookings Institution. <http://muse.jhu.edu/login?uri=/

journals/brookings-wharton_papers_on_urban_affairs/v2001/2001.1currie01.html> accessed 31 May 2010.

Dahlberg, G., Moss, P., and Pence, A. (1999). *Beyond Quality in Early Childhood Education And Care: Postmodern perspectives*. London: RoutledgeFalmer.

Davies, C., and Ritchie, J. (1988). *Tipping the Balance: A study of non-take-up of benefits in an inner city area*. London: HMSO.

Drèze, J. (2006a). 'Universalization with Quality: ICDS in a rights perspective', *Economic and Political Weekly*, 41 (34), 3706–15.

Drèze, J. (2006b). 'Children Under Six: Out of the spotlight', *The Hindu*, 20 October 2006. <http://www.thehindu.com/2006/10/20/stories/2006102002801000.htm> accessed 3 May 2010.

Employees' State Insurance Corporation (2007). Employee State Insurance Act, 1948. <http://esicdelhi.org.in/esiact.php> accessed 21 April 2009.

Fernandes, O. (2007a). The Maternity Benefit (Amendment) Bill, 2007: A Bill further to amend the Maternity Benefit Act, 1961, Bill No. XXXVIII of 2007. <http://prsindia.org/uploads/media/1182409028/1182409028_THE_MATERNITY_BENEFIT__AMENDMENT__BILL__2007.pdf> accessed 21 April 2009.

Fernandes, O. (2007b). The Unorganized Sector Workers' Social Security Bill, 2007: A Bill to provide for the social security and welfare of unorganized sector workers and for other matters connected therewith or incidental thereto, Bill No. LXVII of 2007. <http://prsindia.org/uploads/media/Unorganised%20Sector/1189419973_Unorganised_sector_bill.pdf> accessed 21 April 2009.

George, N. C. (2008). 'Kidding Around with Little Ones: In the absence of adequate childcare facilities in the city, working mothers are leaving their children in unregulated crèches', *Deccan Herald Metro Life*. <http://www.deccanherald.com/Content/Jun92008/metromon2008060872398.asp> accessed 22 April 2009.

Ghosh, S. (1997). 'Integrated Child Development Services Programme – Need for re-appraisal', *Indian Pediatrics*, 34 (10), 911–18.

Gibson, C., and Weisner, T. S. (2002). '"Rational" and Ecocultural Circumstances of Program Take-Up Among Low-Income Working Parents', *Human Organization*, 61 (2), 154–66.

Government of India (1961). Maternity Benefit Act, 1961 (No. 53 of 1961): An Act to regulate the employment of women in certain establishments for certain period before and after child-birth and to provide for maternity benefit and certain other benefits. <http://pblabour.gov.in/pdf/acts_rules/maternity_benefit_act_1961.pdf> accessed 21 April 2009.

Government of India (2005). Rajiv Gandhi National Crèche Scheme for the Children of Working Mothers, 2005. New Delhi: Department of Women and Child Development, Ministry of Human Resource Development. <http://wcd.nic.in/RajivGandhiCrecheScheme.pdf> accessed 22 April 2009.

Gupta, A., Patnaik, B., Singh, D., Sinha, D., Drèze, J., Holla, R., Garg, S., Sundararaman, T., Prasad, V., and Shatrugna, V. (2007). *Strategies for Children Under Six: A Framework for the 11th Plan*, Paper prepared at the request of the Planning Commission. June. <http://www.unicef.org/socialpolicy/files/ChildrenUnderSix.pdf> accessed 30 April 2010.

Hernanz, V. F., Malherbet, F., and Pellizzari, M. (2004). 'Take-Up of Welfare Benefits In OECD Countries: A Review of the evidence', *OECD Social, Employment and Migration Working Papers*, No. 17. France: OECD Publishing.

HM Treasury (2004). *Choice for Parents, the Best Start for Children: A ten year strategy for childcare*. HMT, DfES, DWP, DTI.

Kamerman, S. B. (2006). *A Global History of Early Childhood Education and Care, Background paper prepared for the Education for All Global Monitoring Report 2007, Strong foundations: Early childhood care and education*. Paris: UNESCO. <http://unesdoc.unesco.org/images/0014/001474/147470e.pdf> accessed 28 April 2010.

Kamerman, S. B., and Kahn, A. J. (eds) (1997). *Family Change and Family Policies in Great Britain, Canada, New Zealand and the United States*. Oxford: Clarendon Press.

Katz, L. (1993). *Multiple Perspectives on the Quality of Early Childhood Programs*. ERIC Digests, ED355041.

Kayser, H., and Frick, J. R. (2000). *Take It or Leave It: (Non-) take-up behaviour of social assistance in Germany*. DIW Discussion Paper No. 210. Berlin: DIW.

Lilienfeld, A. M., and Pasamanick, B. (1954). 'Association of Maternal and Fetal Factors with the Development of Epilepsy. 1. Abnormalities in the Prenatal and Paranatal Periods', *Journal of the American Medical Association*, 155 (8), 719–24.

Ministry of Finance, Government of India (2008). 'Social Sectors'. In *Economic Survey 2007–2008*. <http://indiabudget.nic.in/es2007-08/chapt2008/chap108.pdf> accessed 22 April 2009.

Ministry of Women and Child Development (MoWCD) (2007). *Annual Report 2007–08*. New Delhi: Ministry of Women and Child Development, Government of India.

Ministry of Women and Child Development and The World Bank (MoWCD) (2006). *Strengthening ICDS for Reduction of Child Malnutrition: Report of the national consultation on child undernutrition and ICDS in India*. New Delhi: Ministry of Women and Child Development and the World Bank.

Moss, P. (1994). 'Defining Quality: Values, stakeholders and processes'. In P. Moss and A. Pence (eds), *Valuing Quality in Early Childhood Services: New approaches to defining quality*, pp. 1–9. London: Paul Chapman.

National Sample Survey Organisation (NSS), Ministry of Statistics and Programme Implementation, Government of India (2005). *National Sample Survey (61st Round)*, July 2004–June 2005.

NCERT (1993). *Impact of ECE on Retention in Primary Grades – A Longitudinal Study*. New Delhi: NCERT.

NCERT (2006). *Position Paper, National Focus Group on Early Childhood Education*. New Delhi: NCERT. <http://www.ncert.nic.in/html/pdf/schoolcurriculum/position_papers/early_childhood_education.pdf> accessed 27 April 2010.

Nelson, C. A. (2000). 'The Neurobiological Bases of Early Intervention'. In J. P. Shonkoff and S. J. Meisels (eds), *Handbook of Early Childhood Intervention*, 2nd ed., pp. 204–27. Cambridge: Cambridge University Press.

NIPCCD (1992). *National Evaluation of Integrated Child Development Services*. New Delhi: National Institute of Public Cooperation and Child Development.

NIPCCD (2006). *Three Decades of ICDS: An appraisal*. New Delhi: NIPCCD.

Noble, K. (2007). 'Complexities and Compromises', *Australian Journal of Early Childhood*, 32 (1), 24–9.

NUEPA (2010). *Elementary Education in India: Progress towards UEE*. Flash statistics, DISE 2008–9, Provisional. New Delhi: NUEPA.

OECD (2006). *Starting Strong II: Early Childhood Education and Care*. Paris: OECD. <http://www.oecd.org/dataoecd/14/32/37425999.pdf> accessed 27 April 2010.

Oorschot, W. V. (1991). 'Non-Take-Up of Social Security Benefits in Europe', *Journal of European Social Policy*, 1 (1), 15–30.

Pattnaik, J. (1996). 'Early Childhood Education in India: History, trends, issues and achievements', *Early Childhood Education Journal*, 24 (1), 11–16.

Powell, D. R. (1994). 'Parents, Pluralism, and the NAEYC Statement on Developmentally Appropriate Practice'. In B. L. Mallory and R. S. New (eds), *Diversity and Developmentally Appropriate Practices: Challenges for early childhood education*, pp. 166–82. New York: Teachers College Press.

Riphahn, R. T. (2001). 'Rational Poverty or Poor Rationality? The Take-up of social assistance benefits', *Review of Income and Wealth*, 47 (3), 379–98.

Sareen, B. (2004). 'The Status of the Young Indian Child', Submission by FORCES, India to the CRC Day of Discussion on *Implementing Child Rights in Early Childhood*. New Delhi: FORCES. <http://www.crin.org/docs/resources/treaties/crc.37/FORCES_New_Delhi_India.pdf> accessed 2 May 2010.

Saxena, N. C., and Mander, H. (2007). *Seventh Report of the Commissioners of the Supreme Court*, In the case: PUCL v. UOI and Ors. Writ Petition (Civil) No. 196 of 2001. November, 2007. New Delhi.

Sharma, A., Sen, R. S., and Gulati, R. (2008). 'Early Childhood Development Policy and Programming in India: Critical issues and directions for paradigm change', *International Journal of Early Childhood*, 40 (2), 65–83.

Shonkoff, J. P., and Phillips, D. (eds) (2000). *From Neurons to Neighborhoods: The Science of early child development*. 1st ed., Washington, D. C: National Academy Press.

Sinha, S. (2006a). 'Infant Survival: A Political challenge', *Economic and Political Weekly*, 41 (34), 3657–60.

Sinha, D. (2006b). 'Rethinking ICDS: A Rights-based perspective', *Economic and Political Weekly*, 41 (34), 3689–93.

Smith, T. (2007). 'Early Years Services in Britain 1997–2007: A Quiet revolution?' *Journal of Children's Services*, 2 (2), 26–38.

Stafford, B. (2003). 'Service Delivery and the User'. In J. Millar (ed.), *Understanding Social Security: Issues for Policy and Practice*, pp. 213–34. Bristol: Policy Press.

Supreme Court Commissioners (2008). *National Maternity Benefit Scheme*. New Delhi, Office of the Commissioners to the Supreme Court. <http://www.sccommissioners.org/schemes/nmbs> accessed 6 May 2010.

Sylva, K., and Pugh, G. (2005). 'Transforming the Early Years in England', *Oxford Review of Education*, 31 (1), 11–28.

Sylva, K., and Wiltshire, J. (1993). 'The Impact of Early Learning on Children's Later Development'. A review prepared for the RSA inquiry 'Start Right', *European Early Childhood Education Research Journal*, 1 (1), 17–40.

The Consultative Group Secretariat (1992). *Creating Linkages: Women, work and child care, The Coordinators'*, Notebook No.11. The Consultative Group on Early Childhood Care and Development. <http://www.ecdgroup.com/download/cc111aci.pdf> accessed 15 April 2010.

Thukral, E. G. (2005). 'Early Childhood'. In E. G. Thukral, *Status of Children in India Inc*, pp. 31–43. New Delhi: HAQ Centre for Child Rights. <http://www.haqcrc.org/about-us/publication/status-of-indias-children/2005-report.html> accessed 10 April 2010.

UNESCO (1996). *Links between Early Childhood Development and Education and Primary Education*. Action Research in Family and Early Childhood, UNESCO Education Sector Monograph No. 6/1996. Paris: UNESCO.

UNESCO (2010). *Early Childhood Care and Education*. Paris: UNESCO. <http://www.unesco.org/en/early-childhood/> accessed 27 April 2010.

Walker, J. (1991). 'Public Policy and the Supply of Child Care Services'. In D. M. Blau (ed.), *The Economics of Child Care*. New York: Russell Sage Foundation.

Williams, L. R. (1994). 'Developmentally Appropriate Practice and Cultural Values: A Case in point'. In B. L. Mallory and R. S. New (eds), *Diversity and Developmentally*

Appropriate Practices: Challenges for early childhood education, pp. 155–65. New York: Teachers College Press.

World Bank (1999). *Gender and Poverty in India.* Washington, DC: World Bank.

World Bank (2004). *Reaching Out to the Child: An Integrated approach to child development.* New Delhi: Oxford University Press.

World Bank (2010). *World Development Indicators: School enrollment, pre-primary (% Gross)* The World Bank Group. <http://data.worldbank.org/indicator/SE.PRE.ENRR> accessed 29 April 2010.

ANNIKA PISSIN

10 Migration in China: Floating Mothers and Fathers, Left-Behind Girls and Boys

Introduction

Modern China is often approached as a unity. However, comparing the GDP of other countries with the individual counties of China, for example, as the *Economist* recently did, displays great discrepancies within the country (2011), with provinces in eastern China, and above all their urban areas, creating the greatest economic surplus.[1] Paired with, dependent on, and also fuelling the increasing economic activity and surplus is an ever-increasing stream of flexible migrant workers moving from rural areas to cities, deriving mainly from the much poorer regions of western and central China. Among these workers, large numbers are comprised of parents with underage children. Those parents face the choice of either taking their children along with them to their urban destination or leaving them in their rural place of origin, thus rendering their offspring into either *migrant children* or *left-behind children*. This chapter focuses on the latter group.

After providing statistical information concerning internal migration and children, I sum up the major focal points that have emerged in recent years in the discussions concerning left-behind children in contemporary China. Understanding how the problems regarding migration and raising children are perceived, and presented by, mostly urban-based academics and the Chinese public leads to a recognition of how associated issues are solved within China.

1 The discrepancies continue within the provinces, its cities, and within the villages, and to a large extent are based on migration and ethnic background.

Further investigations then show that, while focusing on children in a gender-neutral way, most discussions also put aside, and neglect, the integration the phenomenon of left-behind children within an analysis of the family and family change. I believe that these are two crucial areas of neglect. In the family, as the basic institution of community and the state, gender roles are taught and learned, and it matters very much if a family member is female or male with regard to her or his upbringing, responsibilities and expectations. Changes in family composition, either in the short or long term, also have differing impacts on its male and female members, on mothers, fathers, daughters and sons. Family, approached within a gender framework, and the implicit classification system families refer to, is, therefore, the focus of the remaining part of this chapter.

Internal migration in China

General

China's whole population counted about 1,345,751 million people in 2009 (UNICEF). According to different estimations, about 9 to 12.3 per cent of China's population belong to the category of migrant workers, counting more than 144 million people in that year.[2] The latest estimations from 2010 state a figure of about 211 million migrants (*People's Daily* 2010). A large group of those migrants move from west and central China to the east. Their mean age, which has been declining over the past twenty years, is between twenty and thirty-nine years old. Initially, in the 1980s, this

2 30 million in 1989; 63 million in 1993; 80 million in 2001 (Démurger et al. 2009: 611); 102.6 million in 2004 (Wang and Cai 2009: 26); 132 million in 2006 (Démurger et al. 2009: 611); 12.3 per cent of the population (based on a 1 per cent population sample in 2005, ca. 147.35 million, of which about one third were interprovincial migrants, Du et al. 2007). Increasing by approximately 10 per cent each year (Jin Mou et al. 2011: 213). In December 2010 the *People's Daily* estimated a number of 211 million migrants, approximately 15 per cent of China's whole population.

floating population consisted typically of men, but by the 1990s they were accompanied by women, at first mostly unmarried but now also, increasingly, married. In 2000, the sex ratio of internal migrants was 1.1 males to females (Lou et al. 2004: 208; Fan and Sun 2011: 96).

Reasons for migration are often perceived as primarily economic in nature. Migrated sons and daughters are thought to financially aid their left-behind parents (Du 2007). It is suggested they want to invest in private homes (ibid 2007), and also feel the need to keep up with paying the rising costs of school education and the upbringing of children (see e.g. Saunders et al. 2007; Shang 2008).[3]

Children

The People's Republic of China has ratified the Convention of the Rights of the Child, and thus a child is defined as anybody below the age of eighteen. Nevertheless, in general children are considered to be those up to fifteen years of age, which is the definition that is applied in most information. While the above-stated numbers about migrants are rough estimations, and often calculated on the basis of micro level area research, numbers used in the discourse concerning children are at least as sketchy. Each year about 18,134,000 children are born, of whom about 365,000 will die before they reach the age of five years.[4] The under-fifteens take up 19 per cent of the whole population, counting about 249,482,000 people. The literacy rate of persons between fifteen and twenty-four is 99 per cent, and nearly all girls and boys are enrolled at primary school (UNICEF 2004–8).

3 Visions of the possibility of living in a new house, separated from parents, especially parents-in-law, is in fact the biggest drive for people to migrate (Lou et al. 2004: 218).

4 Most children are born to married couples. In 2010 about 12 million marriage vows were taken, and 1,961 million couples divorced. Sichuan is the leading county for divorces with 169,249 divorces. Based on figures from the last five years, the rate is increasing – see *Chinahush* from February 2011, based on statistics from the Ministry of Civil Affairs. See Li, Zhang, Feldman (2010) on the problems concerning birth registration in China.

Migrant children

The number of migrant children in 2000 was calculated to be 19,820,000, nearly as many as left-behind children in rural areas in the same period (Wang and Zhao 2008: 122; Wang Lu 2008).[5] Most discussions concerning children of migrant parents, no matter whether they focus on migrating or on left-behind children, deal with education, physical health and psychological health. Nevertheless, children who migrate together with their parents face different aspects of the problem than those who stay behind. One big problem is schooling in the urban areas, as in many cases children have no right to free schooling outside their place of registration (see e.g. Li Shuzhuo et al. 2010). In many cases, that leads to the development of private schools with often limited financial resources. Another focus of various discussions is the estrangement of children, caused by the fact that migrant children move around a lot and do not stay in one place for a long time, resulting in an outsider status (Wang and Zhao 2008).

Perception and presentation of left-behind children

The online *People's Daily* stated on 22 December 2010 that approximately 58 million children are now labelled as 'left-behind children'. Forty million of them are below the age of fourteen. This number would account for 20 per cent of all children under fifteen in China, and for 28.2 per cent of all rural children. Among those children, a third of all rural children between infancy and five years of age are left behind. Eight out of ten children are cared for by family and friends (*People's Daily* 2010). Although a high number of left-behind children was mentioned before, most publications, up until recently, worked with figures of 122 million or 100–144 million migrant workers and 22 million left-behind children, of which 18.7 million were thought to be below the age of fourteen (see e.g. Guo 2010). The

5 Wang Lu (2008) suggests a figure of 7–10 million migrant children for 2000.

confirmation of 58 million left-behind children accordingly triggered a range of discussions. A high concentration of these children can be found in Sichuan, Anhui, Henan, Hunan, Jiangxi, Guizhou and Guangdong (*People's Daily*, December 2010).

Generally, the definition of left-behind children encompasses those children whose mother or father or both parents have migrated for work and left the child behind for six months or longer.[6] The definition often implies that it is the biological parents who leave their offspring behind, an interesting implication that I will address in more detail below.[7] In most discussions, the social circumstances under which the children are left behind are of subordinate interest, although care by grandparents is a much-disputed topic.[8]

Reasons for leaving children behind instead of taking them along are manifold (see e.g. Wang and Zhao 2008).[9] In some cases it is related to

6 See e.g. Yang Gao, Li Ping Li et al. (2010), who generally describe left-behind children as 'children staying in their rural home towns and villages', and more specifically rely on the definition of 'children under eighteen who have been left behind at their original residence while one or both parents migrate into other places for work and have been not living together with them for at least six months'. See also the documentary film by Dream Corps International.

7 Children can also become left-behind upon divorce, but usually only when both parents are alive. Orphans (officially, children whose parents are both dead; socially, children whose father has passed away) are not left-behind children although, ideally, both groups are looked after by relatives (on orphans see Shang 2008). Gong Zheng (2007) discusses the case of a ten-year-old boy whose father had developed a mental disorder that made him beat his wife. When the wife left her abusive husband, her son was one year old and came under the care of his paternal grandparents. This boy is also labelled left-behind, although realistically his parents will not return to him. It is implied in the article that his father has a chronic mental disease and that his mother has remarried. There might be a possibility for the boy to live in his mother's new family once he has finished his education.

8 According to the *People's Daily*, 80 per cent of those children whose parents have both migrated for work are taken care of by their (paternal) grandparents. Discussions fail to focus on care by relatives other than grandparents – except in cases of cruel child abuse by aunts or uncles.

9 See, for example, Wang and Zhao (2008), who investigate the reasons for parents to either leave their children in their places of origin or take them along, based on a

greater expense should children join their parents, parents' lack of physical and emotional energy after a long day of work, or payment of extra school fees in urban areas where the child is not registered and where s/he thus is not officially allowed to attend school. Finally, the positive impacts of studying at home are a motivation for leaving children behind (Du 2007). Most children who are given a voice in articles or documentaries state that their parents migrated so that they, the children, could go to school. Indeed, having learned in the cities that education can supply a person with better-paid jobs, parents are willing to migrate in order to afford the rapidly increasing costs that their children's education involves.

The general themes of the problems discussed with regard to left-behind children are similar to those of migrant children: education, health and psychology. Left-behind children, in comparison with rural children living with their parents, are thought to be more prone to injuries and accidents, directing discussions also to security issues. One article mentions that the odds of a left-behind child receiving injuries from burning or scalding, and being involved in traffic accidents or accidents with electricity, as well as drowning, are far higher than for children who grow up in 'normal families' (*Jiancha ribao* nd).[10] Other research points out that due to their weak position left-behind children are often vulnerable to being threatened, robbed, humiliated, beaten, blackmailed, abducted and sold, cheated and kidnapped (Guo 2010). Furthermore, left-behind children's safety is jeopardized because they might be left without a guardian in situations such as disasters or fires (ibid).[11]

One research group, sponsored to investigate left-behind children's situation in Anhui, has defined four areas of deficiency which such children might experience: daily life assistance, mental needs, assistance with

---

survey of over 3,000 migrant workers. They observe regional differences in preferences, and also different preferences of men and women in leaving children behind.

10 The term 'normal family' was used in the article.

11 Guo (2010) lists a number of deadly accidents that have involved left-behind children, among which were three fire accidents in Guangxi and Guangdong at the beginning of 2008, which took the lives of six left-behind children while no other people were killed; during an explosion in a firecracker workshop, thirteen left-behind child workers were killed.

schoolwork, and security (*Jiancha ribao* nd). The same group warns that due to the absence of a concerned guardian, some left-behind children can be more liable to be hurt in accidents and attacked by other people, including the rape of girls (ibid).

When children's voices concerning their own feelings are heard, they usually confirm what the articles argue: namely, that they feel inferior and heartbroken; that, at times, their grandparents do not understand them; and that they feel excluded from the other children at school who are living with their parents.[12] Most of the problems children are facing are perceived and presented as resulting from their care status and, especially, the lack of a motherly presence.

Left-behind children and left-behind elderly: lonely and depressed

Partly due to their cohabitation, and partly due to both groups' dependency on their working parents/adult children, left-behind children are often discussed together with left-behind elderly. Old people and children, alike, are exposed to loneliness (Yang Gao 2010). Statements such as 'parents choose to work in the cities, leaving behind children and old people in solitude and an empty life', are employed frequently (Ying 2010).

Grandparents, however, can be considered from a different angle than children. The speed with which new possibilities and ways of life have opened up in rural China is flabbergasting, and the numbers of people affected by these changes are incredibly high. Confrontation with the rapid change makes it easy to forget what has happened within the lifetime of these grandparents, some of whom might still be affected by traumatic events such as the Great Leap Forward (1958–61).[13] Although school education was heavily promoted by the Communist party in the 1950s and 1960s, the extent and duration of education was far less during this period

12 As shown, for example, in the documentary by Dream Corps.

13 For an account of the different natural and humanitarian disasters during the period of the upbringing of the grandparents' generation, see Shapiro (2001). See also Kleinman and Kleinman (1999) for a summary of Chinese family change based on Yan Yunxiang's *The Flow of Gifts* from 1996.

than from the 1980s onward.[14] The grandparents' generation, then, was confronted with the de-collectivization and land redistribution of 1983, resulting in their own children, the contemporary parents' generation, being left without rationed land. It was thus deemed 'at least unwise, if not suicidal, to invest in children as labourers' (Yan 2003: 208). It is argued that many of these contemporary parents belong to the generation who prefer to live apart from their parents, once they have established their own family.[15]

Based on the numbers stated above, about 46 million children live with their (probably mostly paternal) grandparents. The general theme of most articles runs along the line that grandparents, generally around sixty years of age, do not know how to respond to the problems of their grandchildren. Often illiterate, they cannot provide adequate help with homework.[16] Not being acquainted with school and modern life, they are reported as not being able to communicate with their grandchildren, and having difficulties in understanding the stress children suffer from in completing homework.[17] Furthermore, they are believed not to see the need to buy 'additional materials'.[18] Some specific cases point out neglect and abuse of children by grandparents, and also crude abuse (Yu Linyi 2007; Zheng Qiao 2009).

14 See Stig Thøgersen (2002) for an account of the education of the current grandparents' generation.

15 Yan (2003) states that 'the state privatized the family by destroying traditional communal power and created a new social space for individual development by politicizing the family' (231).

16 This is mentioned in numerous Chinese articles about left-behind children. See also Nyland et al. (2009), on the inadequate nature of 'grandparents as educators and carers' in Shanghai.

17 I have not yet come across a study that focuses on possible linguistic problems of communication, as the children learn Mandarin Chinese at school, which their grandparents, in many cases, might not be comfortable with, because it is not their mother tongue.

18 These materials, also identified as 'incidental expenses' (linghuaqian) by Yan Yunxiang, 'trouble the villagers most: toys, mostly food: candy, soft drinks, ice-cream bars, cookies, fruits, fried instant noodles (which are consumed as snacks by children), and sausages' (Yan 2003: 206).

Left-behind children and criminality

In the general discourse of criminality with regard to left-behind children, extreme violence is linked to and understood to be a result of a chain reaction that derives from a negative mood, including self-abasement, being silent, pessimism and ultimately leading to anti-social behaviour (Du 2007). Mostly argued in psychological terms, left-behind children, who it is argued are vulnerable to developing depression, anxiety and loneliness, and who are thought to lack supervision and education, could potentially become a root of social disharmony and criminality (*Good Guardian* 2007; Guo 2010).

Left-behind girls and boys

Research on the mental health of left-behind children suggest that while girls tend to suffer more than boys from emotional issues, boys are 'more vulnerable to sadness', and tend to harbour 'ideas of suicide' (Yang 2010). However, most articles deal with left-behind children as gender-neutral persons, with one exception, which is discussion about sexual abuse of girls – not boys.[19] Until recent years, the rape of girls by family and community members has not featured much in public discussions and, in fact, was believed to be a rather rare phenomenon.[20]

Although the official opinion holds that girls' education is as important as boys' and that female schoolchildren have the same attention and the same chances, in reality boys are still preferred over girls in that respect. Girls, additionally, are required more often than boys to do household chores, which leads to a reduced focus on school.

19 See, for example, the cases discussed in Zheng Qiao (2009); Ma Huayan (2008); and, as one item of concern among others, in numerous general articles discussing left-behind children.

20 See Ma Huayan (2008) who discusses the case of a seventy-year-old man who raped a distantly related five-year-old girl.

Migrating mothers and fathers

Another gender-sensitive topic is the *missing mother*. While initially it was mostly men who migrated, followed by a period when numbers of migrating unmarried women increased, since at least the late 1990s married women, who are also mothers, have also started to move to cities to work. With the increasing number of migrating mothers, discussions about psychological problems concerning children who grow up without mothers appear to have increased, despite the fact that slightly more fathers than mothers continue to be migrant workers. Concerning child welfare, fathers are mostly mentioned as a suffix to mothers, and are considered to be without much agency. Within the literature, mothers are understood to be the main responsible parent in supervising schoolwork, family education, hygiene and the general psychological wellbeing of a child. However, in published letters written by left-behind children, both fathers and mothers are addressed, and yet Yang Gao's study on the health status of left-behind children, for example, suggests that children become especially vulnerable when their mothers migrate, more so than children who have only experienced their father's migration (Yang Gao 2010).[21] Furthermore, it seems that in recent years several female figures with public authority have emerged as a sort of *public mother*, like the *teacher-mother* and the *police-mother*.[22]

21 See, for example, excerpts from such letters in Guo Ying (2010). See also Linlin (2007).

22 See, for example, Yang Pengfei (2008), Zeng and Huang (2010) and Fang Minjun (2009). It is as yet not entirely clear to me what their actual function is. The so-called 'acting mothers' seem to be state-organized and aim to work against the above-mentioned problems in areas such as schoolwork, security, emotion/psychology, health etc.

Solutions

Faced with tens of millions of left-behind and migrant children, whose numbers, problems, security and future prospects are, as yet, not sufficiently mapped and understood, the state, scholars and NGOs, initially, have merely tried to grasp the quantitative dimensions of this problem. Such efforts have resulted in numerous random, loose investigations of townships and villages throughout the country. Furthermore, newspapers and NGOs report countless touching and shocking narratives of individual children, framed within the quantitative dimension of the left-behind child phenomenon, and often containing messages of empathy for the children. With the establishment of the above-described general fields concerning the mental problems of left-behind children, one fitting solution is seen in the demand for social workers and psychologists at schools, which are largely absent in rural China.

Practical solutions carried out locally and on a small scale by private initiatives or government-backed groups, such as the Women's Federation, are enabling communication with parents by providing phones or ameliorating schools to provide for the psychological wellbeing of left-behind children. Other activities include organizing school outings and fun activities, as well as creating libraries and special spaces for children.[23] The agents of the solutions are usually seen to be the state and its policy-making abilities, the family, consisting of mother and father, the school and society.[24]

23 See the reports of numerous projects throughout rural China on their website. Information about the All-China Women's Federation can be found in Jacka (1997: 90–100), and Sun (2004: 112–16). Several NGOs also concentrate their work around left-behind children, e.g. Dream Corps, Jinan University Rural and Agricultural Association and others.

24 See, for example, an article of 12 January 2011 by the Zhenjiang division of the All-China Women's Federation.

The idea of the lone child

While to a certain degree the above problems concerning left-behind children are true and cannot be underestimated, analysed from a historical and anthropological point of view, some of the areas of problematizing are curious. In the context of this chapter, two questions come to the foreground: why are left-behind children often portrayed as being *alone* although they live together with other family members? And why is the emphasis on missing biological mothers and not so much on missing fathers? In order to answer these questions, which I will not do entirely in this chapter, I first outline the perceived gap between the rural and urban population, as it is mostly urbanites who write about rural people. The voices of the latter group are often not heard with regard to rural life and children and I suspect that several of the perceived problems and sought-for solutions are arranged by urban people, for rural people.

Rural-urban discrepancies

Rural-urban migration in China in general is not perceived in negative terms. As they make up an important part of the motor driving the Chinese economy, migrant workers are basically understood to be necessary. Nevertheless, the urban population who hold the right to live in city areas tend to create a great mental gap between themselves and the rural population. The rural population, labelled as uneducated and poor, is in general pitied, and their problems – discussed in the context of an inadequate social security system, and general poverty due to increasing living costs – are theoretically acknowledged. The discourse is dominated by terms such as 'divide', 'gap', and 'backwardness'.

In attitudes rather similar to the urban members of the eighteenth-century Enlightenment movement, Chinese urbanites see 'peasants as beings living almost in a different world, incapable of understanding [modern ideas] and buried instead in incomprehensible folk superstitions, irrational traditions and religious loyalties' (Outram 1995: 26).[25] Although close contact between urban residents and rural people is nothing new in China, the rapidly increasing number of rural migrants to the city makes them all too visible and they cannot be ignored any longer.[26] Rural people with their rural lives and roots are, thus, approached as *others* by Chinese urban citizens.[27]

With respect to their children, rural parents are believed to treat them cruelly and insensitively, unlike the way that well-educated urban parents treat their children. Physical punishment of children in educational contexts, for example, is seen as something that happens in poorly educated families; thus, mostly, in rural families. Orna Naftali quotes a female urban resident in well-off economic circumstances in Shanghai, who often consults articles by Chinese and Western child psychologists in order 'to understand better her child's wishes and needs'. At the same time, she also emphasizes that this is not typical of parents in other parts of the country. In China's more '"backward (*luohou*) areas", she commented with unmistakable contempt, "people treat their children in shocking ways," which she herself "could not really understand." Unlike "these parents," she assured me, "we [in Shanghai] raise our children with great care"' (Naftali 2010: 601).

Furthermore, sensational picture-series are spread through the internet, portraying deprived and sad childhoods, resulting in very emotional and violent comments by netizens.[28] It is with this basic attitude that many articles about left-behind children are written and read in China. While

25 Instead of 'the Enlightenment' I have substituted 'modern ideas', but the sentiment, as well as the general social conditions of mass migration and daily rural-urban confrontation, is comparable.

26 Seen from within rural areas, Murphy (2002) describes the positive, albeit puzzling, influence of the returnees in terms of the importation of new ideas, but also shows the negative impact of rising inequality in a rural village, due to finances from migration being available to some members of the community and not to others.

27 For a detailed discussion about the process of the 'othering' of peasants and differentiation between the urban and rural population as part of the construction and reproduction of 'dominant national ideas about identity', see Jacka (2006: 31–58).

28 For example, see articles on China Smack, which features translations of the some of the most discussed topics, 'Chinese children tied up while parents work' or 'Yunnan girl child abuse', among many others.

knowledge and motivation exists about the necessity for change in the relationships between the rural and urban populations, it is, again, comparable to the situation during the Enlightenment, 'a task which, simultaneously, they often despaired of completing' (Outram 1995: 26).[29] Peasants and rural migrant workers, it seems, ought to be approached within a framework of development aid from above.

Why does 'left behind' equal 'alone'?

Left-behind children are portrayed as left-alone children, although more than 80 per cent of them are left behind with their grandparents and other relatives. In many cases, grandparents look after the grandchildren of several sons, and thus children grow up together with other children of their kin. The discourse of left-behind children can be better understood when viewed against a background of family change and the urbanization of family.[30]

Public awareness of left-behind children started in the mid-1990s, when the term was used in parenthesis. However, from about 2000 onward, and more so from 2005, the phenomenon of left-behind children was fully established and started to be discussed in the manner outlined above. With respect to rural families, then, the 1980s and 1990s were a period when more and more husband-and-wife-centred families came into existence (Yan 2003: 88). Furthermore, during that period violence against women by husbands received more attention from the media (Jacka 1997: 61). Families thus became privatized (Yan 2003) and public reporting of such grievances, including reports about disassociated children, became part of the mass media culture.

While until the 1980s members of the grandparents' generation could rely – and had to rely – on their families in their daily lives, this has faded

29 See also Gaetano and Jacka (2004: 13–20) for a brief history of rural-urban discrepancies, especially during the twentieth century, in China.

30 Families in urban China changed and started to become more and more nuclear in the nineteenth century, but this became especially prevalent between the 1920s and the 1950s. See Glosser (2003).

away over the two subsequent generations.[31] At least, this is how I understand the articles which present children who are cared for by relatives as left-behind and lonely. This theoretical dismissal of grandparents can be observed in cities as well, where parents are convinced that it would be better to enrol their under-three-year-old child at a pre-school rather than ask the child's grandparents to look after it. However, in Shanghai more than 50 per cent of the children in that age group are taken care of by their grandparents anyway, due to financial constraints, but with the resentment of their parents (Nyland et al. 2009). This conviction is thought to stem from psychological insights about children's education, which have been absorbed by middle-class urban mothers (Nyland et al. 2009; Naftali 2010).

Another conviction, which is not entirely educated-urban, but State- and Party-born, is that a woman's rightful place is next to her child. However, biological parents are not necessarily the best people to raise children, and a biological mother is not necessarily the most important centre-figure in a child's life (Montgomery 2009: 107). Within this context, it is interesting to look at the symbolic function of women in modern China. Duara (1998) convincingly discusses women as fitting objects to take up the role of a national symbol from the beginning of the twentieth century until the 1980s.[32] He points out that 'like many other early twentieth-century patriarchal nationalisms, women were to be liberated for and by the nation. They were to embody the nation to be active agents shaping it' (Duara 1998: 298). A woman's value lay in her 'female virtue and sacrifice', which, as a theme with the power to exert influence on actual lives, ran throughout Chinese written history (see Mou 2004). Parts of this idea are still practised in the approach to women, as can be observed in the discourse of left-behind children.

31 Yan also discusses the individualization of the family members. In that respect, it is interesting to note that the documentary by Dream Corps shows a fourteen-year-old boy who chooses to live alone rather than with his grandparents whose lifestyle he dislikes.

32 He also poses the question about women's symbolic capacity in the era of 'commodification of the symbols of authenticity', the 1990s.

Jacka points out that 'a strong emphasis on the role of woman as mother and nurturer has been a central element in the post-Mao state's attempts to curb social disorder and to promote "spiritual civilisation"' (Jacka 1997: 194). The major organ of the state in spreading this message is the All-China Women's Federation, which also sponsors many activities for left-behind children.[33] Women, in fact, have the role of inculcating children 'with values and standards of behaviour conducive to social stability and modernisation. [...] Bringing children up in a proper way, mentally and physically healthy, maintaining social harmony is a woman's duty' (Jacka 1997: 64). After a widely discussed abuse case concerning a female migrant worker in 1998, the Women's Federation 'advised rural women not to leave their hometown and to seek work locally instead' (Sun 2004: 110). Although women are never openly criticized for not being with their children, they are continuously admonished with such implicit messages about what their authentic role is.[34]

Conclusion

Research about migration is abundant, and increasingly leaves room for the voices of migrant women. However, research focusing on women tends to mention children as a by-product only, although childcare is still to a great extent associated more with women and less with men. As research with children can be problematic regarding ethical concerns, especially in the case of rural left-behind children whose guardianship is not always clear,

33 I could not find many academic articles in Chinese referring to the attachment theory in child development studies, and I thus assume that it is not applied to rural parenting. That theory, in fact, stresses that the biological mother is not necessarily the only person who can assure a securely attached child.

34 Fathers are responsible for providing financially for their parents and guaranteeing them a home. In the context of children, they 'traditionally' pay for expenses due to disease. To do this, they do not need to be together with the family.

not much analytical work concerning their own points of view has been developed, although it is highly desirable.

For setting up a framework to deal with left-behind children academically, a further desideratum is to understand their representation in the media, which is embedded in the bigger issue of child representation and the utilization of the image of *the child* in contemporary Chinese society. Tied to the project of the authenticity of women, children's official representation, albeit probably very different from their daily life experiences, spills over and directs a child's daily life. In order to grasp children's voices, there is a great need to investigate the actual impact and results of this official direction, which is broadcast via television, through mass education and, increasingly, through advertisements about and for children. The representations, then, should be differentiated from the reality of rural life.

One major problem in the discussion of left-behind children is their labelling. Labelling often covers different facets of a phenomenon. In this case, children who are taken care of by grandparents or by other family members, children who take care of their younger siblings, or who live alone in villages until they finish school, while their biological parents are pursuing economic goals for personal independence and education, are labelled as left-behind. However, as regional differences in the patterns of migration and ethnic differences in approaching children exist, so also do differences in the experiences, the expectations and the treatment of left-behind children throughout China. If left-behind children are considered as a homogenous group, with associated traits and problems as discussed, individual approaches are rendered difficult, and problems, other than the grossly circumscribed difficulties in (school) education, health and psychology, are neglected.

Discussing child abuse, Hacking points out that the 'making and molding' of the 'social construction of abuse' has real life consequences for abused people, often in retrospect: 'Child abuse is a new kind that has changed the past of many people, and so changed their very sense of who they are and how they have come to be' (1999: 162). I am not saying that leaving children behind equals child abuse, but that the 'making and molding' of the concept of left-behind children changes the children affected by that label.

Individual cases of left-behind children can be found throughout Chinese history; moreover, even before the 1990s, left-behind children probably existed in large numbers. The *social* construction of left-behind children is not (only) related to their quantity, but also to a change in family perception, individuality and probably to the commercialization of national symbols as women and children, as Duara proposes.[35]

Closely related to this labelling is the practice of contrasting left-behind children with 'normal children' and 'normal families', as is done in numerous articles (e.g. *Jiancha ribao* nd). This practice renders about one in five children abnormal. As the economic drive and the financial needs of adults will probably not change within a short period, it would be more beneficial for these children's situation to be 'normalized' by changing their mode of representation. Normalizing children who live in families that are understood to be incomplete by the lack of presence of the parent generation, however, does not fit into the Chinese state's project of authenticity, which, in turn, is thought to be necessary in creating a harmonious society.

A further concern is the identification of agents, at least in the approach of the All-China Women's Federation, which practically reduces children's agencies to calling their parents from school telephones and going on organized field trips. The real agents in that approach are the state, the family, school, and society – with the family, in fact, being only considered to be the mother and father. Children ought to be protected and educated in all kinds of respects, but there is not much room left for their own voices.[36]

The passivity which is imposed on women is also, and to an even greater extent, part of the presentation and utilization of children. Images of children in imperial China, all images of children playing intelligent games and studying, have been used to carry adult wishes for future success and good

35 See Pissin (forthcoming), in which labelling and its consequences are discussed in more detail within a global context.

36 Although, as I have pointed out above, children do make big decisions and take on responsibilities when they decide to live on their own instead of with their family. However, further research in that direction is required.

fortune and, in fact, for a harmonious household.[37] Therefore, I suggest that the image of studying and happy children is still a powerful symbol of good fortune and harmony. Left-behind children jeopardize this image.

Children out of boundaries, which means children who are not embedded within a two- or three-generation household, confer an image of danger, because they lack the *right* guardian. The dominant social classification system puts children and older people, i.e. grandparents, into the same category of *weak and fragile*. While the role of a child in that system is to be educated and loved, the role of the grandparent is to be taken care of and respected. Both groups are assigned passive positions, while the working adult generation in the middle holds the main power of agency. Accordingly, a grandmother, who is as weak and passive as her grandchild, cannot, within this classification system, be an adequate guardian for a child. Thus, a schoolteacher or a policewoman is a more fitting substitute for a mother, because she belongs to the same generation as the mother; namely, the working adult generation.[38]

References

All-China Women's Federation (2011). <http://www.women.org.cn/> accessed 28 February 2011.

Chinahush (2011). '1.96 Million Couples were Divorced in China Last Year', *Chinahush*, 8 February. <http://www.chinahush.com/2011/02/08/1–96-million-couples-were-divorced-in-china-last-year/#more-7998> accessed 19 February 2011.

37 See Tse Bartholomew, 'One Hundred Children: From boys at play to icons of good fortune'.

38 This chapter draws on knowledge about left-behind children made available up until the beginning of 2011. In 2012, rural left-behind children, alongside rural women and elderly people, were established as an official national problem by the Chinese government. While the above-outlined public discourse is still valid, it is now much more versatile (see Pissin, forthcoming).

Chinasmack (2011). 'Yunnan Savagely Abused by Aunt while Parents Work', *Chinasmack*, 30 October 2009. <http://www.chinasmack.com/2009/pictures/yunan-girl-child-abuse.html> accessed 28 February 2011.

Chinasmack (2011). 'Children on Leashes Tied to the Walls while their Parents Work', *Chinasmack*, 3 May 2010. <http://www.chinasmack.com/2010/pictures/chinese-children-tied-up-while-parents-work-zhejiang.html> accessed 28 February 2011.

Démurger, S., Gurgand, M., Li, S., and Yue X. (2009). 'Migrants as Second-Class Workers in Urban China? A Decomposition analysis', *Journal of Comparative Economics*, 37 (4), 610–28.

Dream Corps International (2008). *Rural China 'Children Left Behind'.* Documentary film. <www.youtube.com/watch?v=l4ooVx6rSLk> accessed 1 March 2011.

Du, P., Li, Y., Wang, P., and Lin, W. (2007). 'The Influence of the Outgoing Migrants on their Families', *Population Journal*, 161 (1), 3–9 (in Chinese).

Duara, P. (1998). 'The Regime of Authenticity: Timelessness, gender, and national history in Modern China', *History and Theory*, 37 (3), 287–308.

Fan, C., and Sun, M. (2011). 'China's Permanent and Temporary Migrants: Differentials and changes, 1990–2000', *The Professional Geographer*, 63 (1), 92–112.

Fang, M. (2009). 'Ji'an: A Policewoman-Mother Cares for "Left Behind Children"', *Road and Traffic Administration*, 4 (in Chinese).

Gaetano, A., and Jacka, T. (2004). 'Introduction: Focusing on migrant women'. In A. Gaetano and T. Jacka (eds), *On the Move: Women in rural-to-urban migration in contemporary China*, pp. 1–38. New York: Columbia University Press.

Glosser, S. (2003). *Chinese Visions of Family and State, 1915–1953*. Berkeley and London: University of California Press.

Gong, Z. (2007). 'Mama, Let Me Somehow Love You Again', *Law and Life*, 1 (2), 14–15 (in Chinese).

Guo, Y. (2010). 'Lonely Left-Behind Children: The Hidden anguish of social harmony', *Jiangxi Education*, 34, 12–14 (in Chinese).

Hacking, I. (1999). *The Social Construction of What?* Cambridge and London: Harvard University Press.

Good Guardian (2007). 'The Acting Guardian: Substituting left-behind children's deficiency of love', *Souhu web*, 01, 22 (in Chinese).

Jacka, T. (2006). *Rural Women in Urban China: Gender, migration, and social change.* New York and London: Sharpe.

Jacka, T. (1997). *Women's Work in Rural China: Change and continuity in an era of reform*. Cambridge, New York and Melbourne: Cambridge University Press.

Jiancha ribao (2008). 'Anhui's Left-Behind Children Number Nearly Four Million. Some Left-behind Girls are Raped', *Xinwen tiandi*, 2 November, 2, 73 (in Chinese).

Jin M., Cheng, J., Griffiths, S., and Wong, S. (2011). 'Internal Migration and Depressive Symptoms among Migrant Factory Workers in Shenzhen, China', *Journal of Community Psychology*, 39 (2), 212–30.

Kleinman, A., and Kleinman, J. (1999). 'The Transformation of Everyday Social Experience: What a mental and social health perspective reveals about Chinese communities under global and local change', *Culture, Medicine and Psychiatry*, 23 (1), 7–24.

Li S., Zhang, Y., and Feldman, M. (2010). 'Birth Registration in China: Practices, problems and policies', *Population Research and Policy Review*, 29 (3), 297–317.

Linlin (2007). 'A Letter from a Left-behind Child Written for her Parents', *A Selection of the Whole Nation's Excellent Literary Compositions*, 9 (in Chinese).

Lou, B., Zheng, Z., Connelly, R., and Roberts, K. (2004). 'Migration Experiences of Young Women from Four Counties'. In A. Gaetano and T. Jacka (eds), *On the Move: Women in rural-to-urban migration in contemporary China*, pp. 207–42. New York: Columbia University Press.

Ma, H. (2008). 'A Seventy Year Old Man Rapes a Five Year Old Girl', *Legal System and Economy*, 4, 38–9 (in Chinese).

Montgomery, H. (2009). *An Introduction to Childhood: Anthropological perspectives on children's lives*. Chichester: Wiley-Blackwell.

Mou, S. (2004). *Gentlemen's Prescriptions for Women's Lives: A Thousand years of biographies of Chinese women*. Armonk and New York: M. E. Sharpe.

Murphy, R. (2002). *How Migrant Labor is Changing Rural China*. Cambridge, New York: Cambridge University Press.

Naftali, O. (2010). 'Recovering Childhood: Play, pedagogy, and the rise of psychological knowledge in contemporary urban China', *Modern China*, 36 (6), 589–616.

Nyland, B., Zeng, X., Nyland, C., and Tran, L. (2009). 'Grandparents as Educators and Carers in China', *Journal of Early Childhood Research*, 7 (1), 46–57.

Outram, D. (1995). *The Enlightenment*. Cambridge, New York: Cambridge University Press.

People's Daily (2010). 'The Number of Left Behind Children is Close to Fifty-Eight Million', 22 December (in Chinese).

Pissin, A. (forthcoming). 'The Global Left Behind Child in China: Unintended consequences in capitalism', *Working Papers in Contemporary Asian Studies*, 39, Lund: Lund University.

Saunders, P., Shang, X., and Li, Z. (2007). 'Using Budget Standards to Estimate the Costs of Children: The Case of Funan County', *Journal of Family Studies*, 13 (1), 57–71.

Shang, X. (2008). 'The Role of Extended Families in Childcare and Protection: The Case of rural China', *International Journal of Social Welfare*, 17 (3), 204–14.

Shapiro, J. (2001). *Mao's War Against Nature: Politics and the environment in revolutionary China.* Cambridge and New York: Cambridge University Press.

Stig, T. (2002). *A County of Culture: Twentieth-century China seen from the village schools of Zouping, Shandong.* Ann Arbor: The University of Michigan Press.

Sun, W. (2004). 'Indoctrination, Fetishization, and Compassion: Media constructions of the migrant woman'. In A. Gaetano and T. Jacka (eds), *On the Move. Women in rural-to-urban migration in contemporary China*, pp. 109–28. New York: Columbia University Press.

The Economist (2011). 'Comparing Chinese Provinces with Countries'. *The Economist*, 24 February. <http://www.economist.com/content/chinese_equivalents> accessed 28 February 2011.

Tse, B. T. (2002). 'One Hundred Children: From boys at play to icons of good fortune'. In A. Wicks (ed.), *Children in Chinese Art*, pp. 57–83. Honolulu: University of Hawaii Press.

UNICEF (2011). *Info by Country: China.* <http://www.unicef.org/infobycountry/china_statistics.html#77> accessed 28 February 2011.

Wang, D., and Cai, F. (2009). 'Migration and Poverty Alleviation in China'. In R. Murphy (ed.), *Labour Migration and Social Development in Contemporary China*, pp. 17–46. New York: Routledge.

Wang, J., and Zhao, J. (2008). 'Upbringing and Education, Pearl River delta', *Social Sciences in China*, 29 (3), 121–35.

Wang, L. (2008). 'The Marginality of Migrant Children in The Urban Chinese Educational System', *British Journal of Sociology of Education*, 29 (6), 691–703.

Yan, Y. (2003). *Private Life Under Socialism: Love, intimacy, and family change in a Chinese village 1949–1999.* Stanford: Stanford University Press.

Yang, G., Li, P., Kim, J., and Congdon, N. (2010). 'The Impact of Parental Migration on Health Status and Health Behaviours Among Left Behind Adolescent School Children in China', *BMC Public Health*, 10 (1), 56.

Yang, P. (2008). 'My Teacher Became my "Acting Mother"', *Jianghuai Rule of Law*, 1, 39–40 (in Chinese).

Yu, L. (2007). 'A Girl Kills a Person: Who cares for the psychological well-being of left-behind children?' *Science and Society*, 5, 46–7 (in Chinese).

Zeng, M., and Huang H. (2010). 'Searching for "Acting Mothers" for Left Behind Children', *Township Forum*, 14 (in Chinese).

Zheng, Q. (2009). 'Concerning the Safety of Girls: The Outcry of left behind girls', *Rural Women*, 7, 6–7 (in Chinese).

BARNEY SHIELS

11 The Equity Approach to Early Childhood Development and Accomplishing the Millennium Development Goals

Introduction

This chapter examines the role of Early Childhood Development (ECD) in achieving the Millennium Development Goals (MDGs) as a set of fixed duration, and fixed target, human developmental paradigms agreed upon by the international community.

Accomplishment of the Millennium Development Goals is one of the most ambitious and significant developmental challenges that has ever been set. The MDGs are, quite simply, too important to fail.

A 2006 United Nations Report on progress towards achieving the eight MDGs reminds us that if we continue to push progress towards 2015:

- More than 300 million people will no longer suffer from hunger,
- 30 million more children will reach their fifth birthday,
- 350 million more people will have access to safe drinking water,
- 650 million fewer people will live without the benefits of basic sanitation,
- Hundreds of millions more women and girls will go to school, will access economic and political opportunity and will have greater security and safety. (2009a)

Every one of these statistics refers to hundreds of thousands of individuals with human faces. Hunger and poverty are the realities of life for the great majority of the world's people. Every child who does not survive until their fifth birthday represents a personal tragedy: a mother without her child; a family in mourning. The push to achieve the MDGs does not come from a desire to reach statistical targets, but the desire to reach millions of people whose opportunities in life are restricted by virtue of the circumstances into which they have been born.

This chapter also stresses the centrality of Early Childhood Care and Education (ECCE) in efforts to achieve MDG 2 and ensure that by 2015 children everywhere (boys and girls alike) will be able to complete a full course of primary education. Finally, the chapter also demonstrates that the most promising strategy in pursuit of this goal is increased focus on equity. This chapter locates its argument within the context of the targets set out in the Millennium Declaration and the policy and practice of UNICEF in the field of early childhood development.

Reviewing that practice to date, in respect of the targets set out by the MDGs, suggests that, while commendable progress has been achieved, the current rate of progress will not satisfy the targets set by the MDGs.

In 2010, UNICEF put forward a conceptual framework which it called *The Equity Agenda*. This framework argued that a heightened focus on equity within country programmes offered the highest possibility of returns (measured as progress towards the targets established by the Millennium Declaration of 2000). The Equity Agenda offered a unique approach to developmental policy and practice and a substantive vehicle for principled progress towards sustainable social development, particularly in some of the most longterm structurally impoverished states of the world.

The Millennium Development Goals and the equity agenda

> These are the world's most vulnerable children. Ten years ago, the United Nations Millennium Declaration reaffirmed our collective responsibility to improve their lives by challenging nations, rich and poor alike, to come together around a set of ambitious goals to build a more peaceful, prosperous and just world.
>
> — UNICEF 2010a: 5

In September 2010, Anthony Lake, Executive Director of UNICEF, reminded attendees of the United Nations High Level Plenary Meeting of the General Assembly in New York, of the commitment that they had made to the world's children in adopting resolution 55/2, the Millennium Declaration.

The Millennium Summit, Declaration and the subsequent MDGs were, by their very nature, ambitious and aspirational. They were founded on a clear recognition that the nations of the world had made significant strides in lifting millions of people from extreme poverty, empowering the most marginalized groups within societies to reach their full potential, and achieving unprecedented global economic growth and social development over the second half of the twentieth century; but that there was more to do to achieve real global justice and development. The MDGs set the most specific, measurable, achievable, realistic and time bound global social and economic developmental targets that had ever been articulated, let alone been committed to by the international community: a clear roadmap for the aspirations of the world at the turn of the twenty-first century. The MDGs set out a clear standard by which the commitments of the governments of the world would be judged. The bar had been set high.

The Millennium Summit and Declaration did not specify the strategies to achieve the MDGs. There were, of course, broad indications of the type of national, bilateral and multilateral commitments that would be necessary to generate the momentum that could push the developmental enterprise towards the new targets it had set itself: debt relief; more generous development assistance; and implementation of international humanitarian and human rights law, amongst others (United Nations 2000). However, these broad undertakings did not constitute the type of programmatic strategies that would achieve the targets the Declaration set out.

Developmental partners, ranging from the state signatories themselves, civil society actors, bilateral and multilateral agencies as well as non-governmental organizations (NGOs), would have to bring together the weight of their collective experience, knowledge and perspectives to identify implementable and context specific strategies to achieve the goals. Like any strategic formulation, the necessary component of monitoring and evaluation was built into the MDG plans and it was through one such mechanism that the equity agenda first came to light in a substantive manner.

In 2010, UNICEF put forward a conceptual framework called *The Equity Agenda* which argued that a heightened focus on equity within country programmes offered the highest possibility of returns. The Equity Agenda offered a unique approach to developmental policy and practice and a substantive vehicle for principled progress towards sustainable social development.

For UNICEF, equity means that all children have an opportunity to survive, develop, and reach their full potential, without discrimination. This interpretation is consistent with the United Nations Convention on the Rights of the Child, which guarantees the fundamental rights of every child regardless of gender, race, religious beliefs, income, physical attributes, disability, geographical location or other status.

Inequity and inequality are distinct concepts. Addressing inequity involves addressing the extent of preventable, and avoidable, inequalities which exist because of (or greatly contributed to by) avoidable factors and elements that combine to embed inequalities that need not be so pronounced, or so rooted in structural global poverty.

Inequities (as opposed to inequalities) arise when certain populations are unfairly deprived of resources that are available to other groups. Whether a disparity can be considered unfair or unjust depends on the context.

For example, young adults tend to be healthier than elderly adults, and female newborns generally have lower birth weight rates than male newborns. These disparities are not inequitable, as the factors that influence them are unavoidable; there are no structural reasons why male newborns are heavier than female, simply biological. However, if young girls and boys show dramatic disparities in access to primary education, that disparity is much more likely to be rooted in social factors and can be seen as unnecessary and avoidable. Gender discrimination is, arguably, the most prevalent inequity within the developmental paradigm; but it is not the only one.

The equity focused approach challenges traditional indicators of human development, measured at the national or regional level. As noted by Vandemoortele and Delamonica (2010: 69): 'Global Targets apply at the global level. Unfortunately, the global MDG canon has turned them into yardsticks for measuring and judging at national level. Measuring progress towards the MDGs can be deceptive, masking real inequities at the sub-national level'.

Equity based approaches to programme and policy, therefore, seek to address the root causes of inequity so that all children have access to education, health care, sanitation and development. Right in practice, and right in principle, the equity agenda challenges practitioners to reach out in substantive ways to the most marginalized groups in societies, and in so doing takes significant strides towards the targets set out by the Millennium Declaration.

ECD, universal primary education and school readiness

Early Childhood Development (ECD) refers to a composite result of the successful fulfilment of children's rights to survival, development, protection and participation during the first eight years of a child's life (United Nations 2010b: 1). One of the factors that contribute to this composite result is that of Early Childhood Care and Education (ECCE), and increasing evidence points to the reality that investment in quality ECCE reaps significant rewards in terms of Universal Primary Education (UPE).

The Second Millennium Development Goal is to ensure that by 2015 all children (boys and girls) will have the opportunity to complete a full course of primary education. The Goal is absolute and universal leaving no room for ambiguity or interpretive bias.

UPE is challenged by a number of obstacles; some represent inequalities and others represent inequities. As early as 2005 the United Nations Millennium Project (an independent advisory panel commissioned by the Secretary General of the UN to propose the strategies that could best achieve the goals and targets set out in the Millennium Declaration) recognized these obstacles.

The United Nations Millennium Project (2005) highlighted the unsurprising reality that poor children were less likely to attend school: '[I]n every country completion rates are lowest for children from poor households. In Western and Central Africa, the median grade completed by the bottom 40 per cent of the income distribution is zero, because less than half of poor children complete even the first year in school' (2005: 2). Other substantive barriers to the accomplishment of UPE were also recognized, including gender disparities, retention rates, children excluded along geographical, ethnic and linguistic lines, children with disabilities and children affected by conflict.

Overwhelming evidence shows that children who are supported in early learning have better school/learning achievements, they are less inclined to drop out of school and have higher productivity later in life. Potentially, the access to quality early childhood education and care could help deprived children to break the cycle of inequity.

Evidence that ECCE interventions offer significantly enhanced cognitive and developmental opportunities and school performances is widespread and compelling. The findings of Nores and Barnett (2009: np), for example, in a meta-analysis of fifty-six studies in twenty-three countries suggest that 'children from different contexts and countries receive substantial benefits from early childhood interventions and these are sustained over time. Interventions that have an educational or stimulation component evidenced the largest cognitive affects'.

Early Childhood services can, and do, play an important role in forming the protective environment around children. Childcare can protect children from family and home-based risk and from the broader detrimental social effects of structuralized poverty. According to analysis undertaken by the National Research Council and Institute of Medicine (2000), measured and appropriate programmatic interventions retain the possibility 'to influence the developmental trajectories of children whose life courses are threatened by socioeconomic disadvantage, family disruption, and diagnosed disabilities' (2000: 309).

The power of investment in the most marginalized is supported by Cleveland and Krashinsky (2003: 12), who point out that, '[a]lthough early childhood education and care benefits all children, much of the evidence suggest that the largest benefits flow to children from the most disadvantaged families [...] good childcare can compensate, at least partially, for a disadvantaged home life'.

One of the major causes of inadequacy in primary education stems from far too many children in the developing world starting school later than the prescribed age, and from children being poorly prepared for school. This leads to high repetition, large numbers of overage learners and high dropout rates; situations that stretch scarce resources and perpetuate the cycle of under-education of a country's children.

It also locks in inequities, forcing disadvantaged children to struggle to keep up with their better-off peers right from the start. Investing in the early years can mitigate inequities that would otherwise only deepen over time; it helps children start primary school at the right age and complete school at the standard time.

UNICEF supports many actions to improve school readiness, including: working within partnerships to help countries; supporting community based early childhood care and development programmes that are linked to other development programmes for women and children; provision of formal pre-school programmes that are linked with primary schools and use national standards for school readiness; implementation of the child-to-child school readiness initiative in which children who are already in school receive lessons and resources they can take home to help get younger siblings ready for school at the right age.

A critical output in this regard is the preparation of children for formal primary education. School readiness reflects a combination of three factors that combine to provide the best educational opportunities for children as they enter into primary education. UNICEF practice in policy stresses the need for ECCE programmes to take all three factors into account.

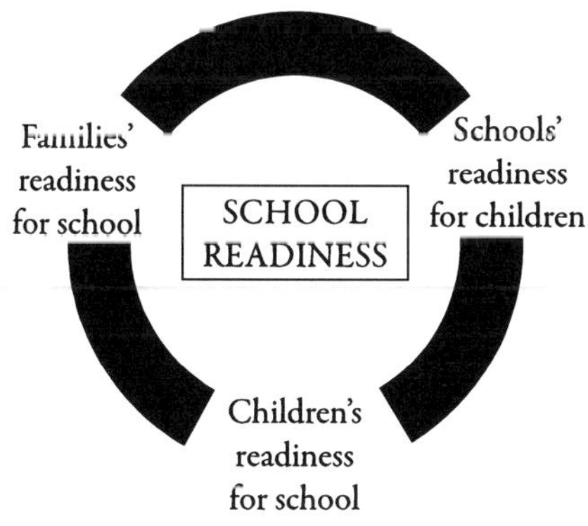

It is, therefore, important to consider schools' readiness for children in terms of ECCE; but in terms of equity it is the other two factors, those of the readiness of children and families, that require the most focus.

The equity approach to ECCE

An equity based approach means targeting disability, gender, marginalized ethnic or racial groups, addressing geographical location, and income levels. The overlap of these factors combine to build an invisible wall that excludes children from education and ECCE opportunities. Girls from rural areas are less likely to attend ECCE programmes, even where they are available. Boys with disabilities are less likely to attend ECCE, even when the nature of the disability presents no substantive practical, or health related, barrier to involvement.

UNICEF's focus on equity highlights the importance of education for any society as a primary tool for empowerment and transformation, and its essential role in breaking inter-generational cycles of poverty and structural disparity.

Equity based approaches to education involve removing barriers to education within and outside formal educational systems and providing equitable education and learning opportunities for all children. This requires particular attention to historically excluded children, for example, through removing barriers to education for girls and expanding on support services, such as ECCE, available to young girls.

The gap between access to education for girls and boys is one of the most prevalent and entrenched forms of inequity across much of the developing world. Girls have less opportunity to avail of educational opportunities for a variety of reasons. There are normative cultural reasons, such as domestic responsibilities that can be considered more important than education and in many cases there is a strong normative sense in which education of girls is somehow perceived to be less valuable than boys' education.

This is reinforced by the entrenched barriers to girls entering into livelihoods outside of marriage, which further reduces the perception that education for girls is an important developmental imperative. There are also vulnerabilities that disproportionally affect girls, such as risk of abuse or violence within the educational context, that combine to entrench barriers to education. Even the onset of menstruation can present an obstacle, when the lack of suitable water, sanitation and hygiene facilities can prevent young girls from completing, or even undertaking formal education.

These unnecessary barriers that prevent girls from availing of their rights to education are clear examples of the types of inequities that UNICEF is trying to address through the equity agenda.

ECCE is essential to enhance children's readiness for primary schooling and beyond. It has the potential to improve retention rates of education systems and the individual learning achievements of children, particularly from poor and disadvantaged households, when they arrive in primary school (Samms-Vaughan 2004). Several good practice cases have developed standards for more integrated, accessible and quality ECD programmes that target groups (such as young girls who have been marginalized).

With regards to equity focused policy and programmatic interventions in education, there is a requirement for more nuanced analytical foundations and needs assessments that accurately reflect contextualized structural inequities, which are different from one country to the next. Evidence based measures that seem to have the most promise in addressing these underlying disparities include: the abolition of school fees; scholarships which enable girls to access (or continue within) educational processes: and the deliberate linking of protective and health based interventions that serve to further incentivize education. Most crucial, however, is the 'nine plus one' years of basic education (which includes one year of early childhood education and one year of lower secondary).

ECCE and ECD are cornerstone strategies to increase primary school enrolment and retention rates, towards the realization of MDG 2. Children who benefit from ECCE access will be more likely to go on into primary education, and also more likely to sustain their involvement within education to the nine plus one years level.

Equity in practice

UNICEF's increased efforts to refocus ECCE policy and programming on equity is guided by four principal hallmarks:

Building evidence for policy development and planning

An equity based approach requires needs assessments and baselines to gather information on target populations, with increased sophistication and focus on children who are traditionally found at the margins of sectoral programmes. UNICEF Multi-Indicator Cluster Surveys (MICS), the principal mechanism through which the organization gathers household information, must be amended to capture more, and more accurate, data on children previously marginalized in such data capture. An equity based approach to ECCE requires that UNICEF MICS more accurately take children on the margins, both geographically and socially, into account.

Integration and convergence of services

ECCE programming that successfully engages inequities must reflect integrated approaches. Efforts to reach out to the most marginalized children must reflect health, education and protection needs. It is in groups that exist on the margins of mainstream strategies that the overlap of these needs is most prevalent. Effective ECCE programmes also recognize the interplay between children's readiness for (primary) school and education, families' readiness for their child's attendance at school and finally, the school's readiness to receive the child. There is a great need for convergence between all sectors to achieve a holistic approach for children and their families.

Empowering families, parents and other caregivers

While there is an understandable tendency within ECCE programming to focus upon the formal education environment (pre-schools, childcare centres, neighbourhood care points, crèches etc.), the integration and convergence discussed above requires that the added value in resourcing parents, families and communities must be fully realized also. A holistic interpretation of early childhood development takes into account the reality that much of the child's development is affected by factors that are active outside the educational context.

Building evidence for policy based development and planning

The design and implementation of research that focuses on the arguments in favour of integrated early childhood development programmes and illustrates the outcomes among children most at risk, will strengthen the argument for equity based interventions, and investment in pre-primary education and care, as well as school readiness.

UNICEF practice in ECD is now reflecting the new equity focus.

Step by Step in Moldova

In Moldova, access to early learning opportunities have been greatly expanded in the past few years thanks, in part, to financial and technical assistance made available through the Education for All – Fast Track Initiative, co-financed by UNICEF. The Moldovan Ministry of Education data suggests a near two-fold increase in the number of children aged three to six enrolled, jumping from an estimated 40,000 in 2001 to 74,000 in 2009 (2010b: np).

Despite these impressive gains, many children remain un-enrolled and many of these children come from economically and socially marginalized backgrounds. To address this inequity the government of Moldova recently approved regulations on creating and running ECD Community Centres for children aged two to six; as well as a guide on establishing ECD Community Centres as a resource for senior management within the system of local public administration. The community centre model, promoted through these resources, aims to promote the development of early educational programmes in places where there are no existing pre-schools or alternative ECCE opportunities.

The model is grounded in the experiences of twenty pilot community centres for children and families created through a UNICEF/UNESCO supported project, in partnership with the Moldovan NGO, Step by Step Moldova, which ran from 2005 to 2007. External evaluation revealed this model to be flexible, cost-effective and crucially an appropriate method of engaging the dynamic demographic situation in the Moldovan context, particularly in rural areas of Moldova where vulnerable populations were being omitted from traditional early childhood educational programmes.

The roll-out of this model offers a significant opportunity for the government of Moldova to increase its coverage of early childhood development services through the promotion of community centres, and thus to address the inequity that currently remains. It is envisioned that this roll-out will result in the establishment of an additional 250 community centres across the country.

Neighbourhood Care Points in Swaziland

In Swaziland, the equity agenda in ECD has been initiated with a view towards children who have been affected by HIV, for example orphans. UNICEF estimates adult HIV prevalence rate is 25.9 per cent (2011: 102), the highest in the world. Furthermore, there are an estimated 14,000 children aged 0–14 living with HIV. HIV plays a significant role in marginalizing huge numbers of children in Swaziland and it is towards these children that UNICEF equity based ECCE interventions have been targeted.

Swaziland has approximately 69,000 children who have been orphaned by AIDS. This figure encompasses maternal orphans, paternal orphans and double-parent orphans, that is, children that have lost both parents to AIDS. It is this last group that are considered the most vulnerable children, often made heads of their households by virtue of their age and left responsible to provide for younger siblings, within a family unit that has lost its primary support mechanism. Vulnerability in the case of AIDS orphans can be loosely defined as: economically vulnerable, sometimes sexually vulnerable or at risk of exposure to HIV, abuse or exploitation, and very often at risk of losing the opportunities in ECD and education. These factors (and others) combine to exclude orphans from many developmental channels.

In Swaziland, there are now more than 600 functioning Neighbourhood Care Points (NCPs), or community based centres (supported by UNICEF and partners including the Swazi government) for orphans, that provide food, psychosocial support and life skills training to orphans and vulnerable children (OVC). These NCPs serve more than 33,000 non-school going children across the country.

NCPs were established to provide day-to-day support to OVC and enable them to be cared for in the communities in which they were raised. Many NCPs provide informal education to children, but more importantly, they highlight the numbers of children who fall outside the formal education system. NCPs have become an effective means of directing children into formal school education. In addition, NCPs provide a safe environment for older siblings to leave younger brothers and sisters so that they may attend school (NERCHA 2007).

NCPs represent a comparatively simple and culturally adaptive intervention in community-based ECCE that offers some of the most vulnerable children in Swaziland a protective environment and a vital avenue into formal educational structures. They represent an application of the equity agenda into practice, that is replicable, sustainable and inexpensive; and that reaches out to some of the most marginalized children in that country.

Conclusion

> We recognise that, in addition to our separate responsibilities to our individual societies, we have a collective responsibility to uphold the principles of human dignity, equality and equity at the global level. As leaders we have a duty therefore to all the world's people, especially the most vulnerable and, in particular, the children of the world, to whom the future belongs.
>
> — UNITED NATIONS 2000: np

The principal of equity was never far removed from the purpose of the Millennium Declaration or the MDGs; in fact, it was enshrined the text of the declaration. A renewed strategic focus on equity now holds the best chance of achieving the ambitious, but worthy, targets which the Declaration articulated.

In the context of MDG 2, the achievement of universal primary education, there is no room for inequity; universality is absolute.

While noting that there is less consensus among policy-makers about the relevance and importance of early childhood care and education programmes than there is over the desire of achieving MDG 2, this chapter argues that de-linking the two makes little policy sense. ECCE programmes have proven aptitude in increasing school readiness and thus in extending primary enrolment and retention.

An equity focused agenda offers the most compelling argument that spreading ECCE programmes to encompass the most marginalized children holds great potential for gains towards MDG 2, and beyond (UNICEF has already begun to make the case that ECCE must form a central pillar of post-2015 educational developmental goals). Simply put, extending ECCE to those children who have never had the opportunity to benefit from it will result in a marked increase in progress towards universal primary enrolment, as well as a huge increase in the potential for development that those individual children may hope to reach. The equity approach in ECCE is right not just in principle but, crucially, also in practice. 'It is increasingly evident that our progress is uneven in many key areas. In fact, compelling data suggests that in the global push to achieve the MDGs, we are leaving behind millions of the world's most disadvantaged, vulnerable and marginalized children: the children who are facing the longest odds' (UNICEF 2010a: 5).

With five years remaining until 2015, the time has come for renewed vigour in our pursuit of the MDGs and, in the case of MDG 2, a focus on ECCE and school readiness remains critical. In order to achieve UPE, and thus MDG 2, the obstacles to equitable access to early ECCE and childhood services have to be overcome and real equity has to be achieved as a matter of urgency.

Developmental programmes and policies must acknowledge within their practice the need to focus on inequity in access to such programmes as a fundamental barrier to accomplishment of all MDGs, and to the emergence of the world envisioned in the Millennium Declaration in which the ideals of human rights, dignity and equity *can* be fully realized, for all children, everywhere.

References

Cleveland, G., and Krashinsky, M. (2003). *Financing ECEC Services in OECD Countries.* Toronto. University of Toronto Press.

National Emergency Response Council on HIV and AIDS (NERCHA) (2007). *Helping Communities Help Themselves: 'Swaziland's innovative community-based response to HIV and AIDS'.* Mbabane: NERCHA.

National Research Council and Institute of Medicine (2000). *From Neurons to Neighbourhoods.* Washington D. C.: National Academy Press.

Nores, M., and Barnett, W. (2010). 'Benefits of Early Childhood Interventions Across the World: (Under)investing in the very young'. Paper presented at the annual meeting of the 54th Annual Conference of the Comparative and International Education Society, Palmer House Hotel, Chicago, Illinois, 28 February.

Samms-Vaughan, M. E. (2004). *Profiles: The Jamaican Preschool Child: The status of early childhood development in Jamaica.* Kingston: Planning Institute of Jamaica.

United Nations (2000). Resolution adopted by the General Assembly 55/2. *United Nations Millennium Declaration, A/Res/55/2, section I–III*, New York: United Nations.

United Nations (2005). *United Nations Millennium Project 2005 Toward Universal Primary Education: Investments, incentives, and institutions.* Task Force on Education and Gender Equality. New York: United Nations.

United Nations (2009). *The Millennium Development Goals Report 2009.* New York: United Nations.

United Nations (2010). *Status of the CRC Report of the Secretary General*, A/65/206 2, August 2010. New York: United Nations.

United Nations Children's Fund (2010a). *Progress for Children, Achieving the MDGs with Equity*, Number 9, New York: UNICEF.

United Nations Children's Fund (2010b). *Early Childhood Development Newsletter – The Best Start in Life for Every Child.* no.44, April/May 2010, New York: UNICEF.

United Nations Children's Fund (2011). *The State of the World's Children 2011: Adolescence, an age of opportunity.* New York: UNICEF.

Vandemoortele, J., and Delamonica, E. (2010). 'Taking the MDGs Beyond 2015: Hasten slowly', *Institute of Development Studies Bulletin*, 41 (1), 60–9. Sussex: Institute of Development Studies.

SECTION 3

Language and Culture: Working with Children

MARY KELLETT

12 Research Methods with Young Children: Extending the Canvas

Introduction

Shifting attitudes towards children's status in society are changing the way we undertake research with young children. Active participation of young children in research began to emerge around the turn of the twenty-first century. Prior to this, young children's social and cognitive competences were regarded as barriers to participation. Research *on* and *about* children prevailed long before research *with* children gained recognition. A key message of the South African Child Gauge Report (UNICEF 2011) is that opportunities need to be created for children of all ages to participate in the spaces which impact on their lives. The responsibility falls on childhood professionals to create supportive, child-friendly environments that facilitate participation. Respect and communication are two-way streets where children are entitled to be treated as equals. Their participation should be integral to any decision-making that affects their lives, including the planning and evaluating phases, and not just the implementation. This requires a fundamental rethinking of children's capabilities, experiences and contributions. Crucially, this necessitates a reappraisal of the research methods we employ with young children to ensure there is genuine engagement and active participation. This chapter explores the rationale behind this shift and maps some examples of research methods with young children from around the globe.

First principles

If we are going to research children and childhood in any meaningful way, careful consideration has to be given to the methodologies employed. We cannot do child research without obtaining data from children. Even when data is collected by adults, this still requires engagement with children. Criticism (e.g. Alderson and Morrow 2004) that some child research is not fit for purpose has arisen because the studies do not generate accurate data. This is because the methods employed are either outside of children's experience or are overlain with power dynamics that get in the way. At the heart of this is imperfect communication. Adults and children exist in parallel spheres where the simplest of enquiries can go awry, as in the example here of an interview where an adult researcher is exploring the closeness of family relationships with a child (Greene and Hill 2005: 10):

> Q: How close are you to your grandfather?
> A: Well, not very close really: I live in Dublin and he lives in Offaly.

There is no reason why tried and tested data collection techniques such as observation, interview and surveys should not work well in early childhood research provided that the methods used are child-centred and age and context appropriate. James (1999: 244) maintains that 'observation, participation and interviewing all entail implicit assumptions about children's competency [...] tools of the trade they might be, but they are far from value free'. With regard to interview situations, Westcott and Littleton (2005: 141) remind us that: '[I]t is easy to forget that children may rarely be spoken to, or seriously listened to, unless they have done something "wrong". Data collection methods need to be about creating joint meaning making so that distinctions can be made between children's lives as lived, experienced and told'. These considerations, among others, have led to a greater focus on participatory methods.

Participatory research techniques

Participatory research techniques have mushroomed in recent years and are known to be effective with young children (Bath 2009). They draw on early work of researchers such as Freire's (1972) Participatory Rural Appraisal (PRA) work in South America which drew on the experiences of rural peasant populations whose illiteracy required imaginative methods to be employed which were not language-dependent. Visual methods, sometimes known as visual anthropology (Prosser 1998), are among the most popular to emerge out of PRA. Drawings and photographs create a representation of a lived experience but the photo itself is only a tool, the real data is generated through the dialogue that it prompts (Ennison and Smith 2000). Other visual records can be created by capturing views, opinions and experiences on stickers (drawings or scribed words) and collating them into montages. A good example of this is the giant message tree that adorns the entrance to Edendale Hospital in Pietermaritzburg, South Africa. Here, health workers supported children suffering from long term health conditions, such as HIV and tuberculosis, to share their views and emotions on stickers and fixed them to the tree.

Participatory techniques enable children to share their perspectives and also to be actively involved in decision-making. Thomas and O'Kane's seminal work (1999) has provided us with many examples that researchers have adopted and adapted successfully with young children. A favourite is 'beans in the pot'. This is an interactive activity whereby children are given a number of beans – counters, dried pasta or conkers work equally well – which they can distribute among pre-labelled pots according to how strongly they feel about, or agree with, something. For example, young children might be asked how they feel at the end of their first day in nursery and presented with a series of pots labelled with pictures to depict happy, sad, frightened, tired etc., and they deposit as few or as many beans as they want to into each pot according to how they feel. This method can also be used to participate in decision-making. Each child can be given one bean to place in the pot of their choice when trying to engage in democratic decision-making, for example, which game to play or which storybook the teacher might read.

Bath (2009) demonstrated the efficacy of participatory techniques in her study exploring young children's experiences of starting school. She devised a number of participatory activities such as 'Who Chooses'. Here small groups of young children were given three different shapes as representations of themselves, their parent and their teacher. Throughout the day, the practitioner asked them a series of 'Who Chooses' questions. Who chooses:

when you get up in the morning?
what you have for breakfast?
what you do at school?
what you play?
what you watch on television?
when you go to bed?

After each question the children indicated who the decision-maker was by placing a sticker into the corresponding shape.

Diamond ranking (Thomas and O'Kane 1999, 2000) is a participatory technique that can be readily adapted for young children. This activity uses the shape of a diamond to construct a ranking of likes and dislikes, while allowing some choices to be ranked equally rather than entirely ordinal. Young children sometimes experience difficulty with the concept that favourite or best is singular and enthusiastically volunteer that several children are their best friend. The diamond template features nine categories or statements. Children choose their top and bottom ranking choices and then equally rank two second choices, three third choices and two fourth choices. An eleven-year-old child researcher, Mitchell Schofield (2008), used this technique to seek his peers' views about attributes of teachers. He brainstormed the topic first and then produced a list of nine characteristic attributes (see Figure 1) for ranking.

Sets fair homework
Exciting
Lots of activities
Encouraging
Happy and smiling
Keeps control of the class
Kind
Fair to everyone
Group work

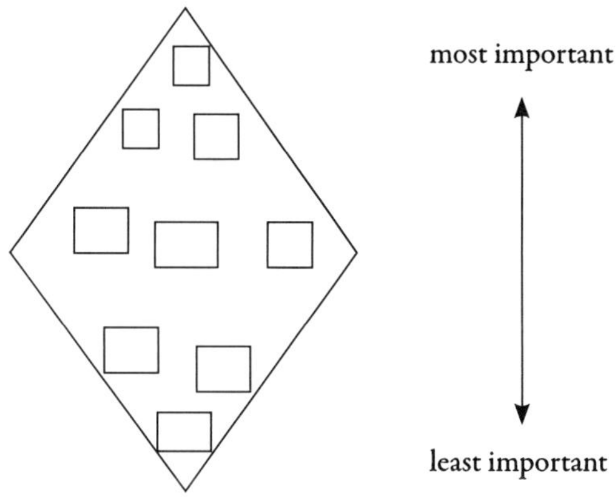

Figure 1 Example of a diamond ranking activity (Schofield 2008: slide 5)

The nine descriptors were written out on small cards. Participating children had lots of fun shuffling the cards around to represent their choices until they were happy with their final rankings. Interestingly, 'happy and smiling' came out at the top of most diamonds with other categories being harder to separate. It is easy to see how the diamond ranking could be used for a multiplicity of purposes and data gathering.

The Mosaic Approach

The Mosaic Approach (Clark and Moss 2001) is arguably the most influential method of the last decade to move forward young children's active involvement in research process. It is a technique that encourages young children to be data collectors as well as participants in research. It is a collection of child-friendly participation activities which together create a 'mosaic' of young children's experiences and has been used successfully in a variety of early years settings to inform our understanding of how young children perceive their nursery environments. In one of the methods, children are given disposable cameras with which to photograph particular aspects of their learning environments that they like or dislike. The photos are used in child interviews as prompts to elicit discussion about experiences of different parts of their environment. Another aspect of the mosaic is where a child takes an adult on a guided tour of his or her early years setting so that the adult sees the milieu through the child's eyes. This is an informative way of accessing children's experiences. The parts of a setting they choose to show to an adult, and how they describe and explain these places, divulges much about their lived experiences. Other parts of the mosaic approach include observations and getting children to draw maps or pictures. The power of the approach is in pulling together multiple sets of information which, in isolation, may only tell part of a story but when pieced together provides a strong mosaic.

Examples of participatory research projects

There are many examples of initiatives that have successfully involved young children in the action parts of research methodology, especially the generation of data.

The Outdoor Learning Project (Waller 2006) was based at a state nursery school located in a mixed housing estate on the outskirts of a large town in the English midlands. Children's views about the outdoor play area were sought using an active participation method. The three and four year-olds were given digital cameras to film and record their perspectives by taking photos of their happy and special places. Through discussion of the photos with a practitioner they then created a learning story:

Zachary's story

One morning red group visited the park shortly after a light snowfall. Zoe noticed some tracks in the snow made by birds.

'Look, look a goblin's foot print', she said.

A small group of children (Charleigh, Jessica, and Zachary) came over to see the footprints. They followed the tracks and Zoe took a photograph on a digital camera. The children followed the track to a pump house where they stopped.

'I think he lives in there', Zoe said – pointing to the pump house.

The children tiptoed over towards a blue door and then stopped.

'You go Julie – we're scared'.

Julie (a practitioner) knocked on the door. The children ran away.

'Don't worry – there is no one at home today'.

Following this the children named the pump house the 'Goblin's House'.

Zachary then collected some sticks and cleared some space on the ground.

'This is for the flowers to grow', he said.

He then placed the sticks around the flowers, as if to protect them. Zachary then said,

'There might be butterflies. I'm making a butterfly garden'.

After a few seconds, he turned and pointed to the steps behind,

'You have to go right up there to see the ducks'.

Zachary drew a picture to represent the goblin's footprints. It is interesting to note that he also drew the Butterfly Garden, which is near to the 'Goblin's House' and is an area of the park to which he has consistently given attention. (Waller 2006: 90)

Ben's story

Ben asked to use the video camera; he picked it up and turned it on. He then walked up the path past a large open meadow.

'I am trying to find dinosaurs. Ssh. Ssh. You have to be very quiet. That looks like where I play football with Mathew – he's my older brother'.

He then walked up the path towards the woods.

'You have to be very quiet to look for dinosaurs. Let me look through the camera to see if I can see any dinosaurs. See here – it's fantastic, you can see them right over there. Look – it's pointing that way'.

He put the camera down and picked up a stick.

> 'This is to beat dinosaurs up with'. Found some nearby dinosaurs.
> Ben ran off into the woods waving his stick in the air.
> 'Ssh. Only I can talk!' (Waller 2006: 91)

In another example, funded by the National Children's Bureau, staff at a nursery in Leeds set out to find out what their young charges felt about nursery staff wearing uniforms. At the time staff wore a 'uniform' that included a T-shirt with the nursery logo on it. In order to access the views of all the children, including babies aged three to sixteen months, the staff created a non-verbal 'listening' activity. They put different items of clothing and fabric into an attractive basket along with some nursery staff T-shirts. Familiar carers supported the children to explore the textures and colours of the items and to express their views. The findings were quite surprising:

- Babies of 3–16 months loved the different textures, bracelets and beads in the basket but showed no interest in wanting to explore the staff T-shirts.
- Toddlers of 16–24 months selected favourite items but staff T-shirts did not feature among any of these.
- Children aged 2–3 years selected and discussed favourite items but showed zero preference for the staff T-shirts.
- Children of 3–5 years dressed up a member of staff to make her look 'beautiful' but eschewed the staff T-shirts in their choices of desirable attire.

The exercise proved invaluable to staff in learning what the children really felt about their 'uniforms'. It helped them to see that the children found individual dress much more interesting and, therefore, they abandoned this policy in favour of the diversity of individual clothing. All the children, whatever their age or cognitive ability, had been able to participate in this consultation (see <www.ncb.org.uk/ycvn>).

A further example relates to accessing young children's feelings and anxieties about their care provision in early years settings. Since 2004, three- and four-year-olds in England have been entitled to twelve and a half hours free early education per week. From 2010 this was increased to fifteen hours of 'flexible' provision and family needs were to be accommodated where possible. Hertfordshire county council was one of the first to offer the fifteen hours' provision and decided to undertake an evaluation of how fifty-eight young children in ten early years' settings were experiencing the new, flexible entitlement.

Play-based methodology was employed to elicit children's views about how young children experienced their early years settings. These included staff observations, puppetry, children guiding adults on walking tours and also using cameras in photo elicitation activities. Findings highlighted many positives about the children's experiences but also uncovered some anxieties. Children were confused about whether they were there for a whole or a half day and were particularly upset about not knowing if they were staying for lunch (a favourite time) and whether or not their friends would be coming that day:

> Am I staying for lunch today?
> Freddy, he's not here, he's gone home?

The findings enabled recommendations to be made about minimizing disruptions, ensuring children were able to spend regular time with friends and staff they knew well and better management of beginnings and ends of differently timed sessions. Outcomes demonstrate that three- and four-year-olds can exercise voice in a meaningful way and influence policy and practice.

Phila Impilo

Participatory research methods with young children are widely practised around the world. I have already alluded to PRA in South America and there are many other valuable activities developed by NGOs and childhood organizations globally. One such is the Phila Impilo project in South Africa

(Chawla and Kruger 2009). The African continent has a distressingly high infant mortality rate and whole swathes of children are ravaged by chronic diseases such as HIV and TB and need long term hospital care. Accessing and understanding their lived experiences is vital if their needs are to be adequately provided for. The video documentary of Phila Impilo makes extensive use of puppetry to generate participatory data. Finger puppets are easy to make and communication can be done entirely via the puppet characters. If there is something a child wants to convey that is distressing or embarrassing, the puppets provide a safe vehicle through which to communicate. Dolls and favourite toys can also become 'voices'. The Phila Impilo children made puppets from brightly patterned socks onto which they sewed large buttons for eyes and then made them talk by placing a thumb in the heel of the sock and fingers in the toe. Here are some of the feelings expressed by the children about their puppets:

> They taught me to remember my treatment.
> They gave me hope when I was tired.
> The puppet was my friend. It let me express what I could not say.
> The puppets helped us to deal with bigger illnesses than chicken pox and flu. (Phila Impilo documentary film 2009)

The film goes on to show a young child talking through his stripy sock puppet about his experiences of living with HIV:

> I was at home when my mother told me that she was HIV positive and that I was too. I was shocked when she told me that I had it. I thought that I did not have it. We were both in bed. My tummy was sore and my mother took me to the clinic. They made me understand why I was sick. I got medicine and then I felt better. Children do not play with me at first. As time passes they play with me. It is better for parents to tell their children what sorts of illnesses they have.

Young children as researchers

Children and young people leading their own research (Kellett 2005; Alderson 2009) is now established as an important source of knowledge about childhoods as generated from children's perspectives. So far, there are very few examples of young children undertaking their own research. Collaborative endeavours such as the Mosaic approach, and others cited in this chapter, are more common. However, this situation is set to change as debates about competencies come under renewed pressure from participation advocates, and greater proliferation of enabling activities that scaffold and support young children to undertake their own research (Frost et al. 2008). This is already happening in the UK and further afield such as China. In 2010, a group of young children in China were supported with research training and then went on to investigate what their peers thought about learning English. Grace Pu (2010), aged seven, completed a small study about this. Her research question was: 'Should Chinese children learn English?'

> I interviewed six children, aged from seven to ten.
> I surveyed six children, aged from seven to nine.
> In total, there are seven girls and five boys.
> They are my classmates, schoolmates, friends and neighbors. (Pu 2010: slide 4)

Through her findings, Grace was able to show that her peers liked learning English and that their favourite English activities were:

> Watching English movies
> Reading English books
> Singing English songs
> Playing English games. (Ibid, slide 8)

Her investigation also revealed that children of her age did not enjoy English writing activities.

Narrative methods

The technique of narrative can be used effectively to involve children in the research process. The format of a story can provide a vehicle to explore ideas and perspectives, for example, by stopping the story part way and inviting children to say what should happen next and why can be a way to access their feelings about different topics. Story can also be a research method in itself, such as Veale's (2005) use of a story game method during a participatory community project in Rwanda to elicit children's experiences of genocide. In the story game each line is contributed by different children orally:

> We ran away and lost our parents. – I was hungry. – I was separated from my parents. – We found a child. – Others died. – There were a lot of bullets shot. – We moved by running. – They brought us into an orphanage. – We met nice people. – When we reached home a child died, – was found, – was buried. – We experienced terrible things. – We met those who carried us. – They brought us back home. (Veale 2005: 260)

Although the contributors in this example were older children, the method is equally valid for young children because of its oral nature and the scaffolding collaboration.

Ethical considerations

Undoubtedly, all research methods that involve young children have to be ethical. I want to take the debate beyond the usual ethical guidance lists, that remind us about informed consent and confidentiality etc., to considerations of children's wellbeing during any research process activity. When children participate in research, either as subjects or co-researchers, there must be no exploitation, however indirect. Exploitation can include causing children to become tired, overworked or anxious. It also relates to the management of expectations. When researchers collect data with or from children they raise expectations in those children that some benefit may accrue either through greater understanding and tolerance of their views or changes that will improve their lives. Too often, researchers fail to return to participants and share their findings, this is even more disappointing when the participants are young children. Cases abound of researchers who interview children in their schools and homes, video-record them or play interactive data generation games with them, but never return to share their findings. We have an ethical duty (and moral imperative) to feed back findings to children who have participated in our research and to do so at an accessible level. Dissemination is frequently omitted from discussions of ethics. This is unfortunate because the dissemination is intricately tied into the nature of the methods used. If children have been involved in the collection of data, there is an ethical obligation to acknowledge their stake in the ownership of the study and involve them in dissemination where possible. Young children are no exception to this. The onus is on adults to make appropriate adaptations to enable them to play an active part should they wish to.

When reflecting on the first decade of the new century, it is evident that better listening and consultation cultures have led to greater participation by young children in many aspects of society, including more active participation in childhood research. The goal of the next decade must surely be to extend the canvas to include more research *by* young children and to share the dissemination arena with them more effectively.

References

Alderson, P. (2009). 'Younger Children's Individual Participation in Matters that Affect them'. In B. Percy-Smith and N. Thomas (eds), *Handbook of Children's Participation*, pp. 88–96. London: Routledge.

Alderson, P., and Morrow, V. (2004). *Ethics, Social Research and Consulting with Children and Young People*. 2nd ed., Ilford: Barnardo's.

Bath, C. (2009). *Learning to Belong: Exploring young children's participation at the start of school.* Abingdon: Routledge.

Chawla, L., and Kruger, J. (2009). *Phila Impilo* (film), <www.icpcn.org.uk>

Clark, A., and Moss, P. (2001). *Listening to Young Children: The Mosaic approach.* London: National Children's Bureau and Joseph Rowntree Foundation.

Ennison, M., and Smith, P. (2000). *Researching the Visual.* London: Sage.

Freire, P. (1972). *Cultural Action for Freedom.* London: Penguin.

Frost, R., Prince, R., and Handscomb, G. (2008). *Active Enquiring Minds.* Essex: Flare.

Greene, S. M., and Hill, M. (2005). 'Researching Children's Experiences: Methods and methodological issues'. In S. M. Greene, and D. M. Hogan (eds), *Researching Children's Experiences*, pp. 1–21. London: Sage.

James, A. (1999). 'Researching Children's Social Competence: Methods and models'. In M. Woodhead, D. Faulkner, and K. Littleton (eds), *Making Sense of Social Development.* London: Routledge in association with The Open University.

Kellett, M. (2005). *How to Develop Children as Researchers: A step by step guide to teaching research process.* London: Sage.

National Children's Bureau. (nd). *Listening as a Way of Life.* Young Children's Voice Network. <www.ncb.org.uk/ycvn> accessed 22 October 2012.

O'Kane, C. (2000). 'The Development of Participatory Techniques'. In P. Christensen, and A. James (eds), *Research with Children.* London: Routledge.

Prosser, J. (ed.) (1998). *Image-Based Research.* London: Falmer.

Pu, G. (2010). *Should Chinese Children Learn English.* <http://childrens-research-centre.ac.uk> accessed 22 October 2012.

Schofield, M. (2008). *11-Year-Olds' Views on School Subjects and Ideal Teacher Qualities.* <http://childrens-research-centre.ac.uk> accessed 22 October 2012.

Thomas, N., and O'Kane, C. (1999). 'Experiences of Decision-Making in Middle Childhood: The Example of children "looked after" by local authorities', *Childhood*, 6 (3), 369–88.

UNICEF (2011). *South African Child Gauge Report.* <www.unicef.org> accessed 22 October 2012.

Veale, A. (2005). 'Creative Methodologies in Research with Children and Young People'. In S. Greene and D. Hogan (eds), *Researching Children's Experience: Approaches and methods*, pp. 253–72. London: Sage.

Waller, T. (2006). '"Don't Come Too Close to My Octopus Tree": Recording and evaluating young children's perspectives of outdoor learning', *Children, Youth and Environments*, 16 (2), 75–104.

Westcott, H. and Littleton, K. (2005). 'Interviewing Children: Context, competence and joint meaning making'. In S. Greene and D. Hogan (eds), *Researching Children's Experience: approaches and methods*, pp. 141–57. London: Sage.

JACQUI O'RIORDAN, DEIRDRE HORGAN, SHIRLEY MARTIN AND MICHAEL BLANEY

13 Day-to-Day Transitions for Children of People Seeking Refugee Status Living in Ireland

Introduction and methodology

This chapter arises out of research carried out in 2011 by a team at University College Cork which examined the experiences of migrant parents in dealing with, and organizing, education provision for their young children. This was an exploratory study, the aim of which was to identify potential supports, as well as barriers, that were presenting to parents and their children as they negotiated the Irish educational system, focusing primarily on the pre- and primary school sectors. Research methods entailed a series of in-depth, semi-structured interviews with nine migrant parents, who were either currently seeking asylum in Ireland, or who had recently received refugee status. Seven of the interview participants were women, who were currently parenting alone, and two were men, who were parenting along with their wives. In the case of the latter, the couples were interviewed together. A major theme from the interviews related to the very stark realities of living in the accommodation made available for those seeking refugee status in Ireland, highlighting the strong relationship between living conditions and children's ability to participate and engage with education.

This chapter focuses on the day-to-day transitions of their children, identified by those research participants who are currently seeking asylum in Ireland, and, therefore, living within the Direct Provision system, a type of accommodation introduced for those seeking refugee status in Ireland in 2000. It draws on a small number of the overall research participants (four) who are of African origin and living in Direct Provision centres, all of whom are mothers, and their children (seven) ranging in age from one to six. Nonetheless, the transitions and experiences that they highlight are important in understanding those factors that influence the educational participation of a particularly marginalized, and invisible, group of migrant children in contemporary Irish society. In the first instance, the daily transitions that children are making are identified and discussed, throwing light on the very complex interactions of accommodation, community and material conditions on children's educational participation. The chapter draws our attention to issues of conflict and continuity in relation to family domains and education settings. It also points to the cultural borders that immigrant families and children face, as education settings may be the first context in which they confront such differences. It is argued that the conditions of living in Direct Provision pose specific barriers to the participation and integration of children. They can be viewed as forming the basis of differentiation and disadvantage, the consequences of which may well have far reaching and negative effects for the children themselves, and for society in general, in obstructing the development of an intercultural and inclusive society.

Transitions: a brief overview

While concepts of transition are increasingly employed in furthering our understanding of childhood experiences, the concept is used in a number of different ways, drawing both on socio-cultural perspectives on childhood and those perspectives that emphasize staged development. Distinctions are made between vertical and horizontal transitions. In general, however, transitions refer to 'key events and/or processes occurring at specific periods or turning points during the life course' (Vogler et al. 2008: 1). We draw on Petrewskyj et al.'s (2005: 1) assertion that they can be viewed as 'multi-layered process[es], involving multiple continuities and discontinuities of experience'. Transitions intersect with common expectations and experiences of growing up and of maturing, and are embodied in the usual or expected ways of progressing through life and of moving from one context to another. They are also associated with changes in 'appearance, activity, status, roles and relationships, as well as associated changes in use of physical and social space, and/or changing contact with cultural beliefs, discourses and practices, especially where these are linked to changes of setting and, in some cases, dominant language' (ibid: 1).

Vertical transitions involve 'key changes from one state or status to another, often associated with 'upward' shifts' (ibid: 2). They can include, for instance, starting and moving on through pre-primary to primary and secondary school, going to university and leaving home. Horizontal transitions refer more to the manner in which we move across social/ physical/environmental/cultural/institutional contexts. In the case of refugee children, the transitions can become quite complex and multi-layered, sometimes involving intersecting transitions of language, culture, physical space and so on. They might involve moving from one country to another, as well as participating and interacting with different education systems.

Studies into children's educational transitions increasingly emphasize the need to make the links between socio-cultural contexts and children's school transition experiences more explicit (e.g. Yeboah 2002). The percentage of new-comer students attending primary schools in Ireland, was estimated at 10 per cent in 2007 (Smyth et al. 2009), largely in line with what would be expected given that census figures in 2011 indicated that migrants constituted approximately 12 per cent of the population. While migration is traditionally dominated by those of working age, the increase in younger and older age groups migrating is worthy of note with the number of children (aged fourteen and under) increasing by 49.7 per cent to 78,600, up from 52,500 in 2006 (CSO 2012).

Our research identifies and attempts to understand children's transitions in relation to their parents' interactions with educational settings. We identify key links between vertical and horizontal transitions, across the conditions of Direct Provision centres and issues arising with their children's education, as faced by children and their parents. We draw attention to the manner in which the lives of children are impacted through the restrictions and associated barriers of living in Direct Provision, *vis-a-vis* the negotiation of the everyday transitions, for instance, from school to home as well as vertical transitions that are viewed as increasingly important for children's social wellbeing and development.

Direct Provision in Ireland

In 2000, the government of Ireland officially introduced a system of Direct Provision to accommodate people seeking asylum. While at the time, this move formalized what had become practice since 1999, it marked a definitive change in support and accommodation for people seeking asylum in Ireland. Through this development accommodation centres were established across the country, some of these are state-owned facilities while others are privately-run centres, sub-contracted to provide accommodation to a growing number of asylum-seekers, while their applications are being considered. At the time, it was suggested that this development would ease societal tensions that had been growing, mostly in and around Dublin, due to an increasing number of people seeking asylum in Ireland since the mid-1990s. The Department of Justice, Equality and Law Reform argued that it brought Ireland's policy in this area in line with other European countries. The proposal was that accommodation, board, and a small financial allowance would be provided to applicants while their applications were processed (RIA 2010).

The development of what has since become known as Direct Provision, at its inception and since, has been the subject of contention. In the early 2000s upwards of 5,500 people were accommodated in Direct Provision accommodation, rising to a peak of 8,080 people in 2005. Right from the beginning, fears about its contribution to marginalization of asylum seekers were raised (Fanning and Mac Éinrí 1999). Although the government has stated that the system of direct provision 'is a humane, fair and effective means of meeting (asylum seekers') basic needs' (Quinn and Hughes 2005: 10), concern has been expressed about its legal basis as well human rights implications, and the long term impacts of segregation on people

(Faughnan and Woods 2000; Collins 2001, 2002; Irish Refugee Council 2001; Brady 2002; Edmond 2003; Fanning and Veale 2004; King 2004; Stewart 2006; Arnold 2012).

For instance, various research sources have drawn attention to its numerous shortcomings in living conditions and catering, isolation from local communities, limited financial support, security, mental health, stress involved in one's life being on hold and a constant fear of deportation as well as the continuing lengthy periods spent by people living under the system (Edmond 2003; FLAC 2010; O'Rourke 2010). Indeed, it is argued that its continuation constitutes a violation of human rights (FLAC 2010; Amnesty 2011; DCYA 2011; UNHCR 2011; Horgan et al. 2012). Arnold (2012: 7), in her recent report for the Irish Refugee Council on Direct Provision, states that 'Direct Provision is an example of a government policy which has not only bred discrimination, social exclusion, enforced poverty and neglect, but has placed children at a real risk'.

When living within Direct Provision, adults are prohibited from employment, and also face restrictions in attempting to further their education. However, children and young people under eighteen are entitled to attend school, similar to children in the broader society. As children and young people under eighteen years of age, safeguarding their welfare comes under the remit of the Health Service Executive (HSE). Under the Child Care Act 1991, the HSE has statutory responsibility for the care and welfare of children who are not receiving adequate care and protection (article 3). As of August 2012, there were 1,725 children living in thirty-seven Direct Provision centres, located throughout Ireland. Of these 1,725 children, 848 were girls and 877 were boys (RIA 2012).

Horizontal transitions in the children's lives

Drawing on our research with parents, key transitions that children in Direct Provision are making include the expected vertical ones of attending crèche, pre-school and primary school. They also include horizontal transitions associated with going to and from: school, from Direct Provision to school, other children's homes, religious and church events, sports and social spaces.

In identifying the barriers presented, in the first instance we examine issues arising regarding living in Direct Provision Centres. Thereafter, we draw attention to issues parents identified as their children transitioned from Direct Provision to pre-school/school and those that arose as they begin to notice their marginalization. We draw attention to the ways that parents attempt to rally resources available to them to protect their children and point to barriers that they have encountered in trying to bridge gaps in these daily transitions. It is argued that 'children are naturally resilient and [that] it must be recognized that "normality" is often what is required rather than any special treatment' (Humphries 2002: 19). Strategies of parents in this regard could be construed as attempts to ease their children's daily transitions and deflect attention from constraints that their living conditions pose. It can be argued that the success of such attempts can be limited and may well not be cognisant of their children's perspectives and full experiences.

We conclude by questioning whether state policy in Ireland, in not seeming to recognize the important intersections between conditions of living and full participation in education, is in practice, further contributing to these children's marginalization. Furthermore, the question arises as to what extent the state is actively contributing to maintaining their marginalization by obstructing efforts parents are making to support these daily transitions.

The experiences of living in Direct Provision centres

A number of factors related to living in Direct Provision were raised by our participants that can be viewed as critically intersecting with children's participation and experiences of education. These include (i) conditions of living in Direct Provision centres themselves, (ii) the often limited sources of information available to parents in making choices about their children's education, and (iii) subsequent obstacles in participating in social and extra-curricular activities.

In the first instance, the conditions of living in Direct Provision, in itself, do not promote the establishment of family privacy, as is now expected in the wider society. Rooms are shared, perhaps with other families, meals and general activities take place either in shared rooms or in public spaces within the centres. This becomes the children's normality; living their lives in close proximity to others in the hostel, living in one room and meeting the other residents in all aspects of their daily lives:

> They are in the same school, in the same place in the same compound [...] they live in the same conditions and the same circumstances, and they all think that all the mummies and daddies have one room, because you know they are born there and they see the parents and the mums in the same room you know. (Research Participant 3)

> They are bored in the hostel. They are there for five or six years so they are tired of the place. A child should not be in that kind of situation for them years, you know, it is too much for them. (Research Participant 1)

This lack of family privacy was also identified by Arnold (2012) as a key concern for families living in Direct Provision. Cooking, in particular was raised as an issue by the mothers; not being able eat in personalized settings, not being able to cook for families as well as lack of variety in food provided, arose as obstacles in this regard. The obstacles presented by these conditions in being able to cook, eat and gather together in personalized family settings constitutes a barrier to the development of personalized lives and as an acute source of stress (Stewart 2006; Foreman 2009; O'Rourke 2010; Arnold 2012):

> [E]verybody, the kids, parents we all have to eat what the centre offers. We are not allowed to cook so we do not cook for the kids. So we have to [...] well put it this way, lunch time it is chips and if the kids don't eat chips that's it, because that is what is offered. I understand that there is like a hundred people in the centre and they can't cook [...] and the chef or the hostel cannot provide for each and every person what they eat or what they do not eat. (Research Participant 3)

Similarly, Arnold (2012) highlights ongoing concerns about the availability of healthy food choices for parents and children in Direct Provision and her work raises concerns about the impact such limited food choices have on the health of children.

Shared cooking and dining facilities are examples of life being lived in public in Direct Provision centres. While there are some limited opportunities for privacy among the residents of Direct Provision centres, at the same time it can be an isolating experience that affords little opportunity for parents to mix and integrate with members of the wider society, impacting on their ability, and their children's ability, to integrate into the wider society. This limits the information sources from which parents can access information about potential schools and pre-schools for their children. Locating a school within easy reach was considered important by participants in this research and this often meant that children from Direct Provision centres attended the same schools, thus decreasing the likelihood of the children widening their social networks.

Furthermore, while living in Direct Provision, one's life seems to be 'on hold' and surrounded by uncertainty. Such circumstances make it very difficult to initiate and maintain interactions and are hampered by the financial constraints associated with living on a low income. The weekly payments of €19.10 for adults and €9.60 for children do not facilitate participation in social or extra-curricular events which have even minimal associated costs, and in some cases this creates difficulties in children's participation in school itself:

> €19.10 for me and the €9 per child that is what they give weekly. So I was just struggling, struggling, struggling how will I put my child to school. So I continue with my €19 and my children's €9 and it is getting difficult, difficult. One time I used to go around begging for clothes and shoes, you know. (Research Participant 1)

Arnold (2012) also identified transport as a barrier to accessing afterschool and extra-curricular activities for children, leading to further marginalization. The result is that lives are lived largely within the confines of the centres, as the following comments indicate:

> We just live in the centre, just in the centre [...] there is nothing to do; there is nothing to do and most of the time we were just being in the rooms [...] the kids tend to be very hyper there. They really tend to be very hyper, because they are confined in these rooms and the pressure is too much, for parents and kids, the pressure is too much. (Research Participant 3)

> No, we don't share, we live in the same room, like this, together. (Research Participant 4)

Such a trend has potential negative implications for children who are attending school and whose social interactions outside of the classroom, with their peers, are restricted. It has also been suggested elsewhere that as children grow older, their differences and, in particular, those differences associated with disadvantage and ethnic minority status, become more visible, and this contributes to further marginalization from education (O'Riordan and FitzGibbon 2004). Furthermore, Curry et al. (2011), in their study on inter-ethnic relations in north inner city Dublin, caution that divides and divisions formed in childhood may well form the basis of future divisions and conflicts in society. They found that migrant children who lived in the same communities and attended the same schools as the majority ethnic children experienced obstacles to integration, based on the children's minority ethnic status. They identified this as a possible source of future conflict. This identified distance and disadvantage is compounded for children living in Direct Provision. For example, the following statement by one of our participants is poignant in this respect. In relation to her children, she stated that 'they live together, they live; it is like, in a bubble they do not know any other thing besides the centre' (Research Participant 3).

Internalizing disadvantages of Direct Provision

Research participants identified that, as their children went to and from school, they began to make friends and socialize informally outside school. This is a very normalized expectation and is often a routinized consequence of school-going. However, in such socializing, and even as children left school on a daily basis to come home, they noticed differences in their living conditions to those of their school friends. They began to ask questions about this. One mother commented that her children:

> say 'my friends in school, they say "we are going home". But we say "we are going to the hostel". And they say, "are we going to be in the hostel forever mommy?"' So you know, like that thing, are we going to stay in the hostel forever, are we going to stay in our own house? Everybody goes to the houses, but we go to the hostel all the time, all the time, mommy. (Research Participant 1)

> he [her child] is seeing it is different, and when the friend comes to my place they are seeing it is different, they see it is different. They say 'where is your bedroom, you do not have a bedroom, where is your kitchen?' You know they are noticing now. (Research Participant 3)

The mothers in our research often found it difficult to explain to their children why they lived in hostels and other children lived in houses. They couldn't tell their children how long more they would stay in the hostels and when, if ever, they would move to their own houses. This uncertainty is reflected in the length of stay of people living in Direct Provision. Minister for Justice and Equality, Alan Shatter, TD, in response to a parliamentary question in April 2012 stated that 3,095 people had made their application for international protection over three years previously and, of these, 272 were waiting over seven years (Shatter 2012).

The mothers were also conscious that their children were aware of the shortcomings of their living conditions and its distance from the normal childhood experiences of growing up in Ireland. At times, mothers indicated that children, themselves, refused to invite school friends home to the hostel.

> They know they stay in a room so they cannot say, 'Can you come to my house?', because they know they do not have a room (Research Participant 1).

> Interviewer: 'Do they [the children] ever invite friends back from school…?' Interviewee: 'No' (Research Participant 4).

They know that they are different, in a deficit way to their school friends, and their circle of friends centres around the hostels, as is illustrated in this comment 'so their circle never really changes, they are always the same ones that go to the Pentecostal church, that go to the same crèche' (Research Participant 3).

A result is that the children were effectively distanced from children in the wider community, confirming findings by White (2010: 13) that 'living in these centres [Direct Provision] isolate and marginalize asylum seekers, setting them apart from local host communities'. Additionally, research undertaken by O'Rourke (2010) found that children living in Direct Provision are reluctant to bring friends back to the centres and they avoid using the term 'asylum seeker'. Furthermore, they are aware of negative stereotypes that associated asylum seeker accommodation with more luxurious accommodation. This is worrying light also of Curry et al.'s (2011) findings on inter-ethnic integration.

Protective factors

Humphries (2002) contends that children are naturally resilient and it must be recognized that 'normality' is often what is required rather than any special treatment. The parents with whom we spoke engaged in a number of strategies to minimize the restrictions of living in Direct Provision through, for instance, developing networks of support with other parents they came in contact with and actively engaging with teachers and school personnel. They also placed a high value on education attainment and were very ambitious for their children, reflecting findings of Curry et al. (2011). In such engagement, it could be argued that these parents were actively engaged in easing the everyday transitions of their children as they moved from Direct Provision, to school environments.

Developing networks of support with other parents

As mentioned above, because of living within Direct Provision, access to information by mothers on potential schools, crèches and pre-schools could be limited. Our research participants sought out information about pre-schools and schools primarily from other parents living in the same centres, and from members of social, advocacy and religious groups with which they were involved. For parents much support was gained from networks within Direct Provision and also from their religious communities:

> [The Christian centre] gives me a chance to see other people, and you know, to know that life is not all about here [Direct Provision]. I think [...] he thinks we are family the way we live there. (Research Participant 3)

Often times they mentioned other African friends, who they identified as particular sources of support to them:

> Well there is an African woman that the children go to the school, so she said that the school is good. (Research Participant 1)

> There was people that are resident in [the centre], their children were going to [name of] school, and they said it was nice. (Research Participant 4)

One mother used whatever contacts and access to information she had, to identify what she considered the most suitable schools for her children: 'I was going around to look for a school for my children and I registered them in different schools [...] it was three or four schools I registered them in. I didn't want them to lose out' (Research Participant 1). She also thought that it would be better if her children attended a school where they were most likely to meet children who were not living in Direct Provision, with the hope that this would facilitate a widening of their social network.

Despite the support of such informal social networks, mothers had limited educational choices for their children and chose schools and pre-schools located nearby the hostels. In such cases, transport might be organized to and from the centre, or parents themselves might co-operate in organizing transport to and from school for their children. One participant recounted that while transport to school was an issue for her, she had come together with others in the centre to pool their resources. She stated that 'we take a friend's car and they join my children with their own children and they help me take my children to school' (Research Participant 1). However, problems arose when the car broke down. While this could be expected in any circumstances, these problems were exacerbated by very limited finances, a small network of friends and a perception that having access to a car might imply that the woman was not eligible for social assistance. This is illustrated by the following comment: '[O]nce the social [welfare] see you riding a car all your allowances will be stopped' (Research Participant 1). This particular comment highlights the surveillance and lack of privacy to which residents in Direct Provision centres feel subjected.

Actively engaging with teachers and school personnel

The mothers to whom we spoke were generally happy with the schools their children were attending, as illustrated by the comment below:

> Yes, I am happy with the school, they teach very well. If there is something wrong they let us know so that we are able to help [the children] as well. They are really nice. If you have any questions to ask they give you chance to ask them any questions. (Research Participant 4)

When issues arose, they engaged in discussions with teachers to resolve them, offering opinions on their children's character. In one instance, where there was an issue about whether her child was misbehaving, his mother listened to the teacher's comments and later, through discussing the incident with her son, she said that she 'just told the teacher he was not a happy child yesterday because he doesn't lie' (Research Participant 1), indicating a willingness and confidence to fully engage with teachers on her child's wellbeing and education. Similar to research by Arnold (2012), parents in this research identified education as a positive influence on the lives of their children which provides them with opportunities for integration.

They were also ambitious for their children, as illustrated in the following comment: 'the level of education should be more than my own' (Research Participant 1). They also viewed participation and achievement in education as a way that their children could integrate into Irish society.

Two participants also identified the manner in which the introduction of the Early Childhood Care and Education (ECCE) scheme, whereby provision is now made for free public access to pre-school care and education for children, has been of assistance to them in facilitating her children's access to pre-school.[1] One mother felt that prior to the introduction of the ECCE scheme her child would have been unable to attend pre-school because of the associated costs:

> I was lucky enough because of the new Government scheme that was introduced, the ECCE scheme they call it [...] So he goes to free pre-school every day. Unlike before, these kids were just staying at home and did not to go to school, obviously they could not afford to take their kids to pre-school. (Research Participant 3)

The introduction of this universal free pre-school scheme has allowed parents and children to extend their social network beyond the Direct Provision centre and the mothers were very conscious of the opportunity for their children to socialize with other children from the broader community. In two of the interviews, mothers discussed the role of the pre-school services in identifying issues related to school-readiness for their children. According to Reynolds and Temple (1998: 232), research on early schooling 'indicates that the initial adjustment to school has significant, and substantial effects on later school success'. One participant mentioned that the pre-school had identified her child's speech delay and helped to organize early intervention with a speech therapist. This intervention was continued when the child started primary school. However, the limitations of this universal pre-school scheme were noted in that following it

1 The Free Pre-School Year in Early Childhood Care and Education (ECCE) scheme was introduced in 2010. Through its provisions, children aged between three and four years (specifically, three years, two months and one day old on 1 September of any given year, but under four years, seven months of age on that date) are entitled to 3.5 hours in designated pre-schools for one year.

participation in further organized classes for children again depended on an ability to pay for them. Crawford and Walker (2007: 48) discuss the potential of protective environments in protecting children from adversities and highlight the role of community support networks, 'particularly those that offer emotional support and practical help and advice', as being beneficial for parents and children. The pre-school setting may be contributing to the creation of such a protective environment and the introduction of a universal pre-school scheme may help contribute to a more inclusive and integrated society. Additionally, research from the Effective Provision of Pre-School Education (EPPE) in the UK, a longitudinal study of early childhood experience, found that children from disadvantaged backgrounds particularly benefited from high quality pre-school provision. In particular, they benefited from provision that catered for children from a variety of socio-economic backgrounds (Sylva et al. 2004: 15).

Conclusion

This research identified regular key transitions children living in Direct Provision are making, strategies parents are making to ease these transitions, as well as key constraints imposed by their living conditions. In acting upon these findings, the Irish state has an opportunity to positively attend to the care and welfare of this group of children. While the discussion is based on the views and experiences of a small number of women living in Direct Provision in Ireland, and does not include the direct voices and opinions of children, the interaction of accommodation, community and associated material conditions is obvious. The findings also support research findings elsewhere that critique the policy of placing families in Direct Provision centres.

Living in Direct Provision contributes to the normalizing of institutional life for children as time periods continue to be lengthy. Children's lives are lived in the public sphere of the other asylum-seeking residents and management of Direct Provision centres, while at the same time generalized expectations of living in family contexts are obstructed. Uncertainty surrounds their 'home' environments; boredom and isolation sets in.

Difficulties are presented for parents in choosing schools, and for children in fully benefiting from participation in the social and academic aspects of education. They are acutely dependent on the provision of transport to access schools and effectively unable to invite friends 'home' from school, as they become aware of the limitations of their environments. Access to space to do their homework is restricted, as is access to extra-curricular activities. They become defined in opposition to, and apart from, their school peers, as a disadvantaged group. The Irish state contributes to constructing their disadvantage. While it is evident that parents actively address issues arising, their capacity to do so is limited because of their own structural and financial positions as people seeking asylum. They have limited access to finances and friends, and can themselves be quite isolated. Furthermore, there is a perception that, at times, strategies they do employ might result in the further loss of state support to which they are entitled, as evidenced by one of our research participants' comments on her access to a car having a negative impact on access to financial state support.

The key role of policy in the marginalization of children of people seeking asylum and the construction of such divisions among children has to be questioned. The lived experiences of children and parents and their current marginalization in Direct Provision raises key concerns about creating the conditions for future social divisions in Irish society. It is worth recalling Curry et al.'s (2011) suggestion that inter-ethnic divisions among children could be viewed as the basis of future divisions in a multi-ethnic Ireland. Addressing disadvantage and marginalization, once established, can be a momentous task.

References

Amnesty International (2011). Submission to the UN Universal Periodic Review, 12th session of the UPR Working Group, October 2011. <http://www.amnesty.ie/sites/default/files/HRII/UPR12,%20Amnesty%20International%20submission%20for%20the%20UPR%20of%20Ireland,%20March%202011.pdf> accessed 1 March 2012.

Arnold, S. (2012). *State Sanctioned Child Poverty and Exclusion: The case of children in state accommodation for asylum seekers*. Irish Refugee Council: Dublin.

Brady, B. (2002). *Strategies to Promote the Inclusion of Refugees and Asylum Seekers*. Dublin: ADM.

Collins, A. (2001). *Meeting the Needs of Asylum Seekers in Tralee*. Tralee: Partnership TráLí.

Collins, A. (2002). *The Needs of Asylum Seekers in Cork*. Cork: Nasc.

Crawford, K., and Walker, J. (2007). *Social Work and Human Development*, 2nd Ed., Exeter: Learning Matters.

CSO (2012). *This is Ireland: Highlights from census 2011, Part 1*. Dublin: Stationary Office.

Curry, P., Gilligan, R., Garratt, L., and Scholtz, L. (2011). *Where to From Here? Inter-ethnic relations among children in Ireland*. Dublin: Trinity College Dublin in Association with Liffey Press.

Edmond, E. (2003). *Direct Discrimination: An analysis of the scheme of direct provision in Ireland*. FLAC Report, Dublin: FLAC.

Fanning, B., and Veale, A. (2004). 'Child Poverty as Public Poverty: Direct provision and asylum seeker children', *Child Care in Practice*, 10 (3), 241–51.

Fanning, B., and Mac Éinrí, P. (1999). *Regional Resettlement of Asylum Seekers: A Strategic approach*. Cork: Irish Centre for Migration Studies.

Faughnan, P., and Woods, M. (2001). *Lives on Hold: Seeking asylum in Ireland*. Dublin: Applied Social Science Research Programme.

FLAC (2010). *One Size Doesn't Fit All: A legal analysis of the system of direct provision and dispersal system in Ireland, 10 years on*. Dublin: FLAC.

Foreman, M. (2009). 'HIV and "Direct Provision": Learning from the Experiences of Asylum Seekers in Ireland', *Translocations: Migration and social change*, An Inter-Disciplinary Open Access E-Journal, 4 (1), 67–85.

Humphries, T. (2002). *Asylum Seeker and Refugee Children Guidance Document, Nottingham City Council*. <http://www.mandaladesign.com.au/startts/may09/Asylum_Seeker_Guidance.pdf> accessed 20 December 2012.

Irish Refugee Council (2001). *Direct Provision and Dispersal, 18 Months On*. Dublin: Irish Refugee Council.

King, D. (2004). *A Needs Analysis of Asylum Seekers Resident in Kilmarnock House*, Killiney. Dublin: Unite Project, Southside Partnership.

NASC (2008). *Hidden Cork: The perspectives of asylum seekers on Direct Provision and the asylum legal system*. Cork: NASC The Immigrant Support Centre.

O'Riordan, J., and FitzGibbon, M. (2004). *An Assessment of Traveller Needs in East Cork*. Cork: HSE Traveller Health Unit and Traveller Visibility Group.

O'Rourke, E. (2010). 'Living in Direct Provision: Resident voices', *JRS: 30 Years of Serving Refugees*, 65. <http://www.workingnotes.ie/index.php/item/living-in-direct-provision-resident-voices> accessed 8 March 2012.

Petrewskyj, A., Thorpe, K., and Taylor, C. (2005). 'Trends in Construction of Transition to School in Three Western Regions, 1990–2004', *International Journal of Early Years Education*, 13 (1), 55–69.

Quinn, E., and Hughes, G. (2005). *Reception Systems, their Capacities and the Social Situation of Asylum Applicants within the Reception System in Ireland*. Dublin: European Migration Network.

Reynolds, A., and Temple, J. (1998). 'Extended Early Childhood Intervention and School Achievement: Age thirteen findings from the Chicago longitudinal study', *Child Development*, 69 (1), 231–46.

RIA (2012). *Reception and Integration Agency, Monthly Statistics Report August 2012*. Dublin: RIA.

Shatter, A. (2012). 'Written Answers. Asylum Support Services', *Dáil Éireann Debates*, 761 (3), Wednesday 18 April 2012.

Smyth, E., Darmody, M., McGinnity, F., and Byrne, D. (2009). *Adapting to Diversity: Irish schools and newcomer students*. ESRI: Dublin.

Smyth, K., and Whyte, J. (2005). *Making a New Life in Ireland: Lone refugee and asylum seeking mothers and their children*. Dublin: Children's Research Centre Trinity College.

Stewart, R. (2006). *The Mental Health Promotion Needs of Asylum Seekers and Refugees: A qualitative study in direct provision centres and private accommodation in Galway City*. Galway: Galway City Development Board, Health Promotion Services, HSE West.

Sylva, K., Melhuish, E., Sammons, P., Siraj-Blatchford, I., and Taggart, B. (2004). *The Effective Provision of Pre-School Education (EPPE) Project: Final Report*. London: Institute of Education/Sure Start.

UNHCR (2011). Submission by the United Nations High Commissioner for Refugees for the Office of the High Commissioner for Human Rights' Compilation

Report – Universal Periodic Review: Ireland. <http://www.unhcr.org/refworld/pdfid/4d8867982.pdf> accessed 20 March 2012.

Vogler, P., Crivello, G., and Woodhead, M. (2008). *Early Childhood Transitions Research: A Review of concepts, theory, and practice*, Working papers in Early Childhood Development. The Hague: Bernard Van Leer Foundation.

Yeboah, D. (2002). 'Enhancing Transition from Early Childhood Phase to Primary Education: Evidence from the research literature', *Early Years: An International journal of research and development*, 22 (1), 51–68.

JOY CHALKE

14 Supporting Children with English as an Additional Language in the Early Years Foundation Stage (UK): Meeting the Challenges

Introduction

Multilingualism and bilingualism are not new features in the world of education, or in the literature, policy and practice associated with the area (Cummins 2000; Conteh 2003). However, there is evidence that the numbers of children entering UK pre-schools, nurseries and schools whose first language is not English is on the increase (DfES 2005; Keat et al. 2009), and these children and families are no longer restricted primarily to urban areas where ethnic populations have historically migrated. In 2005, the Department for Education and Science indicated that the number of children entering education designated as having English as an Additional Language (EAL) had risen by 35 per cent since 1997 (DfES 2005: 3). This growth is forcing an examination of constructs and ideas about practice in engaging and supporting these children and their families.

According to Julios (2008), the impact of globalization has increased the movement of many people and this is clearly seen in the UK. There are growing numbers of families transitioning within the European Union for employment purposes (Duvell 2008). Areas of worldwide conflict continue to produce refugees and asylum seekers; and the presence and challenges associated with these frequently make media headlines, often with negative images and stereotypes attached (Rutter 2006). Additionally, discourses in the media about the perceived threat from fundamentalist Islam since the terrorist attacks in the USA on 9/11 and London on 7/7 can be seen to continue to raise issues of difference within public consciousness (Elgamri 2008), and all these factors may impact our responses to the diversity that we now have within our early childhood settings and schools.

If it is accepted that all learning is culturally mediated within the setting (Conteh 2003), this provides ongoing challenges for understanding the multicultural identities within society in the UK and it seems appropriate at this time to consider the implications for practice this issue may have. Also, within the current economic climate, it is challenging for Local Authorities, schools and other educational establishments to spread a limited resource effectively, and this is likely to be impacting the ability to provide sufficient services such as interpreters and bilingual support assistants at the level required, therefore requiring practitioners, teachers and teaching assistants to fill the gaps.

My experience, over the last eight years, of teaching early years practitioners studying part-time in higher education indicates that they observe that not only are the numbers of children with EAL increasing, but also the numbers of different languages being spoken, so that the demands upon them, as early years teachers, for familiarity with specific cultural variations are also expanding. This chapter explores the views of practitioners working with children and their families regarding their experiences of engaging in this area in the context of practice and pedagogical guidelines within the Early Years Foundation Stage Curriculum (DCSF 2008a) and supporting documentation.

Guidelines for pedagogy within the EYFS and supporting documents

The establishment of the Early Years Foundation Stage curriculum in 2008 gave the opportunity for the needs of young children within the diverse population in the UK to be recognized and planned for. These documents and supporting literature sought to ensure that all providers planned for equality of opportunity and that 'all children, irrespective of ethnicity, culture, religion, home language, family background [...] should have the opportunity to experience a challenging and enjoyable programme of learning and development' (DCSF 2008b: 10). These principles remain enshrined in the revised framework that became statutory in September 2012 (DfE 2012).

The establishment of the Early Years Foundation Stage (EYFS) in 2008, as part of the UK government's ten year childcare strategy to ensure all children have the opportunity to receive high quality care and education from the early years, marked the end of at least a decade of change for those working with children aged 0–5 years. New initiatives and challenges had continually involved adaptations to practice and provision in response to policy and legislative changes for the early years workforce (Kwon 2002; Potter 2007). Many elements from these earlier guidelines and regulations were amalgamated and developed into the guidance and framework documents produced for the EYFS (DCSF 2008a, DCSF 2008b), and indicate that they provide the resources and advice that will enable practitioners to meet not only the legal requirements, but also ensure they are meeting the needs of the individual children in their care.

It is clearly articulated in these documents that young children are viewed as 'unique', as expressed in one of the four key themes (DCSF 2008: 5), this uniqueness is seen positively in terms of children as 'competent learner(s)' who can be 'resilient, capable, confident and self assured'. Staff working with children respond to this by recognizing what individual children bring into the community of the setting, specifically the 'cultural background and range of experience' (DCSF 2008c: 4) from their home environment and previous experiences. The implication of this for pedagogic practice is that time is spent building a relationship with parents to ensure collaborative ways of working that will empower and support the development of self-esteem in the young child, by including the culture and language of the home within the setting. Partnership with parents is, therefore, also a key unpinning principle that informs the work done with children and young families to promote effective learning (DCSF 2007; DCSF 2008a).

It is also very clear in the EYFS that young children's learning is mediated primarily, but not solely, through a play based curriculum (DCSF 2008a), although the difficulties of conceptualizing what play means in different contexts are also acknowledged (DCSF 2008c). Alongside the need for play and playful experiences, there is guidance on the role that language, conversation, questioning and sustained shared thinking play in moving children on in their development and learning (David 2003; DCSF 2008a), and the role the adult plays in ensuring these opportunities are available. It is fairly obvious that language is important to learning and thinking (Potter 2007), playing a key role in assisting each child to move from concrete to abstract thought (David 2003), an essential task for future educational success. The suggestion is that in sharing children's thinking, adults become more aware of children's interests and can, therefore, enable them to develop more effectively by helping them take their ideas forward (DCSF 2008d). The implication of undertaking this type of activity is that it requires a common language for it to be successful.

The quality of adult/child interaction, of which sustained shared thinking is an example, is also identified in many other research and evaluation projects as 'critical to the effective curriculum implementation and long term successful outcomes of children's early learning' (Moyles et al. 2002). Guidance in the EYFS talks about these interactions as the way children's ideas and understanding about the world are shaped and developed (DCSF 2008c: 3). However, in this context it is also acknowledged that it is not just the adult/child interactions within the setting, but the interactions with all those who are important to the child, which include family members and community relationships, as well as peers within the setting, that contribute to learning. The implication, therefore, is that time needs to be spent developing the relationships that are going to promote and sustain these types of interactions.

Learning for the young child is seen as also occurring as a social activity (DCSF 2008c: 3), that develops in specific contexts and utilizes specific relationships (Conteh 2003: 4). Within this context collaborative talk is seen as a valuable and important activity (Conteh 2003). David (2003: 10) highlights collaborative activities as the opportunity for children to engage in learning experiences and problem solving, with talk providing the 'social mode' for thinking and not just a means of communication. Research (Collins 2009) shows that vocabulary acquisition in the pre-school years can be a predictor of reading comprehension in later years and, as suggested by Brown (1980), the ages of four to six are critical to the development of children's communicative speech because this is when they are acquiring command of their first language.

What is best practice guidance for bilingual learners of English?

To some degree the UK is unlike much of the rest of the world as a significant proportion of its population has grown up with only a monolingual experience, with English a dominant and highly valued language worldwide (Gregory and Kelly 1992; Rich and Davis 2007), and this has perhaps influenced a lack of understanding of the valuable nature of bilingualism for children's development (Cummins 2000). In many parts of the world, children are exposed to more than one language from birth within the culture and environment of family and community, or religious life (Pinnock 2009). Smidt (2008: 52) suggests *bilingual* is used as a term to cover children who speak more than one language successfully and generally reflects the fact that children have acquired competency in at least two languages and know when and where to use them, sometimes one of these languages may be English; this is simultaneous bilingualism. She goes on to suggest (Smidt 2008: 21) that these children may not see their languages as separate things, but understand them as language and use them interchangeably. Bilingualism for these children is often a positive experience, if the languages continue to be supported, as there is evidence to suggest that bilingual learners have greater cognitive capacity and abstract thinking skills, and good social skills including increased self-confidence (Conteh and Brock 2006; Han and Bridglall 2009).

Children who are not exposed to more than one language from birth are learning the second language later. This is known as sequential or consecutive bilingualism and it is more difficult for children to learn a language this way (Smidt 2008: 57). Children who are already bilingual on entering educational settings, already have a significant knowledge and understanding about language to draw on and may, therefore, find it easier to acquire the additional language of the classroom (Hammer et al. 2008). Children who have no other language experience to draw on are thrown into a confusing and often bewildering situation (Hammer et al. 2008). The main approaches to EAL that have been evidenced within the UK appear to be either a *submersion* approach, where children are deemed able to pick up the language around them without additional support, or an *immersion* approach where the first language is supported for a short period to enable the child to gain some proficiency in English (Brown 1980; Datta 2000).

Within the immersion approach there are some clear principles for supporting bilingual learners that have been established. However, there are also differences in the ways some of these may be interpreted and developed and in the way the teaching of EAL is predicated (Smidt 2008). It is evident in the language of the EYFS that the child's mother tongue or home language is to be given recognition (Brock and Power 2006: 28; DCSF 2007; Keat et al. 2009: 14). This is deemed important for the child's social and emotional wellbeing and helps to ensure a successful transition into the new culture and language of the setting or classroom. However, it may only be possible to support the language in the setting effectively if there is a speaker of that language available to help model and facilitate interaction with the child or children.

Cummins (2000) suggests that the move to learning through the second language happens too early for many children and there should be more effort made to teach children in their mother tongue for a longer period, as evidence suggests this 'promotes cognitive development and enhances opportunities for learning' (Bjork-Willen 2008: 55). The challenge is the need for children to learn a new language while at the same time being given the opportunity to use their first language to learn new things (Conteh and Brock 2006: 2), and to remain bilingual speakers. Advocates of the use of first language for learning, indicate that it takes children about five years to catch up sufficiently in the target language, to be able to access the academic contexts of the curriculum requirements (Cummins 2000; Pinnock 2009). They also stress the difference between the language needed for conversation or social skills, which children may acquire relatively quickly, and that needed for accessing the curriculum.

The problem, however, is that support for the first language does not presuppose teaching that language (Conteh 2003). So, for many children, responsibility for the first language has to be maintained by the home and community environment, and often children are, therefore, attending heritage or religious schools and experiencing an additional and different culture and approach to the learning of language and literacy. What schools and settings do to support the home or community languages is often limited to practical strategies such as greetings, visual displays and the use of stories, books and rhymes in the first language (Conteh 2003). Bilingual teachers or support assistants may be available for part of the day or week and, in those times, may then assist children to 'catch up' with ideas and concepts through the first language (Ethnic Minority Achievement Services (EMAS) nd).

In summary, therefore, it can be seen that pedagogy around EAL is a complex and contested issue. While there is some general agreement about the use of a child's first language as an essential step in early second language acquisition, the ways in which this may be supported or developed, and the length of time this is required, often depend upon culturally accepted notions of learning (Cummins 2000). It appears the case in the UK that the transitional model is the one that will be found in many settings and on documents (Conteh 2003). However, there is also a growing discussion around the idea that supporting a child as a bilingual learner, by adding English as one of their languages, might be the most effective route to learning and development. This suggestion may be gaining favour as research evidence (Conteh and Brock 2006: 6) suggests transitional bilingualism can lead to restricted concept development and problems with learning. Clearly, children entering settings with EAL deserve to have those who teach them understand some of the complexities and challenges around the task.

What the practitioners say

In order to understand what is actually happening in the settings many of these children are entering, data was gathered from the students I teach regarding their current experiences. The data illustrated here represents the first stage of what could be a potentially larger investigation into current practice. Eighty-four part time students on a Foundation Degree in a university in the south of England, who are also practitioners working in the early years, were encouraged to complete an online questionnaire. This questionnaire allowed them to articulate experiences of working with children learning English as an additional language, the support available for them and any training they had received. The data, from the seventy-four who completed the questionnaire, reveals a mixed picture and raises the issue of the importance of ongoing training, as well as theoretical and pedagogical discussions around this important issue.

At the time of the questionnaire, 63 per cent responded that they were currently working with children in their settings for whom English was not the mother tongue; of those, one student was working with more than ten languages while the majority, 77 per cent, were working with one to three different languages and 22 per cent with four to six languages.

Students were asked if they had ever received support to enable communication with children in the first language. 43 per cent answered in the affirmative, and explained that the majority of the support provided came from the parents themselves, or from the education support service, EMAS. A very small minority also listed siblings (one response), another staff member (two responses), or their own ability to speak the language (two responses) as assisting them in communication. Interestingly, two responses also suggested that training in Makaton (a sign-based communication system) was helpful in aiding communication. One student, who has a number of children in her setting with EAL, reflected that although EMAS was signposted as a resource, they did not always have sufficient staff to respond, or they did not have someone who spoke the language required. On one occasion, she reported the advice she had been given was they 'would have to muddle through as best they could'.

As well as support from other people, students commented on resources they had available within their settings. 57 per cent of those who answered this question had some dual language books, but 33 per cent had none within their setting. This may reflect that currently they have no children with a mother tongue other than English present, but also suggests there are some settings with children with EAL who have no dual language resources, even though they have children for whom English is not the first language. When considering whether there were any examples of scripts available in the mother tongue, 43 per cent said they had none. This appears a significant amount, when one considers the importance of print availability for literacy learning (Hirst 1998; Brock and Power 2006), but also in respect of building ideas among all young children of the importance of understanding difference and diversity. One student said they addressed the issues by 'displaying words, labels and signs [...] translated on the computer'. While the effort to provide the model of different languages is applaudable, there might be hesitation in recommending this as standard practice due to the problems that can occur with online translation.

Responses indicted that there was more confidence in being able to give a greeting in the mother tongue of the child, with 28 per cent of those who answered saying they knew greetings in all languages used and 54 per cent in some. 67 per cent also said that they knew some rhymes, songs or nursery rhymes, which they used with all children. However, that still leaves a significant number where it is possible that no language other than English is heard during the whole of the session from the adults in charge. It could be questioned whether this is something that needs to change if our early childhood establishments are going to engage children with the rich and diverse cultural experiences that make up the UK. It also indicates the probability that currently many practitioners are only monolingual English speakers in many of our settings.

Many responses indicate that visual clues and pictures are also used, with posters, props and pictures being listed as some of the resources available to help make children feel at home and provide familiar resources for them to play with. There was some further indication that technology in the form of music CDs and games on the PC were in evidence in a few settings. Perhaps this is an area that could be further developed as a useful response to providing familiar resources.

Students were also asked to rate a number of categories according to whether they felt it was important that children had opportunities to use their mother tongue for certain daily aspects (Figure 1).

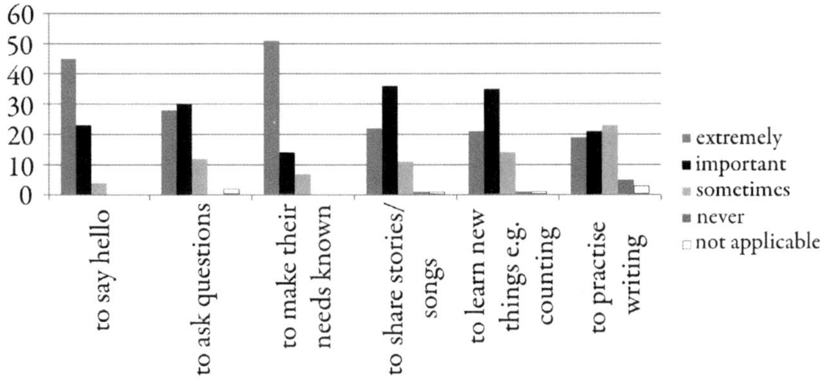

Figure 1 Students rated how important they thought these daily tasks were for children to be able to complete in their mother tongue

The rationale behind this rather simplistic continuum was to gather a snapshot impression about whether practitioners recognize the need for children to use first language, even if no other child or adult may speak that particular language. It can be seen that many practitioners focus on care issues, such as saying hello and making needs known, rather than the curriculum aspects, such as counting and writing. However, these findings are very limited and need further exploration.

In additional responses, it was also recognized that while it might be viewed as important by the practitioner for children to use their mother tongue, it was not always what the parent wanted; a finding that echoes other research (Rich and Davis 2007). A further challenge was highlighted by a practitioner working within schools who suggested 'it is hard to try and achieve educational targets with these children using English, we are coming across lots of barriers at the moment with teaching sounds and numbers', indicting there are not the facilities in place to assess children's gains in their mother tongue.

Finally, the students were asked to comment on any training they had received, or any research they had done in this area. Only 21 per cent reported positively in answer to this question, with many talking about personal research rather than access to specific training opportunities. Of the training opportunities mentioned, some were in the general area of meeting equal opportunities, with only one reporting going on a specific course called 'welcoming children with English as an additional language'. Most of the rest of the training related to in-house experiences from advisors who visited the setting and provided ideas.

Evaluation and conclusion

In summary, the challenges facing early year practitioners in today's changing society include the need to respond to the diversity and difference that they encounter in the lives of the children they care for and educate (Cummins 2000; Conteh 2003; Keat et al. 2009). It has been suggested that it is not always a simple matter to determine the needs of all these children. Nor is it a simple matter to identify appropriate responses that can be made to support their education and ensure they are in a position to receive the 'best possible start in life' (DCSF 2008b); not least if support in the first language is not readily available. The lack of training available to support practitioners in developing skills and confidence in this area has been highlighted in this small scale research and has implications not only for initial training of early childhood practitioners but for ongoing continuing professional development for those already working with young children.

The data gathered from this group of students suggests that there are gaps in provision for children with EAL to support their mother tongue, in a way that has been suggested as good practice in developing bilingualism

(Bjork-Willen 2008). These include a lack of access to the first language, both verbally and with other physical resources, but also possibly, a lack of understanding from practitioners of the importance of the first language support. Challenges of accessing language support remain, but working closely with parents, families and communities provides one way of moving forward. Ideas and strategies to use are available (DCSF 2007) but often require that practitioners research independently, rather than being readily accessible and familiar to them.

The underpinning principle of treating all children as 'unique' (DCSF 2008a), highlighted as good practice within the EYFS, means the practitioner should seek to acquire information not only about the child who is learning EAL, but the language and culture that they bring with them (Crosse 2007). The revised EYFS also indicates that 'providers must take reasonable steps to provide opportunities for children to develop and use their home language in play and learning, supporting their language development at home' (DfE 2012: 6).This, perhaps, also requires flexibility on the part of practitioners as they make efforts to learn words, phrases, and songs and rhymes in the child's first language, as well as seeking to include the variety of languages in the setting in everyday practice. Additionally, practitioners need to ensure opportunities within the settings for children to use their first language with an adult or peer with whom they can develop vocabulary, think about concepts and have their learning extended and enhanced (Brock 2006). Using the first language in this way will provide support for the child's growing identity and, hopefully, avoid the dissonance between home and setting that can easily occur and inhibit the child's first language acquisition. Additionally, settings need to think about ways in which the learning of English can be supported and developed, using all the strategies and ideas promulgated in the literature available, particularly that written specifically for the early years workforce (Crosse 2007; Smidt 2008).

It is suggested that the challenges to successful adoption of these principles include a lack of training and understanding of language learning generally, and second language learning specifically, within the early years workforce (Conteh 2003; Crosse 2007). Although there are now specific texts to help practitioners develop skills and knowledge, my experience is that these are not yet readily accessed to the practitioners. Embedding more specific instruction in early training is, perhaps, an important development for the sector.

Additionally, it has been suggested that the prevalent attitudes towards transitional bilingualism, assimilation and multiculturalism that permeate society in general and some education institutions, specifically (Cummins 2000; Conteh 2003), and which are subject to influence by the media and changing factors in society, often stand in a place of contradiction to the language and practice posited by the curriculum documents. To ensure success for our bilingual children and those learning EAL, these competing influences continually need negotiating by reflective and skilled practitioners.

References

Bjork-Willen, P. (2008). 'Routine Trouble: How preschool children participate in multilingual instruction', *Applied Linguistics*, 29 (4), 555–77.

Brock, A., and Power, M. (2006). 'Promoting Learning in the Early Years'. In J. Conteh (ed.), *Promoting Learning for Bilingual Pupils 3–11. Opening Doors to Success*, pp. 28–41. London: Paul Chapman.

Brown, D. (1980). *Mother Tongue to English*. London: Cambridge University Press.

Collins, M. (2009). 'ELL Preschoolers' English Vocabulary Acquisition from Storybook Reading', *Early Childhood Research Quarterly*, 25 (1), 84–97.

Conteh, J., and Brock A. (2006). 'Principles and Practices for Teaching Bilingual Learners'. In J. Conteh (ed.), *Promoting Learning for Bilingual Pupils 3–11. Opening Doors to Success*, pp. 1–12. London: Paul Chapman.

Conteh, J. (2003). *Succeeding in Diversity, Culture, Language and Learning in Primary Classrooms*. Stoke on Trent: Streetham Books.

Crosse, K. (2007). *Introducing English as an Additional Language to Young Children*. London: Paul Chapman.

Cummins, J. (2000). *Language, Power and Pedagogy. Bilingual Children in the Crossfire*. Clevedon: Multilingual Matters Ltd.

Datta, M. (2000). *Bilinguality and Literacy Principles and Practice*. London: Continuum.

David, T. (2003). *What do we Know about Teaching Young Children?* BERA <http://nationalstrategies.standards.DCSF.gov.uk> accessed 24 October 2010.

DCSF (2007). *Supporting Children Learning English as an Additional Language. Guidance for Practitioners in the Early Years Foundation Stage*. Nottingham: HMSO.

DCSF (2008a). *Practice Guidance for the Foundation Stage*. Nottingham: HMSO.

DCSF (2008b). *Statutory Framework for the Foundation Stage*. Nottingham: HMSO.

DCSF (2008c). *Effective Practice: Play and exploration*. <http://nationalstrategies.standards.dcsf.gov.uk/search/earlyyears/results/nav:46528> accessed 24 February 2010.

DCSF (2008d). *Effective Practice: Creativity and critical thinking*. <http://nationalstrategies.standards.dcsf.gov.uk/search/earlyyears/results/nav:46528> accessed 24 February 2010.

DfE (2012). *Statutory Framework for the Early Years Foundation Stage*. <http://media.education.gov.uk/assets/files/pdf/e/eyfs%20statutory%20framework%20march%202012.pdf> accessed 15 November 2012.

DfES (2005). *Ethnicity and Education: The evidence on minority ethnic pupils*. <http://www.dcsf.gov.uk/research/data/uploadfiles/RTP01–05.pdf> accessed 3 March 2010.

Duvell, F. (2008). 'United Kingdom'. In A. Triandafyllidou and R. Gropas (eds), *European Immigration: A Sourcebook*. Electronic version: Ashgate Publishing.

Elgamri, E. (2008). *Islam in the British Broadsheets: The impact of orientalism on representations of Islam in the British press*. Reading: Ithaca Press.

Ethnic Minority Achievement Service (nd). *Portsmouth City Council Ethnic Minority Achievement* Service. <http://www.emaonline.org.uk/ema/index.cfm?&p=partners,partner&id=15> accessed 15 November 2012.

Gregory, E., and Kelly, C. (1992). 'Bilingualism and Assessment'. In G. M. Blenikin and A. V. Kelly (eds), *Assessment in Early Childhood Education*, pp. 144–62. London: PCP.

Hammer, C., Lawrence, F., and Miccio, A. (2008). 'Exposure to English Before and after Entry into Head Start: Bilingual children's receptive language growth in Spanish and English', *International Journal of Bilingual Education and Bilingualism*, 11 (1), 30–56.

Han, W. J., and Bridglall, B. (2009). 'Assessing School Supports for ELL Students Using the ECLS-K', *Early Childhood Research Quarterly*, 24 (4), 445–62.

Hirst, K. (1998). 'Preschool Literacy Experiences of Children in Punjabi, Urdu and Gujerati Speaking Families in England', *British Educational Research Journal*, 24 (4), 415–29.

Julios, C. (2008). *Contemporary British Identity*. Electronic version: Ashgate Publishing Ltd.

Keat, J., Strickland, M., and Marinak, B. (2009). 'Child Voice: How immigrant children enlightened their teachers with a camera', *Early Childhood Education*, 37 (1), 13–21.

Kwon, Y. (2002). 'Changing Curriculum for Early Childhood Education in England', *Early Childhood Research and Practice*, 4 (2).

Leach, J., and Moon, B. (2008). *The Power of Pedagogy*. London: Sage.

Moyles, J., Adams, S., and Musgrove, A. (2002). *Study of Pedagogical Effectiveness in Early Learning.* DFES Research Briefs. <http://www.dfes.gov.uk/research> accessed 24 February 2010.

Pinnock, H. (2009). *Steps Towards Learning: A guide to overcoming language barriers in children's education*. London: Save the Children.

Potter, C. (2007). 'Developments in UK Early Years Policy and Practice: Can they improve outcomes for disadvantaged children?' *International Journal of Early Years Education*, 15 (2), 171–80.

Rich, S., and Davis, L. (2007). 'Insights into the Strategic Ways in which Two Bilingual Children in the Early Years Seek to Negotiate the Competing Demands on their Identity in their Home and School Worlds', *International Journal of Early Years Education*, 15 (1), 35–47.

Rutter, J. (2006). *Refugee Children in the UK.* London: McGraw Hill.

Smidt, S. (2008). *Supporting Multilingual Learners in the Early Years. Many Languages – Many Children*. London: Routledge.

ANNE M. DOLAN

15 Critically 'Reading the World' through Picture-Books

Introduction

Picture-books feature in all pre-school and early childhood classrooms. As adults, we have memories of special picture-books. Their continued use with children today provides many opportunities for debate, discussion and for critical engagement. Throughout our lives we embark on many different journeys, often through the pages of a book. Books transport us through space and time, and provide children with an opportunity to explore the real and the imagined. Whether the journey is into, and around, the school playground, or to another country, book journeys offer us an opportunity to see through the eyes of another. Picture-books, in particular, provide teachers with a unique opportunity to integrate global, justice and intercultural perspectives effectively into early childhood education programmes. This chapter defines what is meant by *critical literacy* and *picture-books*. The potential of picture-books for incorporating global and justice issues into early childhood education is explored in the context of some specific examples that are presented for illustrative purposes. The chapter looks in detail at the potential of one picture-book, *Mama Panya's Pancakes*, and its accompanying resource. The issue of gender in picture storybooks is also addressed. Ultimately, an argument is made for early childhood educators to choose high quality, engaging multicultural picture-books and to develop strategies for working with these resources, which promote critical literacy and intercultural learning.

Critical literacy

In Ireland, the Department of Education and Skills has produced a strategy for the promotion of literacy and numeracy (DES 2011) following recent reports of reduced literacy standards amongst young people. However, it remains to be seen if literacy and numeracy will be defined in narrow, exclusive or broad terms. Several commentators, such as Comber (2001), argue that simple conceptions of 'literacy', so much promoted today, are inadequate. Comber argues that being critically literate is not only central, but is essential for being literate in a media saturated, diverse world. Children today experience a constant stream of ideas and information online, in print and through electronic games and mass media. Therefore, the term 'literacy' in the twenty-first century is changing and will continue to do so.

Critical literacy has been traced to the work of Paulo Freire who taught adult learners to 'read the word' in order to 'read the world' and to engage in a cycle of reflection and action (Freire and Macedo 1987). According to Wolk (2003: 102), critical literacy is 'about how we see and interact with the world; it is about having as a regular part of one's life, the skills and desire to evaluate society and the world'. That critique is especially focused on issues of power: who has it and who is denied it; how it is used and how it is abused. More specifically, that critique often revolves around issues of race, culture, class, gender, media and the environment, in the hope of creating a more just, humane democratic and equal world. Critical literacy is the ability to actively read text in an active and reflective manner which promotes a deeper understanding of socially constructed concepts, such as power, inequality, and injustice in human relationships.

Critical literacy is more than just understanding what we are reading. It is about asking questions; looking at different points of view, and asking, 'is everyone included in what we are reading?' Promoting critical literacy is now multi-faceted and complex; early childhood educators, including parents and teachers, need to help children develop their own perspectives, as well as understanding the perspectives of others, in order to participate as citizens in our multicultural world. The development of critical literacy skills enables people to interpret messages in the modern world through a critical lens and challenge the power relations within those messages. Early childhood educators who facilitate the development of critical literacy encourage children to interrogate societal issues such as poverty, education, equity, and equality and institutions such as family and school, in order to critique the structures that serve as norms as well as to demonstrate how these norms are not experienced by all members of society. Development educators interpret critical literacy in postmodern terms as a means of highlighting the connection between education and social justice (Fiedler 2008). Critical literacy is not merely about educating children about critical ways of seeing and questioning. It is equally about encouraging what Maxine Greene (1995: 5) calls their 'social imagination' which is 'the capacity to invent visions of what should be and what might be in our deficient society, on the street and in our schools'. Children's literature, including picture-books, provides endless opportunities for teaching critical literacy and for incorporating global and justice perspectives in the classroom.

Picture-books

Typically, a picture-book is thirty-two pages long with a balance between text and illustrations. However, in the better quality picture-books the relationship between text and illustrations is tightly interconnected, complementary and seamless. Both the words and the pictures are 'read'. Therefore, it is this relationship between pictures and words, this inter-animation (Lewis 2001) which makes picture storybooks so special. High quality picture-books contain illustrations which are accomplished works of visual and graphic art, as well as texts which are written in expressive, carefully crafted language. Bader (1976: 1) describes picture-books as follows: 'A picture book is a text, illustrations, total design: an item of manufacture and a commercial product; a social, cultural, historical document; and foremost an experience for the child. As an art form, it hinges on the interdependence of pictures and words, on the simultaneous display of two facing pages and on the drama of the turning page'.

According to the illustrator Uri Schulevitz (1985: 15), a picture-book 'could not for example be read over the radio and be understood fully. In a picture-book the pictures extend, clarify, complement, or take the place of words'. Schulevitz (ibid: 16) highlights the importance of the visual as follows: 'By telling a story visually, instead of through verbal description, a picture-book becomes a dramatic experience: immediate, vivid, moving. A picture-book is closer to theatre and film, silent films in particular, than to other types of books, it is a unique type of book'.

Multicultural literature

Mendoza and Reese (2001: 1) define intercultural and multicultural books as 'picture-books that depict the variety of ethnic, racial, and cultural groups within society'. In recent years picture-books have challenged the under-representation and marginalization of children from different ethnic backgrounds (Gamble and Yates 2008). Mary Hoffman and Caroline Binch's heroine in the picture-book *Amazing Grace* (2007) proves there is no reason why a black female cannot play Peter Pan in the class play. The use of multicultural literature together with intuitive dialogic instruction within safe early childhood education settings can provide children with both a window to other cultures and a mirror reflecting their own (Galda 1998). A child may see his or her life, cultures and values reflected through the mirror of a book. Alternatively, a book may provide a window through which a range of cultural identities and perspectives can be experienced.

While multicultural literature is important for the dominant culture represented in any classroom, it is also beneficial for minority cultures. From reading stories about their own culture, children have opportunities to see how others go through experiences similar to theirs, develop strategies to cope with issues in their lives, and identify themselves with their inherited culture. It is, therefore, important that educators incorporate multicultural literature into the curriculum and make it part of children's everyday life. As well as being a key to unlocking the past and the future, multicultural children's literature also allows children to virtually visit unfamiliar places. Books can demonstrate how children grow up in different places, as well as highlighting sometimes difficult circumstances that children have to endure, perhaps due to war, poverty or extraordinary events (Gamble and Yates 2008).

Multicultural literature can complement children's engagement with many concepts, for example, counting. There are several books from different cultures which reinforce the idea of counting in a creative and entertaining manner. In Laurie Krebs and Julia Cairns' *We all Went on Safari: A Counting Journey through Tanzania* (2004), readers can join Arusha, Mosi, Tumpe and their Maasai friends as they set out on a counting journey through the grasslands of Tanzania. Along the way, the children encounter all sorts of animals including elephants, lions and monkeys, while counting from one to ten in both English and Swahili. The lively, rhyming text is accompanied by an illustrated guide to counting in Swahili, a map, notes about each of the animals, and interesting facts about Tanzania and the Maasai people.

Nevertheless, it is important for teachers to critically assess their choice of picture-books, the images they convey and the potential impact of the story and images on the children in their class. For example, if children are limited to picture-books, such as *My Rows and Piles of Coins* by Tololwa Mollel (1999), or *Elizabeti's Doll* by Stephanie Stuve-Bodeen (1998), both set in Tanzania, they might think that all Tanzanians live in small, rural villages and gain no concept of life there in a big city such as Dar es Salaam. Rather than just working from multicultural and intercultural catalogues of children's picture books, it is important to explore pedagogical approaches and offer interpretive frameworks which will help children to critically engage with core themes and messages of each picture-book.

Culturally diverse early childhood education settings

According to Morris and Coughlan (2005: 10), 'whether you and your children, or the children you work with, live in the multicultural inner city or in the heart of the countryside, the talk, investigation and activity that can be engendered by fine picture-books will lay good foundations for the development of informed and positive attitudes to racial identity – the child's own and that of other groups in our society'. Children learn so much about the world they live in through the books they read, but sometimes they are presented with a limited selection by teachers which are chosen on the basis of their own world-view.

Picture-books include a variety of stories and illustrations from a range of different ethnic groups and cultures around the world. The beauty of the illustrations and the quality of the stories provides a strong visible statement which affirms the importance of valuing diversity. These books can be used to integrate multicultural content into the primary curriculum and in turn can help to create an inclusive classroom atmosphere. However, prior to the 1960s, people who were not white were virtually invisible in children's literature. Sociocultural changes during the 1960s and 1970s fostered renewed interest in multicultural literature for adults and children which reflected 'the diverse life experiences, traditions, histories, values, world-views and perspectives of the diverse cultural groups that make up society' (Grant and Ladson-Billings 1997: 185). It is widely accepted that good multicultural literature can benefit all children in an early childhood classroom (Derman-Sparks et al. 1989). Teachers enhance children's emerging understanding and empathy when they make a point of sharing books that accurately and positively portray the backgrounds of the families in the classroom and that extend children's awareness to the significant groups in their community and the wider world.

Introducing a global perspective into the classroom through picture-books

Picture-books include a variety of stories and illustrations from a range of different ethnic groups and cultures around the world. The beauty of the illustrations and the quality of the stories provides a strong visible statement which affirms the importance of valuing diversity. Increasingly, picture-books are also dealing with a range of complex development issues including interdependence, globalization, justice and unequal distribution of resources in a manner which is accessible for young children.

Children's literature, including picture books, provides children with an opportunity and a method by which teachers can explore a range of development and intercultural themes. Indeed, as Reynolds (2007: 3) comments, 'children's literature provides a curious and paradoxical cultural space: a space that is simultaneously highly regulated and overlooked, orthodox and radical, didactic and subversive'. Within this curious-cultural space, picture-books can bridge the gap between geographically distant places and the lives of the children in the classroom and they can give children an understanding about how and where people have lived in the past, in the present and how they might live in the future (Hannibal, Vasiliev and Lin 2002). Children's literature does make a difference in children's lives, for not only does it entertain, it stretches children's imaginations, reminds them of their humanity and exposes them to other cultures (Temple et al. 2002).

A fundamental step, however, is the choice of high quality, engaging multicultural picture-books which firstly must be appealing to children and secondly should share stories about universal experiences to which children can relate. Dowd (1992: 220) affirms that 'from reading, hearing, and using culturally diverse materials, young people learn that beneath surface differences of colour, culture or ethnicity, all people experience universal feelings of love, sadness, self-worth, justice and kindness'.

Equally, a central concern of development and intercultural education for primary children is to present a world which is constantly changing. While the quality and diversity of picture-books has improved in recent years, so too has their ability to deal with contemporary global issues. The events of 11 September 2001 had a devastating impact all over the world and the date represents a significant milestone in international relations. While the issue was very difficult for teachers to present in classrooms, a number of picture-books were published which highlighted the events in a child-friendly manner, for example, *Fireboat: The Heroic Adventures of the John J. Harvey* (2005) by Maira Kalman, *The Man who Walked Between the Towers* (2007) *by* Mordicai Gerstein, *September Roses* (2004) by Jeanette Winter and *The Little Chapel that Stood* (2003) by A. B. Curtiss. However, it is important to remember the power of the single image (Griffiths and Allbut 2011) or in Marriott's (2002) terms 'the mediated experience'. Therefore, in order to avoid presenting one side of the story, picture-books such as Jeanette Winter's *Nasreen's Secret School: A True Story from Afghanistan* (2009) and *The Librarian of Basra: A True Story from Iraq* (2005) are important for presenting different cultural perspectives. The events of 11 September (2001) had serious implications for a range of cultures all over the world, therefore discussions about events of this nature need to address the multidimensional context in which they take place.

Complex issues such as migration, refugees and asylum seekers can be effectively explored through picture storybooks. The reasons why asylum seekers seek refuge are often misunderstood. Many people do not realize how much asylum seekers, and especially children, have been through. Mary Hoffman's *The Colour of Home* (2002) tells in simple language the story of Hassan, a refugee from Somalia who has witnessed things no child should ever see. When he arrives in England everything is so different and it is very difficult for him to respond to friendliness from his new classmates. His imaginative teacher invites him to paint a picture and in this way Hassan is at last able to communicate the terrible things that happened to his family in Somalia when his home was burnt and his uncle shot. Slowly, through the picture, his teacher and classmates begin to understand his story and why he must try to build a new life a long way from home. The clever use of colour, bright and happy for his home, red and black for anger and war, various tones of grey for his sadness and loss explains Hassan's moods and feelings where words would fail us. Towards the end of the story, colour and hope begins to return to Hassan's life. Another perspective on asylum seekers is provided by Ben Morley. His book, *The Silence Seeker* (2009), tells the story of Joe and his quest to find a quiet place for his new neighbour who is an asylum seeker according to Joe's mother. Joe misunderstands and thinks the boy is a silence seeker especially when Mum adds that he needs peace and quiet. The story shows friendship developing between the two boys, but it also makes Joe realize that he can't find a peaceful and quiet place for his friend and readers are introduced to the threats and tensions which lie in their environment.

Mama Panya's Pancakes: new story sack resource for early childhood education

Research by Ruane et al. (2010), using a picture-book called *Mama Panya's Pancakes*, demonstrates that young people including pre-school and infant children, are capable of engaging with global justice issues, provided the strategies employed are appropriate to the age and cognitive development of each child. This research has led to the creation of a picture-book story sack resource specifically for early childhood educators.

This resource, the *Just Children Story Sack*, was created by Trócaire (an Irish development non-governmental organization) and St Patrick's College of Education in Ireland (Trócaire and CHRCE 2010). This is an excellent example of resources which can promote creative, enquiry-based responses to a picture storybook. This story sack contains a range of resources including Adiko the Puppet. Aimed at pre-school educators and Key Stage One teachers, the sack is built around the colourful children's story *Mama Panya's Pancakes: A Village tale from Kenya* (written by Mary and Richard Chamberlin and illustrated by Julia Cairns). This story provides an opportunity to teach young children about Kenya. The story also enables teachers to bring a global dimension effortlessly into their teaching by highlighting concepts such as diversity and equality.

Mama Panya's Pancakes depicts a young Kenyan boy's experience of visiting the market with his mother. Along the way, Adika invites all their friends for pancakes, causing Mama to worry that she can't afford enough flour to feed the extra guests. However, everyone brings 'gifts' such as milk, butter, and flour so that there is more than enough for everyone. The story highlights the vulnerability of impoverished families, but the use of topics such as 'food' and 'journeys' allow children to identify similarities with their own lives.

The Kenyan landscape is presented in the book, as are sample Swahili words such as 'Jambo' and 'Harambee'. The book contains a map suitable for primary school children which outlines some of the major geographical features located in Kenya, for example, rivers, mountains and major cities. Additional information about village life in Kenya can also be found including: details about animals, insects, reptiles and plants; instructions for pronouncing Kiswahili words, and Mama Panya's pancake recipe. The handbook and resources included in the sack build on this story. Developed in consultation with educators and early education experts, the handbook contains a programme of learning experiences designed to introduce children aged between three and seven to concepts such as: fairness, interdependence, near and far, similarity and difference and another perspective, in a global context. With a puppet, songs, a CD and photographs, the sack provides an example of how education for a just world can begin in preschool and Key Stage One educational settings.

The *Just Children Story Sack* provides resources for early childhood educators to begin exploring with their children concepts, attitudes and perspectives related to global justice. The programme focuses on five dimensions identified as central to education for global justice:

- An understanding of fairness;
- The ability to empathize;
- Openness to and respect for diversity;
- Awareness of the connections between people around the world;
- Awareness of the wider world and of people living in developing countries.

Gender in picture storybooks

Childhood is central to the development of gender identity and children's literature forms one piece in that socialization process. Gooden and Gooden's (2001: 96) study of gender representation in children's books over a five year period found that 'the prevalence of gender stereotypes decreased slightly but the stereotyped images of females are still significant'. Authors such as Mc Cabe et al. (2011) highlight a widespread pattern of under-representation of females in children's literature. Mc Cabe et al. (2011: 198) argue that 'children's books reinforce, legitimate and reproduce a patriarchal gender system'. Adults have a role to play in that they are often responsible for choosing the books which are accessible to children. Hence, it is important to include books which include both female and male characters in a wide range of roles. From a global perspective there are several high quality picture-books which feature the stories of some prominent women, for example, Amelia Earhart, Queen Elizabeth II, Harriet Tubman, Wangari Maathai and Rosa Parks.

Known as the 'Mother of the Civil Rights Movement', Rosa Louise McCauley Parks (4 February, 1913–24 October, 2005) was an African-American civil rights activist. On 1 December, 1955 in Montgomery, Alabama, Rosa Parks, aged forty-two, refused to obey bus driver James Blake's order that she give up her seat to make room for a white passenger. Parks' action sparked the Montgomery Bus Boycott. Parks' act of defiance became an important symbol of the modern Civil Rights Movement and she became an international icon of resistance to racial segregation. She organized and collaborated with civil rights leaders, including boycott leader Martin Luther King, Jr, helping to launch him to national prominence in the civil rights movement. Her story is featured in several picture storybooks for children. Nikki Giovanni and Bryan Collier's book *Rosa* (2005), was written to mark the fiftieth anniversary of her refusal to give up her seat on a Montgomery city bus.

Two books present Rosa's story from the perspective of the bus. Faith Ringold's book *If a Bus Could Talk: The Story of Rosa Parks* (2003) uses the vehicle of a talking bus to narrate Rosa's story. This book opens with a young child called Marcie who believes she is about to take her typical bus ride to school. When she enters the bus, she soon finds out that something is amiss. The bus doesn't have a driver, the passengers are unfamiliar and the bus can talk. In a friendly manner the bus tells Marcie the Rosa Parks story. Beginning with Rosa as a child, the bus takes us through the different stages of her life right up to the infamous moment when she refused to give up her seat. In Jo S. Kittinger's book *Rosa's Bus* (2010) the creative narrative explains the history of Bus #2857 from the streets of Montgomery to its present home in the Henry Ford Museum and describes the injustice of segregation to a generation too young to remember. A boardbook version, *The Story of Rosa Parks* (2007) by Patricia Pingry and illustrated by Stephen Walker, is available for infants and pre-school children. The story begins: 'Do you know Rosa Parks? She is called the mother of civil rights'. Each page has one or two simple sentences stating simple, important information about Rosa Parks. There's enough information for a young child to learn about Rosa without being overwhelmed with details.

Four excellent picture-books have been written based on the life of 2004 Nobel Peace Prize recipient Wangari Maathai: Donna Jo Napoli's *Mama Miti* (2010); Jeanette Winter's *Wangari's Trees of Peace: A True Story from Africa* (2008); Claire Nivola's *Planting the Trees of Kenya: The story of Wangari Maathai* (2008) and Jen Cullerton Johnson's *Seeds of Change* (2010). The first African woman to win the Nobel Peace Prize, Wangari's personal story from veterinary medicine, to the foundation of the Green Belt Movement, to halting deforestation in Kenya is inspirational. *Mama Miti* (the mother of trees) tells Wangari's story aided by Kadir Nelson's stunning collage illustrations. 'Mama Miti' as a young girl was taught by her tribal elders the significance of caring for the natural environment and, especially, for trees. As trees were removed, the foundation of a community was also destroyed. Miti carried this message into adulthood. Wangari grew up in the shadow of Mount Kenya listening to the stories about the people and land around her. Planting trees one by one, she became involved in local community issues. When local women came to her for help with their families she told them to do the same. Soon the countryside was filled with trees. Kenya was strong once more. Wangari had changed her country 'tree by tree'. The books highlight the importance of trees in a global context, their aesthetical value is presented through the beautiful illustrations and the delicate relationship between humans and nature is carefully considered.

For slightly older children (over eight years of age) the book *Amelia to Zora* by Cynthia Chin Lee (2005) celebrates the achievements of twenty-six brave women from all over the world who refused to take 'no' for an answer. She chose twenty-six women whose first names begin with each letter of the alphabet – thus A is for Amelia, pilot Amelia Earhart and Z is for Zora, writer Zora Neale Hurston. Each woman has made a difference in such varied fields as the arts, sports, journalism, science, and entertainment. At the end of the book the author explains why she has chosen given names rather than family names for each woman. 'Family names are usually based on a father's or husband's name. Using a woman's name seemed more personal to me'. She further explains, 'I followed this strategy with Asian names, in which the given name comes after the family name [...] For Daw Aung San Suu Kyi, 'S is for Suu Kyi' (Chin Lee: np). In Burmese, Daw is an honorary title, meaning aunt, Aung San is the family name and Suu Kyi is the given name'.

Clearly, from a gender perspective, there are many excellent picture storybooks which include the stories of powerful women. The challenge remains for educators to ensure that children have access to these books as part of their early childhood education programme.

Conclusion

This chapter demonstrates the potential of picture-books to introduce global and justice perspectives into the Early Childhood Education curriculum for young children. Multicultural literature can provide a mirror and a window for children as they view the world through different lenses and reflect back upon themselves in a new light. However, simply increasing children's access to multicultural literature is not sufficient in itself as a strategy for engaging children with global perspectives. Several early childhood educators struggle with development concepts and do not move beyond superficial descriptions of lifestyles in exotic places. In some cases, reading more about the world can actually negatively influence development or intercultural understanding as negative stereotypes are reinforced. Hence, it is important for early childhood educators to choose books with maximum potential for exploring global and justice perspectives. Educators need to be well versed themselves in the complexities of these perspectives and the political frameworks underpinning these concepts. Children need to be assisted, encouraged and challenged to engage with the issues raised by picture-books in an affirmative, effective and age appropriate manner. Appropriate pedagogical choices need to be made. Resources such as the *Just Children Story Sack* promote active engagement with development issues in the early childhood education setting. Issues such as perspective, power and voice need to be addressed through questions such as whose story is being told and whose story is missing. This is particularly important from a gender point of view. Picture-books such as those highlighted in this chapter can help children engage with global and justice perspectives effectively, efficiently and in an age-appropriate manner.

Note

This chapter is based on a research project funded by Irish Aid through DICE (Development and Intercultural Education), and Mary Immaculate College, Limerick.

References

Bader, B. (1976). *American Picture Books: From Noah's Ark to the beast within*. New York: Macmilllan.

Chin-Lee, C., Halsey, M., and Addy, S. (2008). *Amelia to Zora: 26 Women Who Changed the World*, MA: Charlesbridge Publishing.

Comber, B. (2001). 'Classroom Explorations in Critical Literacy'. In H. Fehring, and P. Green (eds), (2001). *Critical Literacy: A Collection of articles from the Australian Literacy Educators' Association*, pp. 90–111. Newark, Delaware: International Reading Association.

Derman-Sparks, L., and The ABC Task Force (1989). *The Anti-Bias Curriculum: Tools for empowering young children*. Washington, DC: National Association for the Education of Young Children.

DES (2011). *Literacy and Numeracy for Learning and Life. The National Strategy to Improve Literacy and Numeracy among Children and Young People 2011–2020*. Dublin: Department of Education and Skills.

Dowd, F. S. (1992). 'Evaluating Children's Books Portraying Native American and Asian Cultures', *Childhood Education*, 68 (4), 219–24.

Fiedler, M. (2008). 'Teaching and Learning about the World in the Classroom: Development education in culturally diverse settings', *Policy & Practice: A Development Education Review*, 7 (1), 5–17.

Freire, P., and Macedo, D. (1987). *Literacy: Reading the word and the world*. Boulder, CO: Paradigm Publishers.

Galda, L. (1998). 'Mirrors and Windows: Reading as transformation'. In T. E. Raphael and K. H. Au (eds), *Literature-based instruction: Reshaping the curriculum*, pp. 1–11. Norwood, MA: Christopher Gordon Publishers.

Gamble, N., and Yates, S. (2008). *Exploring Children's Literature*. 2nd ed. London: Sage.

Gooden, A. M. and Gooden, M. A. (2001). 'Gender Representation in Notable Children's Picture Books: 1995–1999', Sex Roles, 45(1/2), 89–101.

Grant, C. A., and Ladson-Billings, G. (1997). *Dictionary of Multicultural Education*. Phoenix, AZ: The Oryx Press.

Greene, M. (1995). *Releasing the Imagination: Essays on education, the arts and social change*. San Francisco: Jossey Bass.

Griffiths, H. and Allbut, G. (2011). 'The danger of the Single Image', *Primary Geography*, 75 (summer), 16–17.

Hannibal, M. A., Vasiliev, Z., and Qiuyun, L. (2002). 'Teaching Young Children Basic Concepts of Geography: A Literature-based approach', *Early Childhood Education*, 30 (2), 81–6.

Kittinger, J. S., and Walker, S. (2010). *Rosa's Bus*, Pennsylvania: Boyds Mills Press.

Lewis, D. (2001). *Reading Contemporary Picturebooks: Picturing text*. USA and Canada: Routledge.

McCabe, J., Fairchild, E., Grauerholz, L., Pescosolido, B. A., and Tope, D. (2011). 'Gender in Twentieth-Century Children's Books: Patterns of disparity in titles and central characters', *Gender & Society*, 25 (2), 197–226.

Marriott, S. (2002). 'Red in Tooth and Claw? Images of Nature in Modern Picture Books', *Children's Literature in Education*, 33(3), 175.

Mendoza, J., and Reese, D. (2001). 'Examining Multicultural Picture-Books for the Early Childhood Classroom: Possibilities and pitfalls', *Journal of Early Childhood Research and Practice*, 3 (2), 155–69.

Morris, L., and Coughlan, S. (eds) (2005). *Cross Currents: A Guide to multi-cultural books for young people*. Dublin: IBBY Ireland.

Reynolds, K. (2007). *Radical Children's Literature: Future visions and aesthetic transformations in juvenile fiction*. New York: Palgrave/Macmillan.

Ruane, B., Kavanagh, A. M., Waldron, F., Dillon, S., Casey, M., Maunsell, C., and Prunty, A. (2010). *Young Children's Engagement with Issues of Global Justice: A Report by the Centre for Human Rights and Citizenship Education*, Dublin: St Patrick's College, Drumcondra and Trócaire.

Shulevitz, U. (1985). *Writing with Pictures: How to write and illustrate children's books*. New York: Watson-Guptill.

Temple, C. A., Martinz, M., Yokota, J., and Naylor, A. (1998). *Children's Books in Children's Hands: An Introduction to their literature*. Boston: Allyn and Bacon.

Wolk, S. (2003). 'Teaching for Critical Literacy in Social Studies', *Social Studies*, 95 (3), 101–6.

Children's Books

Chamberlin, M., and Chamberlin, R. (2006). *Mama Panya's Pancakes*. Oxford: Barefoot Books.

Chin-Lee, C., Halsey, M., and Addy, S. (2005). *Amelia to Zora: Twenty-six women who changed the world*. Charlesbridge Pub Inc.

Cullerton Johnson, J., and Lynn-Sadler, S. (2010). *Seeds of Change.* New York: Lee and Low Books Inc.

Curtiss, A. B., and Golino, M. (2003). *The Little Chapel that Stood.* Escondido, CA: Old Castle Publishing.

Gerstein, M. (2007). *The Man who Walked Between the Towers.* New York: Square Fish/Macmillan.

Hoffman, M., and Binch, C. (2007). *Amazing Grace.* London: Frances Lincoln.

Hoffman, M., and Littlewood, K. (2003) *The Colour of Home.* London: Frances Lincoln.

Kalman, M. (2005). *Fireboat: The heroic adventures of the John J. Harvey.* London: Puffin Books.

Krebs, L., and Cairns, J. (2004). *We All Went on Safari.* Oxford: Barefoot Books.

Mollel, T. (1999). *My Rows and Piles Of Coins.* New York: Clarion Books.

Morley, B. (2009). *The Silence Seeker.* London: Transworld Publishers.

Napoli, D. J., and Nelson, K. (2010). *Mama Miti.* Simon and Schuster books for Young Readers.

Nivola, C. (2008). *Planting the Trees of Kenya: The Story of Wangari Maathai.* New York: Farrar, Straus and Giroux/Macmillan.

Pingry, P., and Walker, S. (2007). *The Story of Rosa Parks.* Nashville: Candy Cane Press.

Ringold, F. (2003). *If a Bus Could Talk: The Story of Rosa Parks.* Simon and Schuster Books for Young Readers.

Stuve Bodeen, S. and Hale, C. (2002). *Elizabeth's Doll.* New York: Lee and Low Books.

Winter, J. (2004) *September Roses.* New York: Straus and Giroux/Macmillan.

Winter, J. (2005). *The Librarian of Basra: A true story from Iraq.* San Diego: Harcourt Children's Books.

Winter, J. (2008). *Wangari's Trees of Peace: A true story from Africa.* San Diego: Harcourt Children's Books.

Winter, J. (2009). *Nasreen's Secret School. A true story from Afghanistan.* San Diego: Beach Lane Books.

PAMELA MACKENZIE

16 A Mother Tongue Based Multilingual Curriculum as a Means to Quality Education: Lessons from Minority Language Communities in India and Bangladesh

Introduction

In 1994, the author was invited to visit a remote tribal area of Andhra Pradesh, in India, where a local NGO was planning to set up primary schools as few government schools were available in the area. It soon became clear that most children were unable to understand the content of the curriculum, or the teacher, as Telugu (the state language), which the children could neither speak nor understand, was used exclusively. This resulted in little interaction in teacher dominated classrooms with limited understanding by the children. After discussing the issues with the state education department and realizing that the government was anxious to reduce the extremely high dropout and low achievement levels among tribal communities, the author gathered together linguists from the local universities to discuss how support could be given to the government to alleviate the problems. Thus, this group of linguists, together with the Tribal Welfare Department and Sarva Shiksha Abhiyan, teachers from the local language groups and various consultants, designed and developed an orthography and curriculum for the primary years in eight different languages, using local languages, cultures and the environment (NMRC 2009a).

Following the initial success in increased enrolment, decreased dropout and the enthusiasm of those teachers from the local communities and parents in Andhra Pradesh, the government in Orissa also decided to develop a programme in ten community languages (NMRC 2009b). The author was also closely involved in both NGO and UNDP educational support for indigenous groups in the Chittagong Hill Tracts (CHT) in Bangladesh.[1]

Using lessons learned from this practical experience of working with governments, international agencies, local, national and international NGOs and indigenous communities in India and Bangladesh, this chapter focuses on the need for developing alternative educational programmes for children from ethno-linguistic minority communities and on what is required for successful development and implementation.

The need for a new approach to languages in education

Although many countries in the world are linguistically and culturally diverse, few education systems take that diversity into consideration in the curriculum, promoting instead dominant languages and cultures. Using an inappropriate language for education has a serious negative impact on children's educational achievement and, even though interventions are being made to improve educational provision in an attempt to meet Education For All (EFA) targets and the Millennium Development Goals (MDGs), positive results are likely to be undermined if the languages understood by children are ignored in the process (Pinnock 2009b: 9; UNESCO 2010: 150). Attempting to learn in an unfamiliar language is often so demanding that large numbers of children drop out while others repeat years. A recent report suggests that 221 million children miss out on a positive educational experience simply because they do not speak or understand the language used in school and this is stated as one of the main reasons

1 The UNDP programme began in eight language communities, but so far has only been developed for pre-schools even though it was strongly recommended that MTBMLE be extended to the whole of primary schooling: <http://www.chtdf.org/index.php/focus-areas/education>. Children do not benefit as much from early exit as they do from late exit programmes. NGO MLE in the CHT extends beyond pre-school (Durnnian 2007).

for non-enrolment and irregular attendance (Pinnock 2009b: 16).[2] Added to this, about 54 million children in countries classified as 'highly linguistically fractionalised' are currently not attending school (ibid: 26). Thus, many children are excluded or spend their time struggling to understand, often failing to learn either the school language or the language of their communities, and failing also to learn basic skills and concepts.

The benefits of using the mother tongue in education

Rather than attempting to learn in an unfamiliar language, which hinders progress, investing in mother tongue in the educational process reduces the obstacles to learning experienced by both children and teachers. Although using a child's home language alone may not necessarily lead to better learning outcomes, it has been shown to dramatically improve both children's mother tongue competency and second language skills as well as increase achievement levels across the curriculum (Dumatog and Dekker 2003; UNESCO 2003, 2006, 2008; Benson 2005a).[3] For example, a study carried out in both Andhra Pradesh and Orissa after three to four years implementation of the mother tongue based multilingual education (MTBMLE) programme, revealed that repetition and dropout rates decreased dramatically, providing improved access to education for minority language communities. Achievement levels in all school subjects, including the national official language(s) also improved significantly (NMRC 2011: 13). Besides this, in studies in Africa, it was found that the cost of the provision of education is also reduced (Heugh 2005, 2006a).

2 In Orissa, India, for example, where the author supported the development of programmes for primary education with both the state government and NGOs, figures for 2005 showed that of those that did enrol, 27 per cent of children from indigenous communities dropped out in the first year of schooling, while only one in five survived the primary years to go on to secondary education.

3 Other aspects of a quality education which MTBMLE address include improved classroom practices and appropriate materials.

While large scale and longitudinal research is still required, particularly in developing countries, existing studies (UNESCO 2010) suggest that some conclusions can be made about what children need to become bilingual or multilingual:

Mother tongue is important for children's overall language and cognitive development and for academic achievement. Dutcher (1994) states that the best predictor of both cognitive and academic language development in a second language is the level of development of cognitive and academic language proficiency in L1 (vii; viii; 3–4; 15). She argues that: 'The first language is essential for the initial teaching of reading, and for comprehension of subject matter. It is the necessary foundation for the cognitive development upon which acquisition of the second language is based' (ibid: 36).

Children need to become proficient in the language they grow up in before second language is used as the medium of instruction. Research suggests that this takes a total of twelve years (Dutcher 1994: 2). Therefore, children who have the opportunity to learn in the mother tongue for at least six years of schooling have higher levels of achievement than those who transition too soon (Thomas and Collier 1997, 2004; UNESCO 2006, 2011). The trend towards early-exit from mother tongue based bi/multilingual education and a fast track transition to the state, national or other dominant language (Pinnock 2009) risk causing 'subtractive bilingualism' (Ball 2011: 40). The use of mother tongue is essential to an effective, child friendly learning environment particularly in the early years (UNESCO 2003; Dutcher 2004; Pinnock 2009a). Children develop literacy skills and master content-material more easily in a language in which they think. Cognitive and academic language skills and content-subject material, once acquired, are said to transfer readily from one language to another (Cummins 1984). Children learning in pre-school settings using mother tongue tend to outperform their non-mother tongue peers in almost every competency area. They develop these skills in an environment that involves more child engagement and participation and more integration of local culture in a more child-friendly environment. 'These advantages emerge despite the fact that children in mother-tongue preschools tended to have significantly fewer economic assets, less access to reading materials at home, and teachers with significantly fewer years of experience' (Vijayakumar 2010: 27; see also Pinnock nd: 14).

Mother tongue based instruction promotes a smooth transition between home and school, encouraging emotional stability that leads to better and faster learning and retention of knowledge (Kioko et al. 2008). Children learn the values and knowledge important to the community, creating continuity between one generation and another. It can also improve a child's self-esteem (Benson 2005b; Albo 2006). Inuit students educated in their mother tongue, for example, showed increased self-esteem and cultural pride compared to Inuit children educated only in English or French (Wright and Taylor 1995 cited in Ball 2011: 24). Where language and culture are not valued, linguistic and cultural discontinuity is experienced which reduces self-confidence and self-esteem and interferes with learning (Benson 2005b; Baker and Prys Jones 1998 cited in Ball 2011: 24). This can result in social dysfunction and political instability (Pinnock 2009b: 18). Developing self-esteem, cultural identity and ensuring a place in the community results in a sense of personal worth and value, and reduces alienation.

While the use of mother tongue as a medium of instruction alone cannot ensure educational quality and access for linguistic minorities, it can lead to higher competencies in reading, mathematics, science and the other languages, improved sense of worth and community stability.

Opposition to using first languages in education

Most international agencies have now acknowledged the need for MTBMLE in providing quality education for linguistically diverse countries. However, despite the growing support from the international community, research and experience, there continues to be opposition to using first languages in education, and using local languages as the medium of instruction is still controversial with policy makers. In some cases there is often a lack of political will to change the status quo. In others, choices about which language(s) to use in education are often made on political grounds or assumptions about increased costs, rather than on what is most effective for children's learning needs (Pinnock et al. 2011: 9).

Governments often impose a single language in schools, because they believe it helps to create social cohesion in ethnically and linguistically complex countries, but evidence suggests that opposition to first language education is often a contributing factor in inter-ethnic conflict, while acknowledging local languages can diffuse tensions (Pinnock 2011: 9, 36). Furthermore, investing in adapting school curricula and materials is estimated to add up to 4 per cent or 5 per cent to education budgets (Heugh 2006a: 149) these costs are offset by reduced dropout, repetition and increased achievement levels.

Many parents want their children to learn 'high prestige'–international languages such as English, and believe that enrolling their children in schools that teach in these languages will speed up acquisition. It is presumed to offer greater access to economic opportunity. But many of these schools teach these languages poorly (Graddol 2010: 88) and there is little evidence of long term advantage to an early start in language learning. The teaching of the national language, introduced at upper primary level when children have more advanced learning and language skills, is likely to be more successful (Ball 2010).

Many suggest that children already know their first language and continuing to learn in their mother tongue is of no benefit. But research suggests that at least twelve years are necessary to learn one's first language well, providing a strong foundation for learning other languages (Dutcher 1994).

Some parents suggest that children already know the second language but although children may be adequate in some social communication, a skill which takes only one or two years, it is unlikely that their academic language skills will be sufficiently developed for understanding the curriculum content, mastery of which requires between five and seven years (Cummins 1984).

In areas where several different languages could be taught as the majority language, authorities face a difficult choice. A multiplicity of languages in the community may exacerbate the challenge of providing mother tongue schooling for all children. In such cases alternative solutions need to be found so that children have the best foundation for language learning (Kosenen 2006).

The mother tongue may be an unwritten language and, therefore, not recognized as a legitimate language. The minority language community may have a low status and be subject to discrimination and prejudice, making acceptance of mother tongue instruction difficult, even to the extent of creating reluctance among mother tongue learners to use and demonstrate proficiency in the language. Some argue that terminology for modern academic discourse is not developed and curriculum and educational resources are lacking, but according to Mohanty (2006) this is due mainly to the marginalization of those languages.[4]

There may be a lack of appropriately trained teachers with some teachers not knowing the languages spoken by the children while others will not be sufficiently fluent in the second language. In both cases, changes in recruitment policies may be required and all will need specific first and second language learning training.

Government officials at the various levels of bureaucracy rarely understand the issues or solutions, and, even when they do, frequent changes of those in authority hinder progress. So, as Ball (2011: 44) points out, '[a] s long as there is a lack of political will to create and implement a policy allowing these programmes, the human resource capacity, curriculum and learning resources, popular demand for these programmes will be lacking'.

Donor agencies could also make an important contribution by incorporating mother tongue schooling into their strategies, but 'few donors appear to be promoting good practice' (Pinnock 2009b: 38). If delivery of mother tongue teaching was a focus of their education projects and funding that leads to the promotion of national or international languages, such as English, over local ones was re-evaluated, there might be more progress toward quality education for children from ethno-linguistic minority and indigenous communities. Commitment to developing appropriate language policies and investment in good educational practices will be required if quality basic education is to be delivered and international obligations are to be met.

4 Mohanty (2006) suggests that the 'disabilities and disadvantages associated with minor languages are not inherent; they are socially constructed with institutionalized discriminations in educational, political, economic and other social spheres'.

What is MTBMLE?

Mother tongue based multilingual education begins with what is familiar to the child and builds on that foundation to add new learning. It places the child's language, culture and environment at the centre of the learning process. The child's mother tongue is used as the primary language of instruction across the curriculum. The skills and concepts, usually demanded by the national curriculum, are general; the context for learning is different. A strong foundation in the first language provides a good basis for learning other languages which are gradually introduced as the child progresses through schooling. Oral ability in the new language is developed first, moving on to written forms and then gaining fluency in all language skills (listening, speaking, reading and writing). Evidence suggests that children require five to seven years to become competent users of a second language (Cummins 1984).[5] They need to *learn* the new language before learning *in* the new language and transitioning too early or too abruptly means that neither the mother tongue, nor the second language will be sufficiently strong and children suffer as a result.[6] Those who transition too early experience difficulties, particularly as the curriculum content increases in difficulty and abstraction. Evidence also suggests that only those who continue in the mother tongue throughout their school career are likely to become fully bilingual, or multilingual (Ball 2011: 6). Thus, the mother tongue should not be replaced by the second language or other languages, but other languages should be added so that all languages are used as a resource for learning (Agnihotri 2009).

Table 1 provides an outline for the possible stages of development for first and second language learning beginning with oral language development and moving on to reading and writing. This was developed for children who were starting school knowing only their mother tongue.

5 Some say six to eight years (Collier 1987).

6 Transition programmes promote the mainstreaming of students, eventually using L2 as the medium of instruction, while transfer programmes are what is known as *additive bilingualism* where children continue to learn and learn in L1 as well as L2. See Table one (Ball 2011: 21–2) for a description of different types of bi/multilingual education programmes.

Table 1 Stages of language and concept learning

	Stage 1	Stage 2	Stage 3	Stage 4	Stage 5	Stage 6	Stage 7
L1	Build small children's oral fluency, competence and confidence in L1 Use L1 as the medium of instruction	Use L1 as the medium of instruction Continue to build oral L1 Introduce reading and writing in L1	Use L1 as the medium of instruction Continue to build oral and written L1	Use L1 as the medium of instruction Continue to build oral and written fluency in L1	Continue to build oral and written L1 & L2 for fluency, and learning new concepts	Continue to build fluency & confidence in using L1, L2 and L3 for everyday communication & for learning new concepts	Use all languages for lifelong learning
L2			Introduce Oral L2	Continue to build oral L2 Introduce reading and writing in L2			
L3					Introduce oral L3	Introduce reading and writing in L3	

What is required for a successful mother tongue based MLE programme?

At the beginning of the MTBMLE programme in Andhra Pradesh, a group of linguists who had studied the local languages, including educationalists, government officials and local community teachers, developed an outline plan based on a helpful analysis originally developed by Malone (2010). Besides requiring a positive political environment at the national, and in India, the state level, and agreement at the local level, there were many practical processes and procedures that had to be worked out to ensure the successful development and effective implementation of the multilingual education programme. The components required for the MTBMLE programmes included the need to engage the community and other stakeholders in planning and developing the programmes; the preparation of an appropriate orthography; the development of a culturally relevant curricula; a plan for the acquisition of the state and national languages; the development of textbooks and learning materials; and teacher preparation and support. The processes followed are outlined below, these often happening simultaneously and not in a linear fashion as summarized here:

Survey

Preliminary research was conducted to collect baseline information on educational provision and effectiveness, and information about the languages and their uses in the community. The findings of surveys provided a guide to data collection, language analysis and curriculum development and also as a foundation for evaluation.

Mobilization

Awareness of the programme at all levels of government and amongst all stakeholders is necessary to mobilize resources and ensure support. The frequent changes of government officials can make advocacy and continuity difficult, but where a community itself understands the issues and is engaged, the results are likely to be more positive. Survey and data collection can be a positive way to develop ownership and act as good mobilization activities. The development of materials, literature and dictionaries necessarily involve the local community and participation in workshops act to promote local ownership.

Documenting the language

For unscripted languages, a suitable writing system needs to be developed. In all three programmes, linguists and local community members worked together to develop a suitable and acceptable orthography, which was tested and revised as necessary, and wherever possible using a script acceptable to the local community.[7] The linguistic and cultural data was also used as the foundation for curriculum and literature development.

Working with family and community

Community participation and ownership, along with parental support is critical for successful programmes. Working with the community from the beginning creates a greater awareness of needs and provides support in finding positive resolutions and outcomes. Besides language documentation, community members are the ones who are intimate with the culture and environment, history and stories, which need to be incorporated into the curriculum. Employing local teachers who are part of the community is essential. Furthermore, parents can participate in their children's education, an important feature in early learning, which is rarely possible when there is a disconnect between the home, the community and the school.

7 In India, the script of the state language was used: Telugu script in Andhra Pradesh and Oriya script in Orissa (Odisha). In Bangladesh, traditional scripts were used and Roman script where there were no traditional scripts. One language had developed its own script.

Curriculum development

Using the national curriculum framework of each region as a guide, the knowledge, skills, customs and environment of the local community were used to develop activities for achieving required competencies. Such a culture-based approach values the child and the community and helps children to link their experiences at school with their prior learning.

Children learn best in meaningful contexts, and so a departure from reliance on textbooks, particularly in the early years, was encouraged. The use of an integrated approach that a theme-based curriculum provides was developed. Locally appropriate themes were chosen from seasonal events, daily activities and local environmental characteristics, all of which were familiar to the child. These ideas were then developed into curriculum materials for language, maths and environmental studies. Local artists illustrated the materials according to local culture.

Resource development

Books and learning materials in local languages are important for developing the mother tongue and for learning content. These also contribute to raising the status of the languages spoken by children and their families. Simple second language and dual-language books are important in promoting second language learning and bilingualism. The challenge of preparing reading materials and of designing textbooks for up to five subjects for five or six grades has been successfully met in both Andhra Pradesh and Orissa for eight and ten languages respectively.

For example, textbooks were developed that are used to develop skills and accuracy in language and maths. Activities were then incorporated into teacher's guides to encourage a move away from textbook-based learning so that the skills and concepts are used in everyday contexts familiar to the children. Language activities include *listening stories* for the teacher to read to or tell the students; *children's reading books* with short sentences and pictures that the children can use by themselves or in small groups, *fact sheets* using local knowledge and *big book* stories that are used as whole class reading material. Other materials are made in the classroom by the children and teachers together. These might be, for example, experience stories, stories which are made up using places and characters, experiment write ups and so on. Dictionaries in all eight languages were developed with linguist and community support.[8]

As with language, children learn maths skills and their use through concrete operations and activities. Maths theme webs were developed, using the national curriculum framework of mathematical concepts to gather ideas and activities of maths use in daily life in the communities.

Activities were also developed for science, environmental studies, arts and craft, drama, music and dance, based on local environment, cultural and daily behaviour, and these encouraged the involvement of community members wherever possible.

Literature development

Literature for use as part of the curriculum and for classroom libraries was developed during special writers' workshops. These included oral stories, stories to read aloud, reading books, songs, poems, rhymes, facts and information books related to the cultural themes such as music, plants, animals and work. These formed the beginning of a literature environment where previously there had been none. In all programmes, community leaders, recognized story tellers, artists, teachers, and others were trained in the principles and processes of writing, illustrating, editing, testing and revising.

8 An example of dictionaries and other materials of a partner NGO working in two of the language communities in Andhra Pradesh can be found here: <http://www.gondwana.in/ap/index.htm>.

Effective pedagogy

MLE attempts to be creative and responsive, with a focus on meaning and comprehension, rather than perpetuating a conformist and submissive ethos and its corresponding tradition of rote learning. In order to achieve this, alternative teaching methods needed to be incorporated into curriculum design. Classroom practices need to be closer to community learning practices and the methodology for learning to read and write needs to be adapted to the nature of each language.

Ensuring a good bridging process

There are a number of considerations to take into account when developing a programme for the acquisition of a new language. For young children (up to about age seven), learning a second language differs from the way that older children learn a second language (Nicholas and Lightbown 2008). An informal approach to language learning within daily classroom routines is more effective than formal instruction in the early years. The pace and effectiveness of children's second language learning will vary depending on how much they have developed literacy in their first language (Nicholas and Lightbown 2008; Ball 2010: 28) and how much exposure they have to the new language; therefore the length of the stages outlined in figure 1 above will vary. For older children, the systematic teaching of a new language supports successful mastery of that language, first through formal instruction in the second language as a subject of study, and subsequently, through the use of that language in a gradually increasing number of academic subjects in the curriculum. The achievement levels of those who continue to use both the mother tongue and the second language are better than those who transition to L2 only.

Table 2 is a plan for the gradual transition of curriculum content to the state/national language that takes place over seven years. These plans were developed in India.

Table 2 Possible plan for transition

Pre-sch 1	Pre-sch 2	1st grade	2nd grade	3rd grade	4th grade	5th grade
Language Oral MT	Language Oral MT	Language in MT	Language in MT	Language in MT	MT as subject	MT as subject
Number MT	Number MT	Math in MT	Math in MT	Math in MT with some L2	Math in L2 with MT support	Math in L2 with MT support
Environmental awareness In MT	Environmental awareness In MT	EVS in MT	EVS in MT	EVS in MT with some L2	EVS in MT/L2	EVS in L2 with MT support
Play	Play		L2 oral development	Reading and writing in L2	L2 language development	L2 language development
					Oral L3	Reading and writing in L3

Training teachers

All teachers in the early grades of primary education should be mother tongue speakers of the local language, but some language communities lack trained teachers and the academic level of those who are trained is sometimes limited. In some cases, therefore, mother tongue teaching assistants were employed to work with a non-mother-tongue-speaking trained teacher. Special training programmes were developed to support MTBMLE, incorporating best practices for both first and second language learning and for active classroom participation. Training, however, is rarely enough and continuous support for teachers in practicing new teaching methods is essential for positive outcomes. The provision of teachers guides, including weekly and daily plans, with ideas for activities and designed to transform a good programme of study into positive classroom learning, are helpful in such situations to develop good practices, particularly in the case of teachers operating in remote locations.

Implementation

Piloting and reviewing before upscaling is essential to build a strong MTBMLE programme. In Andhra Pradesh, ten single language schools, with teachers from the same community, in each of eight language groups were identified for a pilot phase. These teachers were trained in contextualizing the curriculum and in using the materials, in activity based learning and child-centred methods, most suited for children of their communities. Orissa, the second state to develop MTBMLE programmes, piloted their curriculum in twenty schools in each of ten language groups. In the Chittagong Hill Tracts in Bangladesh, the programme operated in eight language groups and materials were piloted. The materials were then reviewed by the community and the education department before revising and reprinting. In Andhra Pradesh MTBMLE is currently operating in almost 2,400 schools while Orissa has about 550. Both states are currently (2012) developing orthography and curricula for other language groups.

Monitoring and evaluation

Many communities live in remote areas where difficult terrain and often adverse weather conditions make supervision and support difficult. But MTBMLE will not be successful unless there is a positive monitoring and evaluation system in place. If an evaluation procedure is already in operation this needs to be modified to address the needs of an MTBMLE programme. For example, evaluation schedules for children's learning in mother tongue must be developed and any testing must take the new curriculum into account. Curriculum, textbooks and materials, and teaching methods need to be assessed. The responses of children, teachers and communities to the programme should be considered. Reviews by teachers and observation by resource persons, with time for feedback are essential. Provision of in-service training and/or workshops on a regular basis will build confidence and competence in teachers, facilitate evaluation and enable the further development of necessary literature and curriculum materials.

Conclusion

Developing a mother tongue based multilingual education programme is not easy and, while technically it is not a problem, creating the ideal late-exit programme requires a huge commitment on the part of the government, the communities and supporting agencies. However, where policy, planning, preparation and implementation have been well supported by all the stakeholders, MTBMLE programmes have proved far more successful than traditional non-mother tongue, single language schooling. The outcomes for children from ethno-linguistic minority communities and their families far outweigh the hazards and obstacles that need to be overcome to achieve positive results.

References

Agnihotri, R. K. (2009). 'Multilingualism and a New World Order'. In A. K. Mohanty, M. Panda, R. Phillipson and T. Skutnabb-Kangas (eds), *Multilingual Education and Social Justice: Globalising the Local New Delhi*, pp. 268–77. Orient: Blackswan.

Albo, X. (2006). 'Bolivia Revolutionises Bilingual Education', *id21 Insights Education*, 5, (5), <http://www.multiculturas.com/textos/insightsEdn5_Mother_tongue_first_2006.pdf> accessed November 2012.

Alidou, H., Boly, A., Brock-Utne, B., Diallo, Y., Heugh, K., and Wolf, H. (2006). *Optimizing Learning and Education in Africa – the Language Factor: A Stock-taking research on mother tongue and bilingual education in sub-Saharan Africa Association for the Development of Education in Africa (ADEA).* <http://www.adeanet.org/adeaPortal/adea/downloadcenter/Ouga/B3_1_MTBLE_en.pdf)> accessed November 2012.

Ball, J. (2011). 'Enhancing Learning for Children from Diverse Language Backgrounds: Mother tongue based multilingual education in the early years', Paper commissioned for UNESCO, <http://unesdoc.unesco.org/images/0021/002122/212270e.pdf> accessed November 2012.

Benson, C. (2005a). 'The Importance of Mother Tongue-based Schooling for Educational Quality', Commissioned study for *EFA Global Monitoring Report 2005*, <http://unesdoc.unesco.org/images/0014/001466/146632e.pdf> accessed March 2012.

Benson, C. (2005b). 'Girls, Educational Equity and Mother Tongue-based Teaching'. UNESCO: Bangkok. <http://www.ungei.org/resources/files/unesco_Girls_Edu_mother_tongue.pdf> accessed March 2012.

Collier, V. P. (1987). 'Age and Rate of Acquisition of Second Language for Academic Purposes', *TESOL Quarterly*, 21 (4), 617–41.

Cummins, J. (1984). *Bilingualism and Special Education: Issues in assessment and pedagogy*. Clevedon, UK: Multilingual Matters. No longer available online at <http://www.iteachilearn.com/cummins.bicscalp.htm> but for explanation of Cummins theories see: <http://www.naldic.org.uk/ITTSEAL2/teaching/SLA.cfm> accessed November 2012.

Dumatog, R., and Dekker, D. (2003). *First Language Education in Lubuagan, Northern Philippines.* <http://www.sil.org/asia/ldc/parallel_papers/dumatog_and_dekker.pdf> accessed November 2012.

Durnnian, T. (2007). *Mother Language First*. London: Save the Children. <http://www.lcgbangladesh.org/Education/reports/Mother%20Language%20First%20English.pdf> accessed November 2012.

Dutcher, N. in collaboration with Tucker, G. R. (1994). 'The Use of First and Second Languages in Education: A Review of international experience', *Pacific Island Discussion Paper Series No.1*. Washington, DC: World Bank. <http://www-wds.worldbank.org/external/default/WDSContentServer/WDSP/IB/2000/02/24/000094946_99031910564840/Rendered/PDF/multi_page.pdf> accessed November 2012.

Dutcher, N. (1995). *The Use of First and Second Languages in Education: A Review of international experience*. Washington, D. C: World Bank.

Graddol, D. (2010). *English Next, India: The Future of English in India*. British Council <http://www.britishcouncil.org/learning-english-next-india-2010-book.pdf> accessed November 2012.

Heugh, K. (2005). 'Mother Tongue Education is Best', *HSRC Review*, 3 (3), 6–7. <http://www.hsrc.ac.za/HSRC_Review_Article-14.phtml> accessed November 2012.

Heugh, K. (2006a). 'Cost Implications of the Provision of Mother Tongue and Strong Bilingual Models of Education in Africa'. In H. Alidou, A. Boly, B. Brock-Utne, Y. S. Diallo, K. Heugh, and H. E. Wolff (eds), *Optimizing Learning and Education in Africa – The Language Factor: A Stock-taking research on mother tongue and bilingual education in sub-Saharan Africa*, pp. 138–56. Paris: Association for the Development of Education in Africa, ADEA.

Heugh, K. (2006b). 'Theory and Practice: Language education models in Africa: Research, design, decision-making, outcomes and costs'. In H. Alidou and A. Boly, B. Brock-Utne, Y. S. Diallo, K. Heugh, and H. E. Wolff (eds), *Optimizing Learning and Education in Africa – the Language Factor*, pp. 56–83. Paris: Association for the Development of Education in Africa, ADEA.

Kioko, A., Mutiga, J., Muthwii, M., Schroeder, L., Inyega, H., and Trudell, B. (2008). *Language and Education in Africa: Answering the questions*. Nairobi: A Production of the Multilingual Education Network of Eastern Africa. <http://unesdoc.unesco.org/images/0018/001869/186961e.pdf> accessed November 2012.

Kosenen, K. (2006). 'Multigrade Teaching Among Ethnic Minority Children: The Language issue'. In L. Cornish (ed.), *Reaching EFA Through Multi-Grade Teaching: Issues, contexts and practices*, pp. 239–58. Armidale, NSW, Australia: Kardoorair Press.

McLaughlin, B. (1984). *Second-language Acquisition in Childhood: Volume 1, Preschool Children*. Hillsdale, NJ: Erlbaum.

Malone, S. (2010). *Language Development and Language Education: Components of successful mother tongue based multilingual education programs.* <http://mle-network.org/sites/default/files/Components%20of%20MTB%20MLE%20 programs.pdf> accessed November 2012.

Mohanty, K. (2006). 'Multilingualism of the Unequals and Predicaments of Education in India: Mother tongue or other tongue?' In O. Garcia, T. Skutnabb-Kangas, and M. E. Torres-Guzman, *Imagining Multilingual schools*, pp. 262–79. Clevedon: Multilingual Matters.

Nicholas, H., and Lightbown, P. M. (2008). 'Defining Child Second Language Acquisition: Defining roles for L2 instruction'. In J. Philp, R. Oliver, and A. Mackey (eds), *Child's play: Second language acquisition and the younger learner*, pp. 27–51. Amsterdam: John Benjamins.

NMRC (2009a). *Andhra Pradesh – MLE Status Report.* <http://www.nmrc-jnu.org/nmrc_img/Andhra%20Pradesh-%20MLE%20status%20report.pdf> accessed November 2012.

NMRC (2009b). *Orissa – MLE Status Report.* <http://www.nmrc-jnu.org/nmrc_img/Orissa-%20MLE%20status%20report.pdf> accessed November 2012.

NMRC (2011). *NMRC Newsletter Swara*, 1, 6–7. <http://www.nmrc-jnu.org/nmrc_img/Newsletter_6%20&%207_Proof%206_19%20Nov%202011%20(1).pdf> accessed November 2012.

Pinnock, H., MacKenzie, P., Pearce, E., and Young, C. (2011). *Closer to Home: How to help schools in low- and middle-income countries respond to children's language needs.* CfBT Education Trust and Save the Children International. <https://www.cfbt.com/evidenceforeducation/pdf/CloserToHome.pdf> accessed November 2012.

Pinnock, H. (2009a). *Steps Toward Learning: A Guide to overcoming language barriers in children's education.* London: Save the Children UK. <http://www.savethechildren.org.uk/en/docs/Steps_Towards_Learning_LR.pdf> accessed November 2012.

Pinnock, H. (2009b). *Language and Education: The Missing link.* CfBT and Save the Children Alliance. <http://www.savethechildren.org.uk/en/docs/Language_Education_the_Missing_Link.pdf> accessed November 2012.

Pinnock, H. (nd). *Reflecting Language Diversity in Children's Schooling: Moving from 'Why multilingual education' to 'How?'* CfBT and Save the Children International. <http://www.cfbt.com/evidenceforeducation/pdf/Research%20 Report%20FINAL.pdf> accessed November 2012.

Thomas, W., and Collier, V. (1997). 'School Effectiveness for Language Minority Students', *NCBE Resource Collection Series*, 9. USA: National Clearinghouse for

Bilingual Education, George Mason University. <http://www.thomasandcollier.com/Downloads/1997_Thomas-Collier97.pdf> accessed November 2012.

Thomas, W., and Collier, V. (2002). *A National Study of School Effectiveness for Language Minority Students: Long term academic achievement.* Centre for Research on Education, Diversity, and Excellence (CREDE). George Mason University. <http://www.usc.edu/dept/education/CMMR/CollierThomasExReport.pdf> accessed November 2012.

Vijayakumar, G. (2010). *Getting Ready for School in the Chittagong Hill Tracts: A comparative analysis of mother-tongue-and national-language-based preschools in Adivasi communities.* Research conducted for the SUPER fellowship program, USA: Save the Children.

UNESCO (2003). *Education in a Multilingual World.* Paris: UNESCO. <http://unesdoc.unesco.org/images/0012/001297/129728e.pdf> accessed November 2012.

UNESCO (2006). *Promoting Literacy in Multilingual Settings.* Bangkok: UNESCO. <http://unesdoc.unesco.org/images/0015/001507/150704e.pdf> accessed November 2012.

UNESCO (2008). *Improving the Quality of Mother Tongue-Based Literacy and Learning: Case studies from Asia, Africa, and South America.* Bangkok: UNESCO. <http://unesdoc.unesco.org/images/0017/001777/177738e.pdf> accessed November 2012.

UNESCO (2010). *Global Monitoring Report: Reaching the Marginalised.* UNESCO and Oxford University Press. <http://unesdoc.unesco.org/images/0018/001866/186606E.pdf> accessed November 2012.

SARAH QUINN AND SUE KRAFTSOFF

17 Maintaining the Mother Tongue: An Exploratory Study of Russian-Speaking Immigrant Parents' Opinions on Maintaining their Primary Language in their Children

Introduction

In the last fifteen years, Ireland has seen an influx of immigrants from all over the world, which has ensured Ireland's status as a multi-ethnic and multicultural society. At the time of this study's data collection in 2006, approximately 12.5 per cent (465,330) of the population of Ireland were non-Irish nationals (Central Statistics Office 2007).

The period of high immigration, between 1996 and 2002, saw a 55.3 per cent increase in the number of work permits issued to migrants from the former Eastern Bloc countries in Europe. By 2002, this region of Europe was amongst the top five countries providing migrant workers and asylum seekers to Ireland (Garner 2004). According to the Central Statistics Office (2008), a total of 24,628 Lithuanian nationals and 13,319 Latvian nationals were living in Ireland in 2006. Many immigrants from these countries spoke Russian as their primary language.

The economic downturn in Ireland since 2008 has triggered a sharp fall in immigration. In the third quarter of 2010 the estimated number of non-Irish nationals in the labour force was 276,600, signifying a decrease of 40,900 or almost 13 per cent in the year (Central Statistics Office 2010). However, of the thousands who have remained, many have, by now, made Ireland their home.

It has been seen that as part of moving to a different culture, members of linguistic minorities go through the process of acculturation – from marginalization to integration – in order to become fully functional members of the dominant society (Berry et al. 2002). A practical problem for migrants in moving to a new country is how to integrate with majority culture without losing their own cultural heritage and language (Ng 2007). Studies have found that children of cultural minority groups generally acculturate at a faster pace than their parents (Birman and Trickett 2001), so there is often disharmony between the parents' maintenance of traditional ethnic values and culture and their children's experiences of the host country's culture (Kwak 2003).

Part of the acculturation process involves learning the language of the host country (Ng 2007). While the acquisition of a secondary, majority language may be an essential part of integrating into the host country's culture, studies of Hispanic and Vietnamese minorities in the USA showed that maintenance of the primary, minority language is also very much valued by linguistic minorities (Craig 1996; Young and Tran 1999). Irrespective of their ethnic and social background, these non-English speaking minorities considered maintenance of the primary language in their children as essential to their cultural identity and ethnic pride. Although the first generation of minority groups may work hard to maintain their mother tongue, studies have found that the day-to-day language of choice for subsequent generations (their children) is the dominant language of the culture in which they are immersed (Slavik 2001).

Several factors have been found to be important to primary language maintenance. Bradley (2002) claimed that the attitude of the linguistic minority towards their language is crucial. Burck (2005) placed great importance on achieving the right balance between speaking the majority, secondary language and the primary language. She found that the primary language was more easily lost when the bilingual individual chose to, or was required to, predominantly speak the secondary language. According to Bradley, when the range of social circumstances in which the primary language is spoken is broad, particularly if open to non-family outside speakers of the same language, ongoing maintenance of that language is more likely and any potential language loss is delayed.

While language maintenance may depend on the use of the primary language within the minority community, and the transmission of language values from parent to child, Bradshaw (2006) believed that the education system could support this through its language instruction programmes. Other studies have found that for the primary language to be properly maintained children must learn more than the household vernacular; they need to learn the academic language such as is typically taught in schools (Wong Fillmore 1991; Schiff-Myers 1992; Cummins 1994). For instance, Winsler et al. (1999) found that attendance at a bilingual pre-school supported the development of the primary language.

A common bilingual behaviour is code switching (the alternate use of languages between sentences) (Guiberson et al. 2006). The ideal bilingual is defined as a person who is able to switch from one language to another according to linguistic circumstances but not within the same conversation or sentence. Some believe that this ideal bilingual situation is said to assist bilingual acquisition whereas code-switching prevents successful language acquisition (Ochs and Schieffelin 2006) resulting in language deficiency (Cheng and Butler 1989). Others consider code-switching to be a typical behaviour that occurs at all stages of language development (Backus 1999; Brice and Andersen 1999).

In Ireland, the opportunities to maintain primary minority languages formally within the secondary level education system are limited to a selection of ten modern languages (including English and Irish) that can be taken as Leaving Certificate examinations (though not necessarily taught in the schools). Russian has been included in this subject list since 2003 (Department of Education and Science 2006). At primary level, in 2006, there were 394 primary schools across the country participating in a government initiative to introduce modern European languages into the curriculum; unfortunately, the languages offered were limited to Italian, Spanish, German and French (National Development Plan 2000–6). The National Development Plan 2007–13 aims to build on the success of language initiatives in schools and to continue to invest in language learning.

Despite the increase in linguistic minorities in Ireland in the last decade, and the large number of Russian speakers amongst these, there has been very little research exploring their views on the maintenance of their primary language and its contribution to the preservation of their cultural identity in Ireland. The personal experience of one of the authors of moving to Ireland from Belarus in the late nineties prompted this exploratory study. The study set out to investigate the opinions of parents, who, like those in the literature, attributed importance to maintaining their primary language in their children; how and why they might achieve this within an Irish context, as well as other issues of relevance, were explored.

Methodology

Introduction

The aim of the study was to explore Russian-speaking parents' views on maintaining their mother tongue in their children, including how and why they hoped to do this. Given the dearth of previous Irish-based research, the study was viewed and designed as exploratory in nature and conducted with the aim of informing future related studies in the Irish context.

The study employed a mixed-method design, which used a self-administered questionnaire as a quantitative measure of data collection followed by a focus group as a qualitative measure.

Description of measures

Originally compiled in English and then translated into Russian by a native Russian speaker, many of the questions on the thirteen-item questionnaire were constructed on Likert scales to provide information on a range of strengths of opinions. The questionnaire collected information on the following:

Demographic information on the children, including age, gender, school level.

Parents' perceptions of the importance of Russian and other languages.
Parents' reasons to maintain the primary language.
Parents' strategies to encourage the maintenance of the desired language.

The focus group, conducted post-survey to further explore its main themes, involved a semi-structured group discussion facilitated, through Russian, by the primary researcher. In addition to the issues of why and how parents maintained their children's Russian language, topics discussed were: parents' opinions of different levels of Russian between siblings, children's language preferences and children's ease of cultural assimilation.

Preparatory work

All written information related to the study (participant information leaflet, questionnaire, consent form) was translated from English into Russian by a native Russian speaker.

Following translation, the questionnaire and focus group interview schedule were piloted on two Russian-speaking parents living in Ireland, who did not take part in the study otherwise. Their recommendations were accepted and incorporated into the data collection measures.

The sample and language school

Given the exploratory nature of this study, a sample of convenience was accessed. Parents, whose primary language was Russian and whose children (all under eighteen years) attended a Russian-speaking language school, comprised the study sample. The questionnaire was distributed to one parent of each child attending the Russian language school (N=20 parents). The survey response rate was 80 per cent making a sample size of sixteen parents. These parents reported on a total of twenty-four children. Additionally, five of the surveyed parents participated in the subsequent focus group interview. The language school takes place twice per week from 9.00 to 13.00 hours each Saturday and Sunday. It is supported by the Russian Orthodox Church with the sole purpose of developing and maintaining the primary language of children of Russian-speaking origin and teaches Russian, at elementary and secondary level, following the education curriculum in Russia (Naumov 2008).

Data collection

Having gained permission from the language school principal to access the sample population, all parents of children attending the school were invited to a presentation to introduce and explain the study. At this point written information on the study, together with questionnaires and focus groups consent forms, were distributed to all in attendance (N=20).

Sixteen questionnaires were returned anonymously to a sealed box in the language school. Parents interested in participating in the focus group also returned their contact details to this box but on a separate page to maintain anonymity of the questionnaire. The focus group, consisting of five parents who were native Russian speakers, was audiotaped and was facilitated through Russian by the principal investigator. It lasted approximately an hour and a half.

Methodological rigour

The following measures were undertaken to enhance the credibility of the study's results generally and address reliability and validity issues in the self-designed questionnaire: a thorough description of the study design to support generalization and external validity; the use of a representative sample of questions and piloting to aid content validity (recommended by Peat 2002); and the triangulation of method using qualitative and quantitative measures to improve construct validity (Batavia 2001).

Focus group rigour was ensured by coding and recoding of qualitative data and reflexivity on behalf of the primary researcher.

After both sets of data were translated and transcribed by the researcher they were additionally checked for accuracy by two native Russian speakers, which enhanced the linguistic accuracy, cultural relevance and thus sensitivity of measures.

Ethical approval was granted by the Faculty of Health Science Research Ethics Committee in Trinity College Dublin prior to data collection.

Limitations

There was a potential for sampling bias due to non-randomized selection of the study's sample. This was reduced by not extrapolating beyond the results (Hayes 2000). Although the survey sample size was small, it produced a high response rate, indicating little non-response bias. The addition of the qualitative focus group information, with its required alternative data analysis method, further added to the volume of data and depth of results. The above strategies reduced bias and increased trustworthiness and generalizability of the study (Berg and Latin 2004).

The following section describes the study's findings. As both qualitative and quantitative measures addressed the same issues, findings are presented together under five main headings.

Results

Description of sample

The questionnaire respondents were sixteen Russian-speaking parents who together reported on twenty-four children in total (seventeen boys and seven girls). Twenty-one of these attended primary school and were aged between five to eleven years. The remaining three children were aged between twelve and sixteen years and attending secondary school. Of the sixteen families in the study, half had only one child. There were seven families with two children and only one with three children.

The length of time the families lived in Ireland varied from three to ten and a half years, with an average length of just under seven years. Of the twenty-four children, half were born in Ireland. The following figure (Figure 1) outlines where children were born.

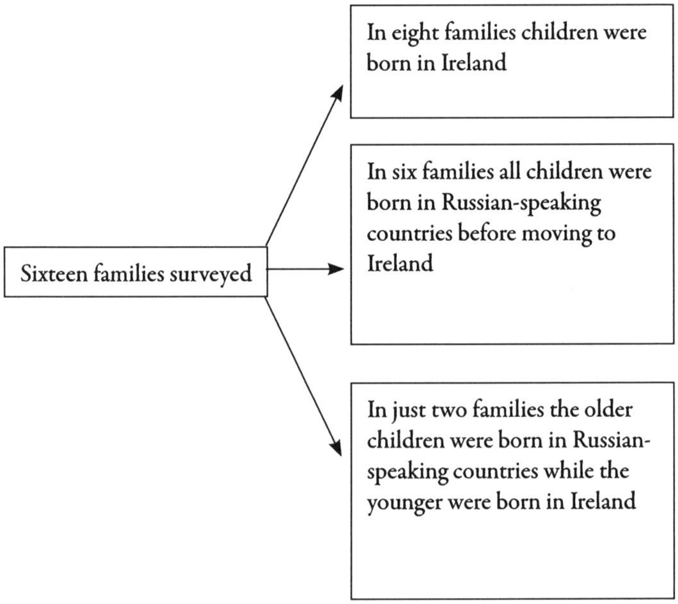

Figure 1 Where children were born – Ireland or Russian-speaking countries

Parents in the focus group were represented by three parents from three families and two parents from the same family, reporting on seven children (six of these were from two sibling families and one was a lone child; and four of the children were born in Ireland).

Status of Russian language in families

Despite a number of families originally hailing from Slavonic countries other than Russia, questionnaire respondents reported that all parents spoke Russian with their children and twenty-three of the children spoke

Russian with their parents (one did not answer this question). Just three children were considered by their parents, in their questionnaire responses, to have sufficient skill to use Russian in Russian-speaking countries. Fifteen were able to communicate with other native Russian speakers (friends and relatives) within the Irish context while eight children spoke Russian within the immediate family only (that is, with parents and siblings).

Exploring children's use of Russian further, focus group participants explained that their children tended to move between Russian and English languages quite freely, often mid-conversation, depending on who they were talking to, but at all times exhibiting an obvious preference for speaking English. Parents claimed to observe children language switching particularly when the use of Russian was not essential, for example when those with limited English proficiency (including parents) were not present and when there was a choice of language available (when interacting with bilinguals). One participant claimed that her children spoke Russian, 'only with those who have bad English; they only speak Russian because they have to'. Another stated that 'when playing [her children] begin to switch to English'.

A focus group parent described how her son had attended the Russian language school for 'the whole year, won't anymore... doesn't show any interest, he didn't understand anything anyway, so all in vain'. This parent went on to say that 'it seems that English is superseding Russian'. She gave an example of her children attempting to translate Russian sayings from Russian cartoons into English.

While all focus group parents considered their children to be fluent English speakers, four also perceived their children to be fluent for their age in spoken Russian. However, the focus group parents also recognized that certain aspects of the language, for example the spoken language, were more developed than others, such as written language. The majority of the questionnaire parents (eleven out of sixteen) seemed doubtful that Leaving Certificate level Russian would be achieved by their children and just five parents were confident their children would actually take the Leaving Certificate Russian exam. Three of the focus group parents specifically attributed their children's failure to develop their Russian language skills to the lack of available tuition in Russian and all focus group parents were unanimous in their support for the introduction of Russian as a secondary school curricular option.

Language differences within families

Parents in the focus group reported that there were often great differences in the level of Russian language competency between siblings. Some believed that their children's Russian language competency was related to the country in which their children's early language had developed; if the child moved to Ireland, having previously lived in a Russian-speaking country and attended school, they felt the child's Russian was at a higher competency level than that of their sibling or friends born in Ireland.

These parents also attribute differences between siblings' levels of language competency to different levels of parental investment in teaching Russian to their children as they grew up. One focus group parent explained that she 'spent more time' with her older daughter, 'working on her Russian'. She went on to say that her older daughter, 'tells more fairy-tales, knows more poems, speaks better, whereas [her younger son] got it harder, he's better off in English'. With regards to age-related differences between siblings, the converse was also true. One parent felt that as her son grew older his English improved while his Russian became weaker while her youngest 'speaks fluent Russian, loves Russian cartoons [...] the oldest doesn't understand Russian films anymore [...] he reads, but doesn't get the expressions at all, what they mean'.

Importance of, and reasons for, maintaining Russian

Questionnaire participants described the importance of their children having fluent Russian and English on a scale of one to four (from 'not at all important' to 'very important'). It was found that while having fluency in Russian was 'very important' to eight parents, these same parents also held the English language in equal importance. The following figure (Figure 2) shows how parents rated language fluency. No parent rated the acquisition of either Russian or English as unimportant.

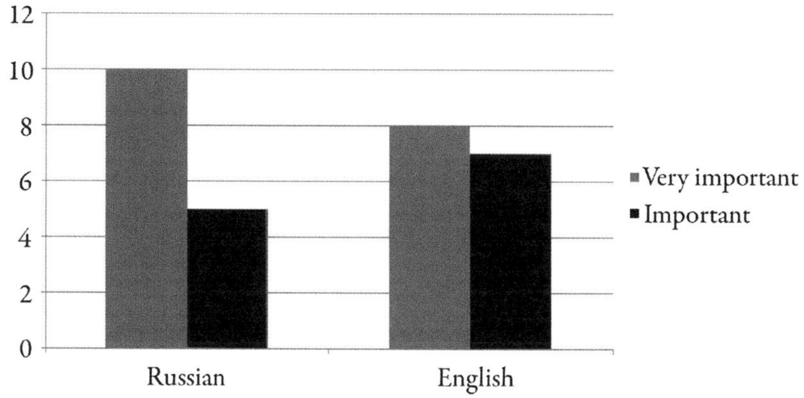

Figure 2 Importance parents attributed to having fluency in English and Russian languages (n=15 as one parent did not answer this question).

Questionnaire respondents were asked to identify the main reason they might value their children's maintenance of Russian. The protection or preservation of their 'cultural heritage' and the 'knowledge of languages' were the key reasons. Two parents valued competency in Russian so that their children might communicate with those in their homeland. Several respondents identified more than one main reason for maintaining their children's Russian so the responses (see Figure 3, see p. 322) are greater in number than the total sample of sixteen parents.

While all parents were keen to maintain their primary language in their children, not all children were similarly focused. One focus group parent explained that '[t]hey don't want to learn. I mean, all they want is to play or do nothing. [To maintain Russian it] becomes necessary to work very hard, of course [...] Sometimes there just isn't enough moral strength [...] but [we, the parents] do our best to give our best effort so that we don't lose it'.

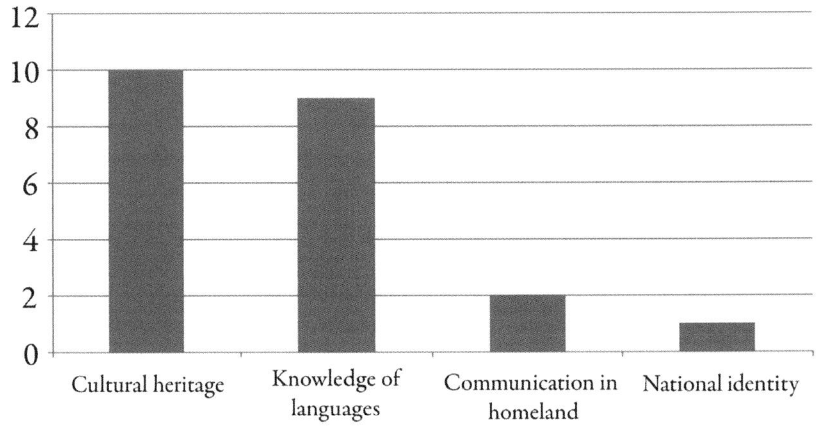

Figure 3 Parents' reasons for maintaining their children's Russian

Strategies parents used to maintain their children's Russian language

All of the focus group participants agreed that they actively encouraged their children to speak Russian through using Russian in their interactions with their children. Of the sixteen questionnaire respondents, fourteen spoke Russian to their children at all times, and the remainder said they 'regularly' used Russian in their interactions with the children. The most frequently used methods of maintaining Russian language, that were also cited as the most readily accessible by parents, were reading (reported by ten parents) and watching TV/DVDs/video games (reported by nine parents). Six parents also gave their children additional homework support or tuition. Other strategies used by focus group parents included: writing, listening to Russian songs and fairytales and learning Russian poems.

Not surprisingly, given the source of the sample, another method of maintaining the Russian language encouraged by all parents was their children's attendance at a weekend Russian-speaking language school. While all of the parents highly valued the educational opportunities the school offered their children, focus group participants were aware of its limitations. Its weekend service, where children usually attend classes on either Saturday or Sunday, fell short when compared to time devoted to teaching and learning other languages within the Irish education system. As one parent said: '[O]f course, [this way of] learning Russian is not sufficient. I would ideally like to have it more often, more of it, and more often'. They wished for more frequent Russian classes to match 'the level in the Russian education system', which was 'about five times more demanding'.

Discussion

In this study, parents cited cultural heritage (the most frequent reason), national identity, and communication in the homeland and with Russian-speaking people among other reasons, for maintaining the primary language – Russian – in their children. These findings were consistent with those of Craig (1996) whose participants, Spanish-speaking parents in the USA, identified reasons such as ethnic pride in their cultural and linguistic roots, cultural maintenance and fear of heritage loss, and communication with family and other Hispanic people as motives for maintaining Spanish in their children.

Measures taken by the Russian-speaking parents in this study to maintain their children's primary language skills, such as attending a Russian-speaking language school, were also comparable with the literature: Young and Tran (1999) found that Vietnamese parents in San Diego (USA) used a Saturday language school run by the Vietnamese community for children to learn the language, culture and customs. Although the majority of parents in this study, and in the literature (for example, Young and Tran 1999), spoke only their primary language in the home environment, children were reported to switch between Russian and English, at times mid-conversation, and at all times favouring the use of English. In this way the term 'ideal bilingual' did not apply to the natural, everyday interactions of these children. This finding was in keeping with that of an experimental study of German-Italian speaking families, which showed that code switching was an inherent part of natural speech of bilinguals, regardless of age, language, or proficiency (Ochs and Schieffelin 2006).

Support for maintaining the primary language by participants in this study was coupled with equally strong support for learning English and consistent with findings of other studies that indicated overall positive attitudes of parents of various ethnic and socio-economic backgrounds towards bilingualism and bilingual education (Craig 1996; Young and Tran 1999). The importance of proficiency in the majority language has already been recognized in the UK, where those applying for naturalization as a British citizen, or indefinite leave to remain (settlement in the UK), must provide evidence of their skill in the English language by taking certain examinations and classes (Border and Immigration Agency 2003). The Irish government has English language fluency as a core goal of its integration policy and hopes to make it one of the criteria for nationalisation in the future (Fanning and Munck 2008). The Office of the Minister for Integration (2009) believes that learning and practising English is very important to improve the quality of life, both socially and economically, for linguistic minorities living in Ireland. The value that the parents in this study placed on their children learning English demonstrated their understanding of its importance in the context of living in a predominantly English-speaking country.

However, it is thought that the case for supporting language development should not be an either/or situation. Instead, Cummins (2001) states that when promoted together, both languages enrich each other rather than subtract from each other, a claim supported by the work of Stagg Peterson and Heywood (2007). Certainly parents in the current study were of the opinion that both Russian and English language development was important for their children. Children who are able to maintain both languages may be better able to retain the values of their original culture, thus becoming bicultural – the most adaptive outcome for a linguistic minority (Romeo et al. 2004).

The focus group parents commented that it was easier to develop and maintain their children's Russian language when it was taught in school.

These parents were also keen to promote the written as well as the oral language. The literature recommends, for true language maintenance, that children should learn their primary language formally, in the cognitive academic way that is typically taught in schools (Wong Fillmore 1991; Schiff-Myers 1992; Cummins 1994). Bradshaw (2006) claimed that the maintenance of minority language requires commitment on several levels; that families have a role to play but so too do schools and other social institutions.

Conclusion

The parents in this study were overwhelmingly in favour of supporting their children's Russian language development. However, many feared that their children's skills and/or motivation to maintain their mother tongue were low. Given the strong link in the literature between primary language development and cultural heritage, ethnic pride, communal and personal identity, and the solid evidence for intergenerational language loss, these parents' interest in language maintenance, and fear for its loss, were both realistic and understandable concerns. With high numbers of immigrants in Ireland from Eastern Europe whose primary language is Russian, there is a demand for some external support for bilingual programmes.

References

Backus, A. (1999). 'Mixed Native Languages: A Challenge to the monolithic view of language', *Topics in Language Disorders*, 19, (4), 11–22.

Batavia, M. (2001). *Clinical Research for Health Professionals: A User-friendly Guide.* Boston: Butterworth-Heinemann.

Berg, K. E., and Latin, R. W. (2004). *Essentials of Research Methods In Health, Physical Education, Exercise Science, and Recreation*. 2nd ed. Philadelphia: Lippincott Williams and Wilkins.

Berry, J. W., Poortinga, Y. H., Segall, M. H., and Dasen, P. R. (2002). *Cross Cultural Psychology: Research and applications*. Cambridge, UK: Cambridge University Press.

Birman, D., and Trickett, E. J. (2001). 'Cultural Transitions in First-Generation Immigrants: Acculturation of Soviet Jewish refugee adolescents and parents', *Journal of Cross-Cultural Psychology*, 32, (4), 456–77.

Border and Immigration Agency. (2003). *Life in the UK Test*. <http://www.lifeintheuktest.gov.uk/htmlsite/background_10.html> accessed 25 February 2011.

Bradley, D. (2002). 'Language Attitudes: The Key factor in language maintenance'. In D. Bradley and M. Bradley (eds), *Language Endangerment and Language Maintenance*, pp. 77–97. London: Routledge Curzon.

Bradshaw, J. (2006). 'Parent and Child Perspectives on Greek Language Education in Australia', *International Journal of Sociology of Language*, 180, 43–54.

Brice, A., and Andersen, R. (1999). 'Code Mixing in a Young Bilingual Child. Communication', *Disorders Quarterly*, 21, (1), 17–22.

Burck, C. (2005). *Multilingual Living: Explorations of language and subjectivity*. Hampshire: Palgrave Macmillan.

Central Statistics Office (2010). *Quarterly National Household Survey*, Quarter 3, 2010. <http://www.cso.ie/releasespublications/documents/labour_market/current/qnhs.pdf>.

Central Statistics Office (2007). *Census 2006. Usual Residence, Migration, Birthplace and Nationalities*. Dublin: Stationary Office.

Central Statistics Office (2008). *Census 2006. Non-Irish Nationals Living in Ireland*. Dublin: Stationary Office.

Cheng, L. R., and Butler, K. (1989). 'Code Switching: A Natural phenomena versus language deficiency', *World Englishes*, 8, 293–309.

Craig, B. (1996). 'Parental Attitudes Toward Bilingualism in a Local Two-Way Immersion Program', *Bilingual Research Journal*, 20, (3–4), 383–410.

Cummins, J. (1994). 'Primary Language Instruction and the Education of Language Minority Students'. In C. Leyba (ed.), *Schooling and Language Minority Students* 2nd ed, pp. 3–46. Los Angeles: Evaluation, Dissemination and Assessment Centre, California State University.

Cummins, J. (2001). *Negotiating Identities: Education for empowerment in a diverse society* 2nd ed. Los Angeles: California State University.

Department of Education and Science (2006). *State Examinations Commission. Leaving Certificate Examination 2006. Chief Examiner's Report.*

<http://www.examinations.ie/archive/examiners_reports/cer_2006/CE_REPORT_2006RussianLC.pdf> accessed 25 February 2011.

Fanning, B., and Munck, R. (2008). 'Editorial', *Translocations*, 3, (1), 1–4.

Garner, S. (2004). *Racism in the Irish Experience*. Dublin: Pluto Press.

Guiberson, M. M., Barrett, K. C., Jancosek, E. G., and Yoshinaga Itano, C. (2006). 'Language Maintenance and Loss in Preschool-Age Children of Mexican Immigrants: Longitudinal study', *Communication Disorders Quarterly*, 28, 4–17.

Hayes, N. (2000). *Doing Psychological Research: Gathering and analysing data*. Buckingham: Open University Press.

Kwak, K. (2003). 'Adolescents and their Parents: A Review of intergenerational family relations for immigrant and non-immigrant families', *Human Development*, 46, (2–3), 15–136.

National Development Plan 2000–2006 (2007). *Modern Languages In Primary Schools Initiative*. <http://www.ndp.ie/docs/Language_Initiative/478.htm> accessed 25 February 2011.

National Development Plan 2007–2013 (2007) *Transforming Ireland: A Better quality of life for all*. <http://www.ndp.ie/documents/ndp2007–2013/NDP-2007–2013-English.pdf> accessed 25 February 2011.

Naumov, A. (2008). 'The Emerald Isle'. In *Russkiy Mir Foundation*. <http://russkiymir.org/en/publications/index.php?id4=3532> accessed 25 February 2011.

Ng, S. H. (2007). 'From Language Acculturation to Communication Acculturation: Addressee orientations and communication brokering in conversations', *Journal of Language and Social Psychology*, 26, (1), 75–90.

Ochs, E., and Schieffelin, B. (2006). 'The Impact of Language Socialisation on Grammatical Development'. In C. Jourdan and K. Tuite (eds), *Language, Culture And Society: Key topics in linguistic anthropology*, pp. 168–89. Cambridge: Cambridge University Press.

Office of the Minister for Integration (2009). *Learning English*. <http://www.integration.ie/website/omi/omiwebv6.nsf/page/infoformigrantslearningenglish-en> accessed 25 February 2011.

Peat, J. (2002). *Health Science Research: A Handbook of quantitative methods*. London: Sage Publications.

Romero, A. J., Robinson, T. N., Haydel, K., Farish, B. A., Mendoza, F., and Killen, J. D. (2004). 'Associations Among Familism, Language Preference, and Education in Mexican-American Mothers and Their Children', *Journal of Developmental and Behavioural Pediatrics*, 25, (1), 34–40.

Schiff-Myers, N. B. (1992). 'Considering Arrested Language Development and Language Loss in the Assessment of Second Language Learners', *Language, Speech, and Hearing Services in Schools*, 23, 28–33.

Slavik, H. (2001). 'Language Maintenance and Shift Among Maltese Migrants in Ontario and British Columbia', *International Journal of the Sociology of Language*, 152, 131–52.

Stagg Peterson, S., and Heywood, D. (2007). 'Contributions of Families' Linguistic, Social, and Cultural Capital to Minority-Language Children's Literacy: Parents', teachers', and principals' perspectives', *The Canadian Modern Language Review*, 63, 517–37.

Winsler, A., Diaz, R. M., Espinosa, L., and Rodriguez, J. L. (1999). 'When Learning a Second Language does not Mean Losing the First: Bilingual language development in low- income, Spanish speaking children attending bilingual preschool', *Child Development*, 70 (2), 349–62.

Wong Fillmore, L. (1991). 'When Learning a Second Language Means Losing the First', *Early Childhood Research Quarterly*, 6 (3), 323–46.

Young, R. L., and Tran, M. T. (1999). 'Vietnamese Parent Attitudes Toward Bilingual Education', *Bilingual Research Journal*, 23 (2–3), 113–21.

Notes on Contributors

MICHAEL BLANEY studied Social Policy and Criminology at the Open University where he gained his primary degree. He completed a Masters in Social Policy at University College Cork in 2009. He is an outreach worker with asylum seekers and refugees in Cork.

JOY CHALKE (BEd, MA) is a Principal Lecturer in the School of Education and Continuing Studies at the University of Portsmouth, specializing in early childhood education. She has worked on a range of research projects with early years practitioners who are her students, investigating the attitudes and experiences of educators within the sector. Her doctoral study is an exploration of ideas around personal and professional identities in the field of Early Childhood Education.

JOHANNA DAVIS, a native of Germany, began to work for and with children in 2003 in a musical project in Argentina. An academic career in early childhood was soon to follow in her new adopted home country of Ireland. This has turned a love of children into a passion for childhood, which permeates her work in teaching, research, advocacy and practice in early childhood. Particular areas of interest include quality and equality issues, early childhood development aid and the development of creativity in children as well as adults who work with children. Her professional life is dedicated to the improvement of children's lives from micro-interactions to macro-policies.

ANNE M. DOLAN is a Lecturer in Primary Geography with the Department of Learning, Society and Religious Education at Mary Immaculate College, Limerick. She has recently conducted research into picture-books and their applicability to global education and is the author of *You, Me and Diversity: The potential of picture-books for teaching development and intercultural education* (in press).

ROSARII GRIFFIN specializes in international and comparative education and is currently a Lecturer in Adult Continuing Education at University College Cork, as well as working in Finance. She is Co-Chair of CREATE, a UCC (HISRC)-Malawi project based on an EU FP7 €3.5 project. Since 2011, she has been an executive and founding member of the Centre for Global Development at UCC. From 2008–11, she directed the Centre for Global Development through Education (CGDE) at the University of Limerick, based on an €1.5m Irish Aid and Higher Education Authority (HEA) funding award. As Director of the Centre, she led six international projects in partnership with twelve Irish Higher Education Institutes and four African HEIs and Ministries. A former EU, UK and Oxford scholar, she has published four books and is currently working on a fifth book about international and comparative global educational issues (2013).

DEIRDRE HORGAN is a Lecturer in Social Policy in the School of Applied Social Studies and Director of the multi-disciplinary BA (Early Years and Childhood Studies) at University College Cork. Her research interests include childhood well-being and citizenship, within the broad framework of diversity. She has recently undertaken research on child trafficking and separated children in Ireland and is currently Principal Investigator on a government-funded research project on children and young people's participation in their homes, schools and communities.

MARY KELLETT is Professor of Childhood and Youth and Director of the Childhood, Youth and Education Programme at the Open University. Perhaps best known for her pioneering work to empower children as researchers, she founded the Children's Research Centre to train and support children and young people to undertake their own research. She has over thirty-five years' experience of working with children and young people as a social worker, primary teacher and academic. She holds a number of Adjunct Professorships in Australia and Europe and sits on several national and international advisory panels. She has written widely on a range of childhood and education issues, most notably on children's participation and voice and on child-led research.

MATEMOHO KHATLELI holds an MEd in Management of Special Education in Developing Countries and a BPhil Ed in Special Education – Visual Impairment. She is a Lecturer in the Department of Special Education at the Lesotho College of Education, Maseru and previously worked with the Department of Education and Training as an assistant inspector in the Special Education Unit. She was a member of the research team on the CGDE/LCE project on Identification and Assessment for children with disabilities in Lesotho.

SUE KRAFTSOFF is an Occupational Therapist, currently working with children with disabilities in Dublin Mid-Leinster. She completed her undergraduate degree in Occupational Therapy in Trinity College Dublin in 2007 and has been working in the Health Service Executive since. In 2011, she graduated with distinction from a postgraduate Masters in Disability Studies course from the National Institute for Intellectual Disability, Trinity College Dublin. She hopes to continue pursuing postgraduate academic studies in line with her work as an Occupational Therapist.

FLORENCE KYAKUDYA is a Lecturer in the Department of Special Education at the Lesotho College of Education, Maseru.

STELLA LONG is a Lecturer in Special Education at Mary Immaculate College, Limerick. She has undertaken research on special education in Lesotho and has presented nationally and internationally on this topic. She is co-author (with Jacqui O'Riordan, James Urwick and Maria Campbell) of the chapter 'Towards a holistic understanding of special educational needs', in *Teacher Education in Sub-Saharan Africa: Closer perspectives* (edited by Rosarii Griffin, 2012). In addition to her interest in development education, her expertise is in gifted education, dyspraxia, co-teaching and teaching mathematics to pupils with special educational needs. She is currently a PhD candidate at Trinity College Dublin.

SUSAN MCKAY is a psychologist, nurse and Arts and Sciences Distinguished Emeritus Professor at the University of Wyoming in Laramie, Wyoming. For almost two decades, she has taught and researched issues focused upon women, girls and armed conflict, women and peacebuilding, and feminist issues in peace psychology. She has published more than seventy-five books, book chapters and articles. Recent books include *Where Are the Girls? Girls in Fighting Forces in Northern Uganda, Sierra Leone, and Mozambique, Their Lives During and After War* (2004). Her recent funding comes from the Oak Foundation to study participatory strategies to promote reintegration of formerly-abducted girl soldiers in Northern Uganda, Sierra Leone and Liberia who return from fighting forces with children. She is past President of the Division of Peace Psychology of the American Psychological Association.

PAMELA MACKENZIE worked for several years as a primary teacher in the UK and in the Yemen Arab Republic, with a focus on both first and second language learning in education. She was awarded a PhD in Education from the University of Reading in 1994. Since then she has been supporting the development of multilingual education (MLE) and literacy programmes together with government, academic institutions, NGOs and international agencies. She is currently an education consultant where her main focus is on research, training, planning, supporting and evaluating the development of programmes which focus on language and education. She presents widely on issues relating to education in minority language communities, relating to both policy and practice, and is involved in international multi-agency advocacy to ensure quality education for marginalized groups.

NTHABELENG MAKETELA is associated with deaf education in Lesotho, where she has been engaged in teaching and supervising teacher trainees in Special Education at post-secondary institutions. She has worked at the Ministry of Education and Training as a general teacher and later on joined the Special Education Unit where she worked as an itinerant teacher. She has worked closely with teachers at Early Childhood Centres, primary schools and secondary schools to support learners with disabilities/SEN in Lesotho. She has taken part in research, particularly focusing on the education of learners with disabilities/SEN in Lesotho. She is also a member of the National Association of the Deaf in Lesotho (NADL).

SHIRLEY MARTIN has been a Lecturer in Social Policy at the School of Applied Social Studies, University College Cork, since 2004. Her main research interest is in the well-being of children and the focus of her research relates to key areas of children's lives, such as early years care and education, educational disadvantage and participatory research with children and young people. She is currently leading a government-funded research project examining young people's experiences of child and youth participation initiatives.

MAHIMA MITRA is reading for a DPhil in Social Policy in the University of Oxford's Department of Social Policy and Intervention. She completed an MPhil in Comparative Social Policy at Oxford in 2010 and an MSc in Child Development at the University of Delhi in 2006. She has worked as a Qualitative Research Analyst for the World Bank's New Delhi office for over two years and as a Lecturer for undergraduates in Human Development and Childhood Studies at the University of Delhi. Her research interests span family welfare policy, and early years and higher education policy.

UNA MURRAY is an international development consultant who provides expert and specialized consultancy services for a range of development organizations including the United Nations, Irish Aid and various NGOs. She works across a range of development areas including policy processes, mainstreaming issues in development institutions, gender analysis, child labour and small enterprise development. She has undertaken many evaluations, including those focused on child labour and policy implemented through the UN International Labour Organization (ILO). She is a lecturer providing modules on development-related issues in Irish universities, including University College Cork (UCC), and has also lectured in Ethiopia for UCC collaborative training initiatives. She has worked on development topics in Kenya, Tanzania, Uganda, Malawi, Ghana, Laos, Iran, Thailand, Sri Lanka and the Philippines.

GRACE NTAOTE holds a PhD in Education and is a Lecturer in the Department of Special Education at the Lesotho College of Education, Maseru.

SAMUEL OKYERE, a child rights advocate, recently completed his PhD at the University of Nottingham. His thesis was entitled *Understanding Child Labour: The Case of Children Working in Artisanal Gold Mining at Kenyasi, Ghana.* The thesis used the accounts of a group of children working in artisanal gold mining to examine the dominant representations of and legislation on children's involvement in precarious work. He conducted the fieldwork for this study as part of his role as research assistant on the project. He is currently a postdoctoral research fellow at the Centre for Advanced Studies at the University of Nottingham and mainly supports the university's Children and Childhood network.

JACQUI O'RIORDAN lectures in the School of Applied Social Studies at University College Cork. She has extensive experience in a range of equality concerns, through her research in Tanzania in the mid-1990s, as well as a number of community sector research consultancies undertaken in Ireland. Her research interests include gendered lives and livelihoods, analysis of care and caring and, more recently, examination of aspects of childhood and children's lives. She has recently undertaken research on trafficking in children and on children living in direct provision in Ireland.

HELEN PENN is Professor of Early Childhood and co-Director of the International Centre for the Study of the Mixed Economy of Childcare (ICMEC) at the Cass School of Education, University of East London. She has undertaken consultancies on early childhood education and care policies and practice for many international development agencies, including Save the Children, ISSA, UNESCO, UNICEF and the Asian Development Bank, as well as OECD and the EU. She has a particular interest in Southern Africa and Central Asia. She is the author of over 100 publications, including books, journal articles and chapters in books, as well as many development agency reports.

ANNIKA PISSIN is a Researcher at the Centre for East and South-East Asian Studies, Lund University. She studies children in imperial and contemporary China, with her main interest in the study of marginalized children and the use of child representation by political and economic actors.

SARAH QUINN has been an Assistant Professor in the discipline of Occupational Therapy at Trinity College Dublin since 2002. As well as having worked clinically in a variety of settings, including working privately with children with autism, she has more recently become involved in outreach work at a women's prison. Her current research interests are in exploring student development in community-based learning experiences. Her research MPhil was in the area of early childhood care and education.

BARNEY SHIELS is an experienced development practitioner with an extensive understanding of early childhood development (ECD) programming in the developing world. Previously, he managed a large Irish Aid funded programme in South Africa's Eastern Cape, focusing on community-based responses to HIV and AIDS, with a particular focus on ECD. Since leaving South Africa in 2010, he has focused on human rights, development policy and effectiveness – initially as Advocacy Officer with UNICEF Ireland, and most recently as Research, Learning and Advocacy Advisor with Irish Aid in Lusaka, Zambia.

JAMES URWICK is a specialist in educational policy and planning who has worked in various higher education institutions in Africa for long periods. His more recent research has focused on issues of basic education, teacher provision and educational quality that are relevant to the achievement of the Dakar goals in low-income countries. In 2009–10 he was a research fellow in the Centre for Global Development through Education at Mary Immaculate College, Limerick, Ireland.

ANGELA VEALE is a Lecturer in Applied Psychology at University College Cork. Her research and publications focus on participatory research, children and families in post conflict contexts, transnational families and psychological perspectives on globalization and migration. She was a Fulbright Scholar in the Program on Forced Migration and Health at Columbia University and a visiting professional in the Victim Participation and Reparation Unit at the International Criminal Court in The Hague.

KAREN WELLS is Senior Lecturer and Programme Director for International Childhood Studies at Birkbeck College. She is the author of *Childhood in a Global Perspective* (2009). Her research is on the intersection of international political economy (e.g. war, international law, global capitalism) with practices of childhood. She is currently researching the social networks of young refugees and is the Principal Investigator for the ESRC seminar series 'Violence and childhood: international perspectives'.

MICHAEL WESSELLS is Professor at Columbia University in the Program on Forced Migration and Health. A long-time psychosocial and child protection practitioner, he is former Co-Chair of the IASC Task Force on Mental Health and Psychosocial Support in Emergency Settings. Recently, he was co-focal point on mental health and psychosocial support for the revision of the Sphere humanitarian standards. He has conducted extensive research on the holistic impacts of war and political violence on children, and he is the author of *Child soldiers: From violence to protection* (2006). Currently, he is lead researcher on inter-agency, multi-country research on community-driven interventions for strengthening linkages with government-led aspects of national child protection systems. He regularly advises UN agencies, governments, and donors on issues of child protection and psychosocial support, including in communities and schools. Throughout Africa and Asia, he helps to develop community-based, culturally grounded programmes that assist people affected by armed conflict and natural disasters.

MIRANDA WORTHEN is Assistant Professor in Health Sciences at San Jose State University. She earned her PhD in Epidemiology from the University of California, Berkeley. She earned her BA from Harvard and her MPhil in International Development from Oxford University. Her research has primarily been in conflict or post-conflict countries in several countries in Africa, Asia and Europe. She has been working with young mothers who were child soldiers since 2003 and was a co-coordinator of a multiyear participatory action research study on young mothers formerly associated with armed groups in Sierra Leone, Liberia and northern Uganda.

She has also published on her research on prostitution and sex trafficking in Nepal and India. Her current research is a multidisciplinary study examining mental health and anger problems among United States military service members and veterans, and she is collaborating with colleagues to conduct a longitudinal study of Reserve and National Guard service members and their mental health needs.

Index

abduction 29, 30
Acholi customary law 32
adoption, illegal 19, 21
  transnational 11, 16, 18–22
advocacy 28, 102
Africa 291
  Central 16, 207–8
  East 16
  Southern 93
  Sub-Saharan 15, 20, 22, 32–3, 34, 51
  West 15–16, 48
  see also individual countries
agriculture 35
  children working in 51, 57–60
aid, indirect 115–16
aid projects 101
  drawbacks of 108, 109–10
aid workers *see* development practitioners
Alber, E. 17–18, 19
All-China Women's Federation 196, 198
Amazing Grace, Hoffman 274
Amelia to Zora, Chin-Lee 283
Annan, J. 28
anxiety 29, 189
Apio, E. 32
Appreciative Inquiry (AI) 120
apprenticeships 75
Archambault, C. 18
armed forces 27, 28
Arnold, S. 239, 241–3, 247
Asset-based Community Development (ABCD) 116
asylum seekers in Ireland 235, 238, 249–50
  accommodation 238, 241
  depictions of in picture books 278–9
  marginalization of 238–41, 243–5, 250
  social networks 246–7
  terminology 245
attachment theory 39
Australia 88

Baatombu children 17, 19
Badcock-Walters, P., Kelly, M. and Görgens, M. 135
Bader, B. 273–4
Bakker, I. and Gill, S. 12, 13
Baland, J. M. and Robinson, J. A. 69
Baldi, S. and MacKenzie, M. 28, 30–1
Ball, J. 295
Bangladesh 53, 70, 290, 304
Basotho nation 136, 138, 140
Bath, C. 224
Belarus 314
belonging 32, 36
Benin, North 17, 18
bikas 112–13
bilingualism 259–61, 267, 292, 300, 312, 324
  code switching 313, 323–4
  definition of 313
bilingual support assistants 256
Boller, K., Ross, C. and Paulsell, D. 100
Boothby, N. *et al* 32
Bose-O'Reilly, S. *et al* 74
Bosnia 86
Botswana 97, 134
Bourdillon, M. 53–4, 68

boys 29, 138, 183, 204
  child soldiers 32
  with disabilities 210
  left-behind 189
  work 17, 54, 73, 74
  see also gender
Bradley, D. 312
Bradshaw, J. 313, 325
brain development 99
Brazil 21, 71
Brett, R. and Specht, I. 28
Brown, D. 259
Brundtland Report 114–15
Burck, C. 312
Burman, E. and McKay, S. 32

Canagarajah, S. and Coulombe, H. 70–1
Canterbury University Childhood Research Centre 102
capitalism 12, 14, 21
Cardoso, A. R. and Verner, D. 71
care chains, global 14–15, 21
Carlson, H. L. and Stenmalm-Sjöblom, L. 171
Carlson, K. and Mazurana, D. 29–30
Carnegie, Andrew 89
Carr-Hill, R., Katabaro, K. J., Katahoire, A. R. and Oulai, D. 135
Carsten, J. 36, 38, 40
cash transfers 56, 91
Ceglowski, D. and Bacigalupa, C. 170, 173
Central Social Welfare Board, India 163
Centre for Equity Studies, India 167
Chad 19
charities 86–8
Charity Commission 90
child
  abuse 197
  circulation 16–17, 18, 22
  definition of 69, 183
  economic exploitation 18, 20, 52
  mortality rates 85, 108, 111, 183, 203–4
  relationship to mother 17, 18, 27, 32, 195
  well-being 94–5, 148, 167, 190, 247, 257
child labour *47–61, 67–77*, 111
  definition of 47, 49–50, 51, 53
  elimination of 52, 53, 59–61, 67
  statistics 48, 50
  supply factors 57
  types of work 48, 51, 53, 58
'child mothers' *see* mothers, formerly associated with armed forces
child work 53, 61, 70–1
  definition of 50–1, 53–4, 69
  positive aspects of 75–7
  trade unions 55
childcare 139, 196, 208
  government strategies 163–4, 166–7, 257
  private 96–7, 146, 167
  quality of 169
  statistics 165, 166
  see also crèches
Child Care Act 1991, Ireland 239
childhood 11, 69
  anthropology of 99
  definition of 54, 161, 183
  experience 244, 249, 281
  settings 255–6, 284
children
  abandoned 31, 32
  data collectors 225
  illegitimate 31
  migrant 181, 184
  left-behind *see* left-behind children
  participation in research 222–30, 232
  researchers 224–5, 231
  in social reproduction theory 13
children associated with armed forces or armed groups (CAAFAG) 27, 28–32, 34, 37–8

'children of bad memories' *see* children associated with armed forces or armed groups (CAAFAG)
Children's Investment Fund Foundation (CIFF) 89–90, 100
children's rights 59, 61, 85
China 231
  internal immigration 96, 181–3
  left-behind children *see* left-behind children
  rural 187, 191–3
  women in 195–6
  see also Great Leap Forward
  civil rights movement, America 281–2
  Cleveland, G. and Krashinsky, M. 208
  Cockburn, J. 71
  Collier, Paul 87
  Collingwood, C. 117
  Colour of Home, The, Hoffman 278
  Comber, B. 272
  community activities 34–5, 40
  community links 35
  Convention on the Rights of the Child, United Nations 124, 126, 161
  principles of 118, 206
  signatories 52, 147, 163, 183
Coombe, C. 135
Cooper-Huhn, Chris 89
Council for Assisting Academic Refugees (CARA) 88
Crawford, K. and Walker, J. 249
crèches 139, 165, 166
critical literacy 272–3
Crosswell, M. 110
Cryer, D., Tietze, W. and Wessels, H. 171
Cuba 94
Cummins, J. 260–1, 324
Currie, J. 172
Curry, P. *et al* 243, 245, 250
Dakar Agreement on Education for All 147
Dakar Framework for Education 132
data, collection of 95–6, 100, 102, 110, 122–3, 212
Davis, Johanna 5
de Sousa Santos, B. 110–11, 112
Democratic Republic of Congo 31
Department for Education and Science, UK 255
Department for International Development, UK (DfID) 87
  DfID *Young Lives Project* 100
Department of Education and Skills, Ireland 272
depression 29, 189
developing countries *see* global North/global South
Development and Change 96
development
  definition of 113, 213
  economics and 112–13
  educators 273
  measurement of 94, 99, 114, 134–5, 205, 206
  personal 118
  practices 112–13, 116, 120–6, 206
  sustainable 114–15, 132–3, 204
development economics 91, 97, 98
development practitioners
  Irish 107, 121–3
Developmentally Appropriate Practice 119
diamond ranking 224–5
Direct Provision 238–9
  education and 239–40, 242–5, 246–7; *see also* pre-school readiness
  statistics of 239, 242, 244
  centres 239, 240–1, 248
disability 210
  assessment of 155–6

disability, *cont.*
  education and 132
  pre-school 155
  statistics in Lesotho 146, *150–6*
  stigma 153
disarmament, demobilization and reintegration programmes (DDR) 30
discourses, hegemonic 119
diversity, responses to 255–6
domestic workers 14, 18
Dowd, F. S. 277
drug abuse 70
Dutcher, N. 292

Early Childhood Care and Development (ECCD) 139
Early Childhood Care and Education (ECCE) 93, 204, 207
  benefits of 4–5, 98, 248
  policy 5–6
  problems with 5
Early Childhood Care and Education Scheme, Ireland 4
Early Childhood Development (ECD) 5, 98, 108, 211
  benefits of 117–18
  community centres in Moldova 214
  definition of 93–5, 117, 207
  problems with 108–14, 118–19, 215
Early Childhood Education and Care (ECEC) 93, 95, 161–4, 168, 172–3
  parental perceptions of 170
  service quality 169–70
Early Childhood in Developing World Contexts International Conference 1
Early Years Foundation Stage Curriculum 256–8, 260, 266
economic productivity of individuals 98–9, 118

education 33, 49, 59
  development and 131–40; *see also* HIV/AIDS
  lack of 19, 28
  languages 290–1
  mother tongue 291–305; *see also* MTBMLE
  multicultural books 276; *see also* picture books
  primary 131–40, 289
  right to 55–7, 131
Education for All Campaign 70, 138, 213, 290
Edwards, M. 91–2
EFA Global Monitoring Report 134
Effective Provision of Pre-school Education (EPPE) 249
Egypt 58
Elizabeti's Doll, Stuve-Bodeen 275
employment 33, *47–60*; *see also* child labour *and* child work
  minimum age 47, 50, 52, 67
empowerment 102
England 21
English as an additional language (EAL) 255–6, 260, 261–5
English language 294
Enlightenment, Age of 111, 112, 192, 194
Equity Agenda, the 204
equity approach 203–17
equity, definitions of 206
Ethiopia 21, 58
Europe 18, 59, 94, 95, 111; *see also individual countries*
European Union 93, 98
'evidence based policy' 87, 100

families 18, 19, 36
  multiple 22
  rejection by 37–8

  reunification of 28
  transnational 4, 11, 16
family kinship 36
Fan, C. 70
Farmer, Paul 102
fathers 15, 96
  migrating 190, 192
feminism 13
'filles meres' *see* mothers, formerly associated with armed forces
Fireboat, Kalman 278
Fleischman, J. 89
Ford Foundation, the 89
fostering 16
  international 18–21; *see also* adoption, transnational
Foucault, M. 111
France 88, 131
Freire, Paulo 272
Fyfe, A. 70

Gates Foundation, Bill and Melinda 89
gender 29, 93, 96–8, 132, 182, 281–7
  equality 14, 132
  inequity 13, 97, 206, 210–11
  parity 138
  roles 54, 57, 73, 182
  stereotypes 281
Germany 135
Ghana 71
gift exchange of children 17
'girl mothers' *see* mothers, formerly associated with armed forces
girls
  associated with armed forces 27, 29, 30–2, 34, 37, 38; *see also* mothers, formerly associated with armed forces
  left-behind 189
  education of 56, 138, 183, 203, 210–11
  statistics of 55, 56, 239
  see also gender
Global Child Development steering group 28
Global Monitoring Report 138
global North 22, 94, 101, 107, 117, 119
global South 22, 15, 97, 107, 132
globalization 18, 255
gold-mining 70, 71–4
Gooden, A. M. and Gooden, M. A. 281
Goody, Esther 15
grandparents 15, 40, 187–8, 194–5, 199
Grantham-McGregor, S. 2
Greany, C. and Elliott, C. 120
Great Leap Forward, the 187–8
Green Belt Movement 282
Greene, Maxine 273
Gross Domestic Product (GDP) 114
Guarcello, L. *et al* 70
Guardian Aid Project, the 92–3

Hacking, I. 197
Haiti 102
Hancock, G. 90
Harriss-White, B. 56
Harvey, P. and Lauren, R. 69
Hashim, I. M. 72
Heymann, J. 96
Heady, C. 70
health 15, 16, 35, 39
  asylum seekers 242
  safety and 70, 74, 186
  statistics 87
  training 35
Health Service Executive, Ireland (HSE) 239
healthcare, free 102
Heckman, James 98
Hernanz, V. F. *et al* 171–2
Herz, N. 89, 90
Hindman, H. D. 69
Hinton, R. 54

HIV/AIDS 30, 102, 214–15, 230
  education 134–7, 139
  statistics 136–7
HIV Sentinel Survey Report 136–7
homelessness 20
Hulme, David 91
human capital 98–100
Human Development Index (HDI) 114–15, 145
human ecology 102
human rights 239
Humphries, T. 245
Hunan Province *see* China

IECCD (International Economic Cooperation Coordination Division) 145–7
If a Bus Could Talk, Ringold 281–2
illiteracy 56, 223
immigration 86, 96
  children 312
Impact of HIV/AIDS on Education and Institutionalizing Preventive Education: Education in the context of HIV/AIDS 135
India 48, 54, 85, 162–8
  Andhra Pradesh 58, 289–90, 291, 298, 300, 304
  education 56, 162
  Orissa 289–90, 291, 300, 304
inequality, global 85
infant mortality 11, 83, 85
infertility 17
INGOs *see* NGOs
Institute of Education, London University 88
Institute of Fiscal Studies 97
Integrated Child Development Services, India 163–4, 167
inter-ethnic integration 242–3, 245, 248, 250, 294
International Aid *85–102*
  funding chains 88
  projects 91
  tenders 88
International Labour Organization (ILO) 48, 49, 67, 68, 70, 73
  ILO Child Labour Programme 60
  ILO Convention 138 on Minimum Age of Workers 52, 67–8
  ILO Convention 182 on Minimum Age of Workers 52
  ILO Convention on Domestic Work 52
internet 193
Inuit 293
investment, private 89–90
International Pharmaceutical Excipient Councils 60
Iraq 88, 91
Ireland
  asylum seekers in *235–50*
  linguistic minorities 324
  Russian immigrants to 311, 313–14, 318, 320, 325
Irish Refugee Council 239
Irish-Aid 88

Jacka, T. 196
James, A. 222
Janani Suraksha Yojana (JSY) 165
Japan 135
Jones, N. *et al* 60
Jonglei Canal Project 113
Julios, C. 255
Just Children Story Sack 279–80, 284

Kamaiya 48
Kampala 86
Katz, L. 169, 173
Kenya 280
Kotze, H. 151, 153

Kuru Art Project 91
Kwankye, S. O. *et al* 72

labour
  bonded 48
  forced 47, 49
  see also child labour
Lake, Anthony 205
Lancet, The 97, 98, 100
language
  competency 320
  primary 311–16, 321, 323–5; *see also* mother tongue
  schools 304, 315–16, 319, 322–3
  stages of learning 297
Latin America 70, 95
Latino migration 14
Least Developed Countries (LDC) 133–4
left-behind children 15, 21–2, 182, 183, 185–6, 197
  definition of 185, 194–5, 197
  gender 189
  parents of 190, 195–6; *see also* mothers
  representation of 197, 198–9
  risks 186–9
  statistics 184–5
left-behind elderly 187–8
Lesotho *131–40*
  College of Education 148
  Council of Women 147
  Daycare and Community Centre 147
  disabled schools 151
  Education Act 2010 139
  Ministry of Education and Training 139
  National Disability and Rehabilitation Policy 154
  National Federation of Organisations for the Disabled 153
  Population and Housing Census 146
  Pre-school and Daycare Centre 147
LeVine, R. and New, R. 99
Levy, V. 58
Liberia 28, 34, 37, 41
Librarian of Basra, The, Winter 278
Liebel, M. 54, 55
Likert scales 318
literacy 131, 261, 263, 272, 292; *see also* critical literacy *and* illiteracy
  rates 87, 110, 151, 183
Little Chapel that Stood, The, Curtiss and Golino 278
Live Aid 85
Living Conditions Among People with Disabilities in Lesotho 151
Lord's Resistance Army (LRA) 29, 30

Maasai 18
Maathi, Wangari 282
macro grants 35
Madonna 19
majority world *see* global South
Makaton 262
Malawi 19
malnutrition 20
Malone, S. 298
Mama Miti, Napoli 282–3
Mama Panya's Pancakes, Chamberlin 279–80
Man who Walked between the Towers, The, Gerstein 278
marginalization, economic 27, 31, 32
marriage, forced 32
Marriot, S. 278
Maternal Mortality Rate (MMR) 165
maternity benefits, India 164–5
Mbekenga, C. *et al* 33
McCabe, C. *et al* 281
McKechnie, J. and Hobbs, S. 53
McKnight, J. L. 116
Mendoza, J. and Reese, D. 274
menstruation 211

microcredit 35
migration 11, 14–15, 21–2, 96, *181–99*, 237, 278
  children's independent 72, 76
  internal 15, 182–4
Milanovic, Branco 85–6
Millennium Development Goal Two 207, 211, 216–17, 290
Millennium Development Goals 70, 132, 137–8, *203–17*
Millennium Summit and Declaration 205, 216, 217
minority world *see* global North
mobility 11
modernity 111
Mohanty, K. 295
Mokoena, N. 152, 153
Moldova 213–4
Mongolia 87
monitoring and evaluation 305
Montessori 156
Morris, L. and Coughlan, S. 276
Mosaic Approach 225
mother tongue *289–305*
  benefits in education 291–2, 296
  immigrants 312
  importance of 260, 320–1
  opposition to 293–5
  statistics 262, 263–5
  see also language
Mother Tongue Based Multilingual Education (MTBMLE) 298; *see also* pedagogical practice
  components of 298–302
  definition of 296
mothers 27, 29–31, 40, 97
  birth mothers 17–18, 22
  formerly associated with armed forces *27–42*; *see also* children associated with armed forces or armed groups (CAAFAG)
  migrating 13, 15, 21, 190, 192
  role of 12
  working 97, 166
Mozambique 32
multiculturalism
  languages 256–8
  books 274–5, 283–4
Multi-Indicator Cluster Surveys 212
My Rows and Piles of Coins, Mollel 275

Naftali, Orna 193
National Children's Bureau, UK 228
National Development Plan, Ireland 313
National Maternity Benefit Scheme, India 165
National Research Council and Institute of Medicine 208
Nazareen's Secret School, Winter 278
neglect, parental 18
Neighbourhood Care Points 215
Nepal 48, 112–13
Netherlands, The 134
NGOs 34–5, 153–4, 155, 173, 205, 289–90
  methods of 18, 94, 101, 116, 191
  drawbacks of 19, 20, 53–4, 99
  funds 90, 92, 166
  international 7, 20, 53, 87, 94, 97–8
  Moldovan 214
Nicaragua 55
Nigeria, Maiduguri 56
Nores, M. and Barnett, W. 208
North America 59, 89, 99, 101, 171, 172
nutrition 28

O'Rourke, E. 245
OECD (Organisation for Economic Cooperation and Development) 88, 93, 98, 161
  Family Database 100
Office of the Minister for Integration, Ireland 324
Open Society Foundation 95
orphans 19–20, 139, 214–15

Outdoor Learning Project 226
Oxfam 109, 116
Oz-Aid 88

Pakistan 56
parents 5, 17, 20, 34, 167, 172–3, 187–8
  adoptive 17–18, 19, 20–2
  biological 195, 197
  of children with disabilities 149, 155–6
  expectations 146, 195, 294
  isolation of 242–3, 246–9
  left-behind 183
  perspectives 168, 170–1, 240, 266, 272
  primary language *311–25*
  rural 193
  working 161, 181, 187, 191
  parental
  care 15, 18
  characteristic factors 57
  empowerment 213
  migration 14, 15, 184–6, *235–50*; *see also* mothers *and* fathers
  practices 117, 245
  role 146, 262, 299
Parks, Rosa 281–2
Parreñas, R. S. 13
Participation Action Research (PAR) 33–6
participatory activities 223–4
Participatory Rural Appraisal 223
Partner to Poor, Farmer 102
pedagogical practice 256–8, 284, 302
  and language 257–9, 261, 263, 296–7, 298
  MTBMLE 302, 303
Peru 55
Phila Impilo 229–30
philanthropy 89
Philippines 14, 70
picture books 271, 273
  asylum seekers 278–9
  counting 275
  multicultural books 274–7
  racism 281
  world events 278
Planting the Trees of Kenya, Nivola 282
play 54
play-based learning 258
Pogge, T. 90
post traumatic stress disorder 29
post-colonial studies 111–12
poverty 30, 32, 47, 69
pregnancy 30
  forced 31
prejudice 27
pre-school readiness *207–17*, 248
prostitution 30, 48, 70
Psacharopoulos, G. 70
psychoanalysis 22
psychology 22, 94
Pu, Grace 231
public mother 190
public services 98
puppets 229–30, 279, 280

Rajiv Gandhi National Crèche Scheme 166
rape 29–30, 187, 189
Razavi, S. 97
'rebel babies' *see* children associated with armed forces or armed groups (CAAFAG)
reintegration 29–30, 36
relatedness 36–40, 42
research methodologies *222–33*, 235, 316–17
  ethics 232–3
  narrative 232
  play based 229
Reynolds, K. 277
Reynolds, A. and Temple, J. 248
Richardson, D. 98
Roma 95
Rosa, Giovanni and Collier 281

Rosa's Bus, Kittinger 282
Ruane, B. *et al* 279
rural 15, 210
  China 191–3
  education 138, 147
  HIV/AIDS 137
  Moldova 214, 223
Russell, C. 109–10, 115–16
Russia 87, 102
Russian language *313–25*
Rwanda 102, 232

Sachs, W. 112
Said, Edward 111
Salmon, C. 57
San People 91
Sardar, Z. 119
Sarva Shiksha Abhiyan 289
Save the Children 31, 32, 53, 85
scheme take-up *161–73*
  impacting factors 171
Schofield, Mitchell 224
school
  attendance 33
  meals, free 138, 140
  readiness 209, 212, 248, 249
Schulevitz, Uri 274
Schumacher, E. F. 115
Sedlacek, G. *et al* 70
Seeds of Change, Cullerton Johnson 282
Sefeane, Kekesto 136
Senegal 132
September Roses, Winter 278
sex
  transactional 30, 31
  violent 29, 31
sexually transmitted diseases 30, 136
Sharma, A. *et al* 162
Shatter, Alan 244
Shrestha, N. 112–13
Sierra Leone 28, 29, 30, 31, 34, 37, 39, 41
Silence Seeker, The, Morley 279
SINTEF (Stiftelsen for Industriell og Teknisk Forskning) 151, 152
Skillshare International 152
Smidt, S. 259
social reproduction 11–22
Somalia 278
South Africa 16, 94, 223
South African Child Gauge Report (UNICEF) 221
South America 97
special education needs (SEN) 148, 150–4
  teacher training 148–9, 150, 152, 157–8
St Patrick's College of Education, Ireland 279
Stagg Peterson, S. 324
Steer, A. 110, 114
Step by Step Moldova 214
Stern, E. 88
Story of Rosa Parks, The, Pingry and Walker 282
Sudan 113
Sustainable Global Development Conference 109
Swahili 275
Swaziland 214–15
Sweden 171

Tabassum, F. and Baig, L. 56
Tanzania 33, 138, 275
teachers
  languages 256, 262–6
  training 265–7, 295, 304
Thailand 86
Thomas, N. and O'Kane, C. 223
'tomorrow's rebels' *see* children associated with armed forces or armed groups (CAAFAG)
trade unions 55
trafficking 18, 19, 48
transitions 236–8, 239–40, 255, 292, 293
Treaty of Versailles 67
Tribal Welfare Department, India 289

Trócaire 279
tuberculosis 136
Tucker, V. 113
Twi 72

Uganda *28–41*, 30, 92–7
Uganda People's Defence Force 30
Unesco 70, 93, 132, 147, 149
United Nations (UN) 31, 132, 134
  Committee on the Rights of the Child 118
  Convention on Rights of the Child 126, 147, 161, 206
  Convention on the Rights of Persons with Disabilities 154
  Development Programme Action Plan 87, 115, 135
  Family Division 98
  Millennium Project 207
  Study on Women, Peace and Security 31
UNICEF 49, 70, 87, 88, 148, 204–6, *209–17*
United Kingdom 134, 226–9, 259
Universal Declaration on Human Rights 55
Universal Primary Education 133–4, 138, 207–10
universal truth 124, 125, 126
University College Cork, Ireland 235
University College London Development Economics Department 97
urban 4, 15
  HIV/AIDS 137
  China 192–3
Urwick, J. and Elliott, J. 138
Urwick, J. and Griffin, R. 147–8
USAID Agency for International Development 110
USAID Health Profile Lesotho 136

Vandemoortele, J. and Delamonica, E. 206
Veale, A. 232
violence against women 194

wages 110–11
  Aid staff 90
  children's 74
Walker, James 170
Walker, S. P. 97, 98
Wangari's Trees of Peace, Winter 282
war 21, 27, 111
We all went on Safari, Krebs and Cairns 275
welfare state, absence of 22
wellbeing outcomes 15
Westcott, H. and Littleton, K. 222
What is Aid? 109
White Paper on Irish Aid 116
WHO Lesotho; summary country profile for HIV/AIDS treatment scale-up 136
Winsler, A. *et al* 313
Wolk, S. 272
women 12, 13, 27, 96–7, 101, 283
  India 162, 163
  role 195–6
Women's Federation of China 191
work
  accidents 48, 50
  domestic 51, 52
working children's movements/organizations 54
World Bank 70, 85, 87, 93, 94, 99, 114, 115
World Conference on Education for All 161
World Education Forum 132, 161

Yang, Gao 190
Young, R. L. and Tran, M. T. 323